# Shelf Life

**Also by Gideon Haigh**

*The Night Was a Bright Moonlight and I Could See a Man Quite Plain: An Edwardian Cricket Murder* (2021)
*The Brilliant Boy: Doc Evatt and the Great Australian Dissent* (2021)
*The Momentous, Uneventful Day: A Requiem for the Office* (2020)
*Cricket in Mind* (2020)
*This is How I Will Strangle You: An Incest Survivor's Story* (2019)
*The Standard Bearers: Australia v India, Pakistan & Sri Lanka 2018–19* (2019)
*Crossing the Line: How Australian Cricket Lost Its Way* (2018)
*From Flock to Baggy Green* (2018)
*Shadows on the Pitch: The Long Summer of 2017–18* (2018)
*A Scandal in Bohemia: The Life and Death of Mollie Dean* (2018)
*An Eye on Cricket* (2017)
*Stroke of Genius: Victor Trumper and the Shot That Changed Cricket* (2016)
*Certain Admissions: A Beach, A Body and a Lifetime of Secrets* (2015)
*Ashes to Ashes: How Australia Came Back and England Came Unstuck, 2013–14* (2014)
*Uncertain Corridors: Writings on Modern Cricket* (2013)
*End of the Road?* (2013)
*The Deserted Newsroom* (2012)
*On Warne* (2012)
*The Office: A Hardworking History* (2012)
*Out of the Running: The Ashes 2010–11* (2011)
*Sphere of Influence: Writings on cricket and its discontents* (2010)
*Good Enough: The Ashes 2009* (2009)
*Inside Out: Writings on Cricket Culture* (2008)
*The Racket: How Abortion Became Legal in Australia* (2008)
*The Green & Golden Age: Writings on Australian Cricket Today* (2007)
*All Out: The Ashes 2006–07* (2007)
*Silent Revolutions: Writings on Cricket History* (2006)
*Asbestos House: The Secret History of James Hardie Industries* (2006)
*A Fair Field and No Favour: The Ashes of 2005* (2005)
*Game for Anything: Writings on Cricket* (2004)
*The Tencyclopedia* (2004)
*Bad Company: The Strange Cult of the CEO* (2004)
*The Uncyclopedia* (2003)
*The Vincibles: A Suburban Cricket Season* (2002)
*The Big Ship: Warwick Armstrong and the Making of Modern Cricket* (2001)
*One of a Kind: The Story of Bankers Trust Australia 1969–1999* (1999)
*Mystery Spinner: The Story of Jack Iverson* (1999)
*The Summer Game: Australian Cricket in the 1950s and 1960s* (1997)
*One Summer Every Summer: An Ashes Journal* (1995)
*The Border Years* (1994)
*The Cricket War: The Inside Story of Kerry Packer's World Series Cricket* (1993)
*The Battle for BHP* (1987)

With David Frith
*Inside Story: Unlocking Australian Cricket's Archives* (2007)

With Cecilia Haigh
*Father and Daughter* (2017)

By Cecilia Haigh and Harvey Behrendorff
*The Dictionary of Made-Up Creatures* (2019)

# Shelf Life

## Journalism 2000–2021

GIDEON HAIGH

Edited by Russell Jackson

SCRIBNER

SCRIBNER

First published in Australia in 2020 by Gideon Haigh
This edition published in Australia in 2021 by Scribner, an imprint of Simon & Schuster Australia
Suite 19A, Level 1, Building C, 450 Miller Street, Cammeray, NSW 2062

Sydney New York London Toronto New Delhi
Visit our website at www.simonandschuster.com.au



10 9 8 7 6 5 4 3 2 1



NATIONAL LIBRARY OF AUSTRALIA
A catalogue record for this book is available from the National Library of Australia

9781761105234 (paperback)
9781761105241 (ebook)

Cover and interior design by Anne-Marie Reeves
Cover image: © Cecilia Haigh 2020
Typeset in Adobe Jenson Pro
Printed and bound in Australia by Griffin Press

FSC
MIX
Paper
FSC® C009448

The paper this book is printed on is certified against the Forest Stewardship Council® Standards. Griffin Press holds FSC® chain of custody certification SGSHK-COC-005088. FSC® promotes environmentally responsible, socially beneficial and economically viable management of the world's forests.

# CONTENTS

# EDITOR'S NOTE

Unlike many volumes of collected journalism, this book is not the product of vanity or self-importance. In one sense, it exists despite its author, coming after years of badgering on my behalf that Gideon Haigh collect the best of his journalism on topics other than sport. He wouldn't do it, so I have.

Gideon's resigned nod of assent is welcome news to ardent Haighophiles. It also addresses the needs of the strange but important subset of readers who adore the most acclaimed cricket writer in the world but couldn't care less about cricket.

The American editor Robert Gottlieb once said that publishing is the act of making one's enthusiasms public. Gideon does this better than most. Inevitably, I find, the topics he enthuses about in epigrammatic sentences over lunch will soon appear on the page. Such is the clarity of his thought, the rigour of his research and the precise transfer of them through the keyboard, the output is of remarkably consistent quality. Whittling them down was tough.

The articles in this collection exhibit a broad-gauge mind and an incisive journalistic talent. They span decades and range in subject matter from high finance to low culture. They reveal not only a totally committed journalist who works endlessly at his craft, but a humane and principled man whose curiosity is unwaning. With his usual self-deprecation, Gideon describes items herein as 'ephemeral'. Even the offcuts would be the pride and joy of many other journalists. He can make almost any topic seem interesting.

Introducing another of Gideon's books, I strained to describe his style and settled on 'ornamental non-fiction'. That makes me cringe now, because it is not just wrong, but the opposite of the truth. Words serve a very specific purpose in Gideon's journalism – none are merely decorative and none are out of place. As Gideon's career progresses, words work with ever greater efficiency. Points are never laboured. Given the chance, he would murder half the characters in this paragraph and ruthlessly interrogate the survivors.

My selection combines articles short and long, on topics serious and unserious. As a rule, Gideon tends to write at greater length on topics he approaches earnestly. Book reviews and shorter columns have been his primary outlet for fun and flourishes. Even there, he's never one for didacticism, but unfavourable critiques can be withering, their targets many and varied: crooked CEOs, inept bureaucrats, preening writers, dopey reviewers, spivs and charlatans of all stripes. More so, he draws our attention to characters of hidden depth and events of unexplained consequences.

There is a trend in journalism towards ostentatious acknowledgment of the 'contribution' certain individuals make to the field. Quite often, this is merely a case of celebrating the ubiquity of their work, its importance to other journalists, and how high it pushes them in the media pecking order – much more so than the work's impact on those who consume it, or on society at large.

I will leave it to others to judge the contribution Gideon's work makes towards public faith in journalism, and its ability to inspire others to greater heights. What I can comment on is Gideon's unseen mentorship and quiet encouragement of scores of younger journalists and writers – a role he performs for no personal gain, and to no adulation. Like few of his generation, he has taken it upon himself to fill certain gaps created by the shortcomings of the tertiary education system, and the newsroom cutbacks that have placed an ever-diminishing pool of young journalists in the hands of mentors who are either overworked, or, quite frankly, not up to it.

Whatever pride Gideon feels in this remains hidden to the many beneficiaries of his wise counsel, just as you the reader will have no sense of writerly self-satisfaction in the words that follow. Reading them, and appraising a talent so formidable yet free of ego, we're presented with an irony: he's exactly the sort of person Gideon Haigh would write about.

Russell Jackson

# INTRODUCTION

About twenty-five years ago, soon after leaving the office behind for freelance journalism, my afternoon's work was disturbed by the knock of a middle-aged woman, who proved to be a door-to-door market researcher. She looked a little forlorn and footsore, so I invited her and her folder in for a cup of tea.

I fear I was little use to her. I recognised none of the brands she showed me, could identify none of the slogans she reeled off. But the time passed quite pleasantly in my office until she concluded her survey by asking which of a range of alternatives described my work. Running my eye down the list, I couldn't see anything that *really* fitted, and settled for ticking the box labelled 'semi-skilled trade'.

The researcher glanced around the book-lined room. 'So what *is* it you do exactly?' she asked.

'I'm a journalist,' I answered.

'Ah,' she nodded. 'Journalist. That's a profession.'

I shook my head. 'Not the way I do it ma'am,' I said.

And I haven't. Professions have qualifications. I don't. Professions have binding codes of practice. I've never read one worth a damn. Professions have venerable institutions. Journalism has organisations, almost identically dumb. Professions encourage orderly progress to higher levels of seniority and prestige. Me, I've carried on doing the same thing year after year since 1984, with only a yen to do what I do better than before. Which may make the job sound tedious – in fact, it's what has made my working life precisely the opposite. Titles, ranks, postings, sinecures – all these have seemed to involve *obligations*, which leave me feeling slightly uneasy. I like doing my own thing, and journalism has let me. And while the basics of the trade are pretty simple, being a good journalist is hard, and a very good journalist harder still – it is something to which one can fruitfully dedicate a life.

Thus *Shelf Life*, a sample of some of my journalism from the last couple of decades, sympathetically sifted by my friend Russell Jackson, whose idea this has been for some time, and from whose gentle proddings there was, during COVID, finally no distraction. Well, sure, why not? I've always been partial to such collections. My shelves contain a host, from Hazlitt to Hitchens, Didion to Dyer, Chesterton to Chaudhuri. I like Martin Amis' introduction to *The Moronic Inferno* where he offers the book 'with all generic humility', although mine is a little more particular. Reading some of what Russell disinterred during his survey was like stumbling on a teenage diary. Did I *really* write that? Did I ever even *think* that? Ah, well, I did my best at the time, and, as I'm always telling my daughter, that's all we can ever do. Cecilia took the cover photo, by the way, making it my favourite part of the book.

The bits and bobs very loosely grouped in *Shelf Life* were published first in *The Australian, The Age, The Bulletin, The Guardian, The Monthly, The Global Mail, Meanjin, Business Review Weekly, Australian Book Review, Australian Doctor* and *Air*. Generally they reflect my own serial impulses – the desire to find out more about *that thing*, or to share my fascination with that *other thing*, which always beats waiting around for someone else to do it.

I'm sometimes asked how I reconcile my cricket journalism with the rest of what I shall eloquently call my 'other stuff'. It's probably simplest to say that the former involves knowing a lot about a little, the latter a little about a lot. I have a journalist's general knowledge – isolated peaks of awareness separated by huge vistas of ignorance – which I try to redeem with a journalist's curiosity and enthusiasm. I fall hard for my stories, and have always been sorry to part with them. Yet I am not so in love with writing that I wish they could go on forever; journalism has conditioned me to think of completion by publication, however obscure the journal and minimal the reception. I sometimes worry that I've published too much, and am ever mindful of David Foster Wallace's exasperated sigh about John Updike, that the sonofabitch must never have had an unpublished thought. But I also identify with Geoff Dyer's self-explanation – that he writes his books in order to finish them and place them on a shelf, never to be revisted. Thus my title, actually, which involves both a bad pun, and the twin connotations contained in 'shelf life', of perishability and perpetuity. Journalism is the business of always moving on, with the hope of, every now and again, leaving something solid behind.

So I shall thank Russell, a fine journalist in his own right whose progress has given me great satisfaction and whose work down the track will be well worth collecting, for taking such trouble over this otherwise rather thankless task. I'm also grateful to my friend Anne-Marie Reeves for her sterling design efforts, to my mother Isabel for her unflagging proof reading, to my partner Caroline for sticking with a distance relationship through lockdown hell, and also, quite sincerely, you, the reader, for supporting a little lo-fi something in this era of clamorous everythings.

Gideon Haigh

# 'NOT WITH A BANG'

## *Nevil Shute's* On The Beach (2018)

Nevil Shute Norway was an engineer. His business was aeroplanes. Writing? A 'pansy occupation'. His brother, Fred: now *there* was a writer. Then Fred was killed in France, aged nineteen. 'If Fred had lived we might have had some real books one day, not the sort of stuff that I turn out,' said Nevil. 'For he had more literature in his little finger than I have in my whole body.' Nevil Shute Norway dispensed with his surname for his writing, fearful that 'hard-bitten professional engineers might consider such a man not a serious person'.

Yet, just over sixty years ago, Shute published arguably Australia's most important novel – important in the sense of confronting a mass international audience with the defining issue of the age. *On the Beach*, the story of humankind's thermonuclear extinction, has since sold more than four million copies. Shute was the first genuinely popular mainstream novelist to envision apocalypse, and one of only a handful to see the horrific mission through by leaving no survivors – just a silent irradiated planet, adrift in space.

Shute was a Briton. But no novel could be more explicitly Australian than *On the Beach*, set in his new home town of Melbourne. Nor could any novel make such provocative creative use of our distance from the rest of the world: as the last habitable continent, Australia is suddenly the most important place on Earth, at the very moment of its greatest impotence and ignorance, awaiting dooming winds from an incomprehensible war in the northern hemisphere.

Australians were shocked to see themselves so cast. Helen Caldicott, then a nineteen-year-old medical student, was radicalised into a lifetime of anti-nuclear activism: 'Shute's story haunted me…Nowhere was safe. I felt so alone, so unprotected by the adults, who seemed to be unaware of the danger.' But it was in the United States that the book had its greatest impact, rousing readers from an uneasy stupor and becoming one of the Cold War's most powerful cultural artefacts.

Early on 22 July 1957, a false alarm of nuclear attack sounded in

Schenectady, New York. Only one man, reported *Harper's*, roused and evacuated his family. Everyone else, including civil-defence officials, emulated the mayor, who 'rolled over and went back to sleep'.

Into this eerily somnolent world was *On the Beach* released. Debate was underway in the US about fallout from nuclear testing in Nevada, and Shute's publishers had brought forward the book's release, sensing its topicality. Shute was pessimistic. A decade had passed since the Bulletin of Atomic Scientists set its famous Doomsday Clock ticking, and the incident at Schenectady epitomised the apathy and complaisance of the times: thus Einstein's observation that nuclear weapons had changed 'everything except the nature of man'. The atomic bomb was still identified with resolving World War II; the five-year-old hydrogen bomb was seen as a lesser scourge than communism. The public seemed unshockable.

Advance copies of *On the Beach* had been sent to a host of politicians, including the next American president, John F. Kennedy, and to senior military officials. Some had offered startlingly candid endorsements, including consecutive secretaries of the US Air Force, Stuart Symington and Thomas Finletter. 'Every American should read *On the Beach*,' stated Symington, at the time Joseph McCarthy's Senate nemesis. 'I hope it is fiction,' responded Finletter, later Kennedy's ambassador to NATO. 'Are you sure it is?' Readers wanted to find out. Selling 100,000 copies in its first six weeks, *On the Beach* even displaced *Peyton Place* from the top of bestseller lists.

Some critics complained that the book's resolutely low-key depiction of human extinction was unconvincing: people just wouldn't die that way. Yet readers identified readily with the characters' quiet dignity. This conventional novel about unconventional weapons became 'the most influential work of its kind for the next quarter of a century and the only one most people ever read' – as the critic Paul Brians puts it – precisely by being simple:

> Shute directly addresses the most primal fears of the human race which has spent most of its history denying or compensating for the fact of personal death, and does so with a relentlessness which the complex technique of a more sophisticated writer might have muted. For once there are no distractions: no invading aliens, no super fallout shelters to

> protect the protagonists, no struggle back from a dreadful but exciting postwar barbarism. There are simply a man and a woman reaching the agonizing decision to kill their only child in its crib as the rest of the human race expires round them.

The passages Brians describes, where the Australian naval officer Peter Holmes seeks to persuade his wife that this act may be necessary, are the more harrowing for the constancy and devotion the couple exhibit elsewhere:

> 'Let me get this straight,' she said, and now there was an edge in her voice. 'Are you trying to tell me what I've got to do to kill Jennifer?'
>
> He knew that there was trouble coming, but he had to face it. 'That's right,' he said. 'If it becomes necessary you'll have to do it.'
>
> She flared suddenly into anger. 'I think you're crazy,' she exclaimed. 'I'd never do a thing like that, however ill she was. I'd nurse her to the end. You must be absolutely mad. The trouble is that you don't love her. You never have loved her. She's always been a nuisance to you. Well, she's not a nuisance to me. It's you that's the nuisance. And now it's reached the stage that you're trying to tell me how to murder her.' She got to her feet, white with rage. 'If you say one more word, I'll murder you!'

By September 1957, *On the Beach* had been serialised by no fewer than forty American newspapers, and acquired for screen adaptation by the director of the moment, Stanley Kramer. Shot on location in Melbourne, starring Gregory Peck and Ava Gardner, it would become the first American film screened in the USSR.

Shute loathed the film. Nonetheless, on 12 January 1960, a few weeks after its release, he wrote to an admirer: 'A popular novelist can often play the part of the *enfant terrible* in raising for the first time subjects which ought to be discussed in public and which no statesman cares to approach. In this way, an entertainer may serve a useful purpose.' The next day, seated behind his favourite old roll-top desk, he finished a sentence in his next novel, *Incident at Eucla*, gazed out on the towering cypress pine that dominated his immaculate English-style garden, and suffered a lethal stroke.

*

Devotees of Nevil Shute call themselves Shutists. Since a first conference in Alberquerque on the centenary of Shute's birth, members of the Nevil Shute Norway Foundation have held nine worldwide gatherings: their next is scheduled for May 2020 in Devon, home of his parents, and a setting for his novel *Most Secret* (1945). Nonetheless, Shute languishes in something very like obscurity – for reasons not far to seek. His twenty-three novels are plain, staid, even chaste: they proceed sedately towards broadly positive conclusions; they contain no bad language, no villains of note and almost no sex. His characters are usually ordinary middle-class people who face extraordinary situations; their customs and conventions are evoked with a clear but kindly eye. Who can forget the telegram in *A Town Like Alice* (1950) that the heroine sends the hero, whom she had feared dead at the hands of their Japanese captors in Malaya?

> HEARD OF YOUR RECOVERY FROM KUANTAN ATROCITY
> QUITE RECENTLY PERFECTLY DELIGHTED STOP

The decline of Shute's reputation is unremarkable: it simply attests the perishability of popular art. Shute sold fifteen million books in his lifetime, but he aspired to neither literary immortality nor critical approval: 'The book which thrills the reviewer with its artistic perfection will probably not be accepted by the public, while a book which the public value for its contents will probably seem trivial and worthless artistically to the reviewer.' His obscurity also reflects the contours of the book market: the middle-class, middlebrow novelist of ideas is a discontinued line.

Shute's views, moreover, would today exclude him from any self-respecting liberal intelligentsia. He was a rock-ribbed conservative, a monarchist, a meritocrat, an ex-serviceman, a self-made millionaire. He was indulgent of colonialism, loathed the welfare state, rather disapproved of democracy's coarsening influence, and vehemently opposed state support for creative writers, informing Sir Robert Menzies that it turned them into pretentious snobs: 'It encourages him [the writer] to take an inflated view of his own genius, an attitude which places him out of sympathy with his potential readers...I see no point in subsidising young writers to produce what the public does not want to read.' He loathed 'modern art' and read little fiction, starting Patrick White's *Voss* (1957) but losing interest; he much preferred the young Geoffrey Blainey's Tasmanian mining history, *The Peaks of Lyell* (1954).

Not that Shute was a controversialist; suffering from a stammer, he was a diffident public speaker and a reluctant interviewee. But he was shy rather than timid. He travelled constantly, and to some of Australia's remotest reaches; his diaries and notebooks teem with factual detail and anthropological observations. He flew planes, sailed boats, raced cars and rejoiced in machines of all kinds, even owning Australia's first dishwasher. Such values as he held, he felt, were simply the fruit of experience – and they were the values that led him to *On the Beach*.

*

Nevil Shute Norway was born in West Ealing on 17 January 1899. His fascination with aircraft was fostered by living between two aerodromes; his love of machinery originated in a visit, as a schoolboy truant, to London's Science Museum. Otherwise, his life was unexceptional until he enrolled at Shropshire's famous public school, Shrewsbury, then run by the charismatic young Cyril Argentine Alington. Like many public schools during World War I, Shrewsbury nurtured a patriotic cult of death. Shute's older brother, Fred, a brilliant classicist, was an early disciple: he was commissioned as a lieutenant in the Duke of Cornwall's Regiment and died on the Western Front within weeks. The effect on Nevil, which he later described without rancour or self-pity, was profound:

> For the remainder of my time at Shrewsbury, I don't think I had the slightest interest in a career or any adult life; I was born to one end, which was to go into the army and do the best I could before getting killed. The time at school was a time for contemplation of the realities that were coming and for spiritual preparation for death, and in this

> atmosphere the masculine, restrained services in the school chapel under Alington played an enormous part.

That Shute should have felt a kinship with characters facing death, then, should not surprise. *On the Beach*'s original epigraph was from one of Alington's famous evening-service addresses, published as a story in *Shrewsbury Fables* (1917): 'I will deprive men of the foreknowledge of death which they possess at present. This power Prometheus has received my order to take from them.' In the story, 'A Dream', the speaker is a stranger with a machine able to recreate the past or foretell the future. Alington says he would like to see how his boys turn out, until the stranger explains that some will be 'absent': dead. 'Perhaps it would be safer to stick to the past after all,' Alington decides. The stranger nods: 'Yes, you are all like that when it comes to the point.'

That Shute did not join the absent was due to his stammer, which frustrated his quest for a commission; by the time he enlisted as an infantryman, the war had only months to run. This arbitrary prolongation of his life became almost a source of perplexity:

> For four years of my adolescence I had lived in a world that was growing steadily bleaker and grimmer, and in that four years I had grown to accept the fact that in a very short time I should probably be dead. I cannot remember any particular resentment at this prospect; indeed, in some ways it was even stimulating. It has puzzled many people to imagine how the Japanese produced their kamikazes or suicide pilots in the last war. It has never been much of a puzzle to me, however; in 1918, anybody could have made a kamikaze out of me.

After gaining a third in engineering, Shute gravitated to the aviation infantry, which he joined as a junior dogsbody. Its mixture of boffins, adventurers, spivs and speculators would provide a rich stock of characters for the Buchanesque adventure novels for which he would originally be known. These, however, he considered purely recreational: 'To write a book is a very easy matter for the man or woman who really wants to do so. No training is necessary.' It was aviation that for the next fifteen years provided Shute with a satisfaction 'almost amounting to a religious experience'. It stretched his imagination, leading him to design the first British plane with a retractable undercarriage; it defined his personal life, introducing him to his future wife at the Yorkshire Aeroplane Club, which he founded and ran; it informed his politics, in a formative experience of state ownership.

Anxious to put its stamp on the burgeoning lighter-than-air market, Britain's first Labour government commissioned two airship designs: the private sector R100, built by Vickers Ltd, and the R101, directed by the Air Ministry. As Shute put it: 'I joined the capitalist team.' The R100 crossed the Atlantic both ways in a pioneering journey, with Shute among the crew; the R101, lavished with money but dogged by an exorbitantly incompetent bureaucracy, crashed on its maiden voyage. Shute thereafter regarded dirigisme as the worst of ideological sins, and politicians and civil servants as 'arrogant fools' unless otherwise demonstrated.

Having joined one capitalist team, Shute then decided to run his own. Airspeed Ltd was not just the source of his wealth; it made him believe in its pursuit. 'From beginning to end,' notes the American academic Julian Smith in his monograph *Nevil Shute* (1976), 'Shute and his characters were never shy about making money, for money is the surest sign that a man is doing what the world wants done.' By 1938, Shute himself was rich enough not to work and too young to retire. What to do? His fifth book, he decided, should be useful: 'No man can see into the future, but unless somebody makes a guess from time to time and publishes it to stimulate discussion it seems to me that we are drifting in the dark, not knowing where we want to go or how to get there.' In spirit and intensity, *What Happened to the Corbetts* (1938), a vision of a Britain ravaged by strategic bombing, strongly anticipates *On the Beach*.

The Corbetts, Peter and Joan and their three children, are Shute archetypes, trying to do right in the face of egregious wrong. 'We're not famous people and we've not done much,' says Joan. 'Nobody knows anything about us. But we've lived quietly and decently and we've done our job.' They aren't alone. In this novel, even the dying, like the wife of their builder neighbour Littlejohn, do their best:

> The bomb had fallen on or near their greenhouse. A flying fragment of the glass had sheared through all her clothes and wounded her behind the knee. She had bled to death, quietly and unostentatiously, as in everything that she had done...Presently the builder picked her up in his arms and, staggering a little, carried her into the house and upstairs to the bedroom where the candle was still burning, he laid her on the ornate, gilded iron bed beneath a picture of 'The Stag at Bay' and a text in a wood Oxford frame that told them 'God is Love', and covered her with a counterpane.

*What Happened,* like *On the Beach,* is a conventional novel on an unconventional, very nearly taboo, subject: the civilian experience of war, with its trials of disaster and displacement. It is not, however, an anti-war novel. To write against war when its coming was inevitable would have struck Shute as pointless posturing. He was arguing not for peace but for preparedness, to ready Britons 'for the terrible things that you, and I, and all the citizens of the cities in this country may one day have to face together'. On the novel's release in April 1939, a thousand copies were distributed to workers in Air Raid Precautions. It was 'the entertainer serving a useful purpose'.

When bombs began falling on Britain six months later, Shute returned to uniform in the Royal Navy Volunteer Reserve. 'I have no respect at all for the writer of any age or sex,' he explained, 'who thinks he can serve his country best in war time by sitting still and writing.' In fact, Shute continued writing, his war novels being among his most successful: *Pied Piper* (1942), an adventure; *Landfall* (1940) and *Pastoral* (1944), romances; and the aforementioned *Most Secret* (1945), a palpably propagandistic thriller. But he did his sitting mainly in the Department of Miscellaneous Weapons Development, among Admiralty boffins developing experimental weapons, some of which worked, some of which didn't.

Shute is primarily associated with one of the latter, the Great Panjandrum: a 4,000-pound barrel of high explosive to be propelled up the beaches of

France by two giant Catherine wheels. Its ignominious failure, scattering a bridge of admirals sent to supervise its testing, became proverbial, even inspiring an episode of *Dad's Army*. For Shute, however, weapons were a serious business. On D-Day eve, he philosophised: 'We engineers are apt to lie awake these days wondering whether in our old age, if we survive to see it, we shall regret these years of work upon the weapons that have made a desperate adventure possible.' And a successful weapon, Shute discovered, could prove even more problematic than a failed one.

*

To Shute, a graver plague even than war was visited on Britain by the July 1945 election of a Labour government. He regarded the welfare state with growing horror. *No Highway* (1948), whose theme of aviation safety showed off all Shute's technical acumen, was a runaway bestseller and then an improbable star vehicle for Jimmy Stewart and Marlene Dietrich, but much of the income was soaked up by Labour's punitive taxes on the wealthy. Feeling increasingly a stranger in his own country, Shute invited the novelist James Riddell to join him on a continent-hopping journey to and from Australia in his single-engine Percival Proctor monoplane.

In this last efflorescence of the *Pax Britannica*, the pair took a route that now seems unimaginable: Lebanon, Iraq, Kuwait, Pakistan, Burma. Shute was rejuvenated. In Sumatra, he met a perky Dutch woman, Geysel Vonck; in Normanton, he encountered the laconic ringer Jimmie Edwards. He would entwine their stories of incarceration by the Japanese in *A Town Like Alice* (1950). In Rangoon, he visited a former Royal Engineer turned Buddhist priest: U. Prajnananda's predictions of a coming prophet inspired Shute's most intellectually adventurous novel, *Round the Bend* (1951), in which an aeronautic engineer becomes a middle eastern mystic with a creed based on precision maintenance. Both would sell and sell: initial print runs of 150,000 became his norm. Above all, Shute was captivated by the splendour of the Australian landscape and the sunny good nature of its people, noting their uninhibited esteem for things British.

This immediate kinship was probably as much about Shute as Australia.

Riddell loathed the country on sight, thinking it conformist, casually racist, disquietingly martial: Bondi's marching lifesavers reminded him of 'the Hitler Youth'. But Shute liked the obvious prosperity of Melbourne, where he stayed at the Melbourne Club. Taking the election of Robert Menzies in December 1949 as a harbinger of political common sense, Shute made his choice. The *Sydney Morning Herald*'s front page of 7 June 1950 bore the headline: 'Nevil Shute To Live in Australia.' 'Britain is not a very good country for a successful man,' the new arrival explained. 'I believe Australia is going to be the most prosperous part of the Commonwealth.'

Shute marked the move with two of his slighter novels: *The Far Country* (1952) and *In the Wet* (1953). The latter is genuinely odd: a prophecy of the Commonwealth in 1984, in which England's decline has been so abject, and Australia's emergence so irresistible, that the Queen decides to base the throne in Canberra. It argues vigorously against the equalising forces of democracy, Australia's rise being linked to its adoption of 'multiple voting': additional votes for the successful and wealthy. Sweeping away the 'tub-thumping nonentities and union bosses', multiple voting has left Australian politics to 'real men'.

Both novels reflect Shute's excitement at Australian possibility. And by now, after fifteen years in engineering and fifteen not, Shute was probably this country's wealthiest creative artist. At his new 200-acre property in Langwarrin, south-east of Melbourne, he was a novelist before lunch and a gentleman farmer after. The area was then so isolated that his house needed its own generator and a lofty tank to provide water at gravity pressure. For a man who delighted in the mechanical, these were pleasures as much as necessities. And with *Alice* set to become the fifth of his novels adapted for the screen, he could afford to take a few chances. Thus did the end of the world come to Melbourne.

*

Shute's first inspiration for *On the Beach* was an article in *Time* just before Christmas in 1954 reporting on a paper delivered at the French Academy of Sciences. In 'The Cumulative Effects of Thermonuclear Explosions on the

Surface of the Globe', the physicist Charles-Noel Martin identified a number of ways in which neutrons and atmospheric debris from bomb tests 'may upset the natural conditions to which [human] life has become adapted'. *Time* soberly noted: 'Physicist Martin, who is pro-American, is not making Communist propaganda.' Shute the conservative dutifully copied this down; Shute the engineer brooded on the inference.

He was actually about to start another novel, *Beyond the Black Stump* (1956) – an unusually ambivalent story in which the romance goes unconsummated and the promise of wealth remains unfulfilled – and might well have been distracted: his taste for prophecy had been pricked. Notes for what was then called 'The Last Day', now in the National Library of Australia, suggest that he continued researching it throughout this period. They include the text of a speech to the British Medical Association by his friend Major General Kingsley Norris, Australia's senior military medico. 'It Could Happen to Us' candidly discussed the casualties of a nuclear war and the near impossibility of their treatment. Norris, another Melbourne Club member, would act as Shute's adviser on radiation-related illness.

Shute may have felt a particular urgency about 'The Last Day'. In London in November 1955, he suffered a heart attack. It was not his first, but this one felt different: a personal *memento mori* for the man composing a global one. Soon after, he 'suddenly went crazy' and placed an order for a Jaguar XK140, a classic marque of which only a dozen were built each year. He would have his scientist Osborne respond the same way to impending mortality in *On the Beach*, buying a 'venomously fast' red Ferrari.

*On the Beach* obtained an additional personal dimension from being the only novel Shute set principally where he was living at the time. The terrain is his neighbourhood: the beaches, farms, railway stations and pubs of the Mornington Peninsula, most of them identifiable. 'Falmouth' is seaside Frankston; rural Berwick and Harkaway appear under their own names; directions to the Holmes' house are so exact that a visitor can study the bay from what would have been their view. Among Shute's manuscripts, jotted in pencil on an envelope, are his observations of the route to Barwon Heads: the headlong flight of expiring Moira Davidson that concludes *On the Beach*.

It is as though the book's theme was so pressing that it consumed all of Shute's imagination.

The epigraph was sifted from a page of possibilities, Alington finally giving way to lines from T. S. Eliot's 'The Hollow Men' – which also offered a title, nodding to the naval expression for awaiting reassignment:

> In this last of meeting places
> We grope together
> And avoid speech
> Gathered on this beach of the tumid river...
> This is the way the world ends
> Not with a bang but a whimper.

Chief among Shute's technical sources was *Facing the Atomic Future* (1956), by Sir Ernest Titterton, the Australian National University's British-born guru of nuclear physics – an irony, as Titterton was an outspoken apologist for weapons testing in Australia. Shute specially noted Titterton's chapter on 'radiological warfare', specifically the so-called cobalt bomb: a thermonuclear device whose destructive capacity was based chiefly on radioactivity rather than explosive force.

The cobalt bomb had been mooted by the Manhattan Project's disillusioned Leo Szilard in February 1950 to evoke nuclear warfare's alarming potentialities; it would be championed by his hawkish contemporary Edward Teller, perversely, as a means of scaring mankind straight: 'The cobalt bomb is...the product of the imagination of high-minded people who want to use this spectre to frighten us into a heaven of peace.' Even Titterton could see that the 'heaven' promised by radiological warfare was not on earth:

> If some madman decided that he wished to poison the whole of the human race with radioactivity...it would be possible to arrange for a shell of cobalt around a fission or fusion bomb to absorb the excess neutrons and make radiocobalt...The slow decay of radiocobalt (half-life 5.3 years) would make this contamination much more serious than in the fission product case.

For various technical reasons, the cobalt bomb flourished only in fiction, reaching its apotheosis in *Dr Strangelove* (1964) and *Planet of the Apes* (1968). And, truth be told, the science of *On the Beach* is flawed at best: thermonuclear fallout would not distribute itself evenly around the world; shelter *would* be possible. But Shute had chosen his weapon wisely.

The physics and the fiction of Armageddon have a longstanding relationship: Szilard was famously inspired by H. G. Wells, who coined the phrase 'atomic bombs' in *The World Set Free* (1913). But the subdued public reaction to Hiroshima had been echoed in a kind of creative moratorium, nuclear weapons reverting to the stuff of science fiction, where most tales were frivolous or upbeat. In this environment, strategic speculations flourished. The Eisenhower doctrine of massive retaliation committed the United States to revenging any nuclear attack by disproportionate force. Yet hawks argued that the only way not to lose a nuclear exchange was to win it, waging a pre-emptive war with superior weaponry. While Shute was writing his manuscript, between '13.3.56 and 23.9.56', Australia's government was abetting British efforts to refine such weaponry by hosting nuclear tests in the Monte Bello Islands and at Maralinga.

With the cobalt bomb, Shute reminded readers of the destructive capacities of weapons whose use was in danger of being normalised, maximising the helplessness of victims, minimising the doubt that future war would involve an unprecedented calculus of death. As that most erudite of physicists Freeman Dyson has argued:

> *On the Beach*...is technically flawed in many ways. Almost all the details are wrong...Nevertheless, the myth did what Shute intended it to do. On the fundamental human level, in spite of the technical inaccuracies, it spoke truth. It told the world, in language that everyone could understand, that nuclear war means death. And the world listened.

*

*On the Beach* is neither stylistically ambitious nor philosophically sophisticated. The dialogue almost seems there to kill time – as, indeed, it is. Shute's coup is to begin the novel when it is already too late: the events of *On the Beach* span the period from Christmas 1962, fourteen months after the 'short, bewildering war' of thirty-seven days, to the end of August 1963. That war is introduced almost by the way, so much the defining fact of life has it become. Australian knowledge of it is fragmentary, either anecdotal or seismographic. All that is clear is that a tit-for-tat regional skirmish spread from the Middle East. Political leaders were among the first casualties: most of the orders were given by underlings without superiors to countermand them. Australia, we learn, experienced panics after the war; there remain riotous incidents. But *On the Beach*'s characters have reached differing degrees of acceptance of their common fate; the novel's poignancy springs from the tenderness with which they collude in each other's means of coping.

Perhaps because Shute wrote it in roughly the same amount of time that it covers, without flashbacks or digressions and in continuous chapters of equal length, *On the Beach* forces the reader to live in the instant with the characters. These characters, moreover, have a familiar quality. Lieutenant-Commander Peter Holmes, of the Royal Australian Navy, and his wife, Mary, are the Corbetts redux: good people in dark times. But where war uprooted the Corbetts, war confines the Holmeses to a shrinking world, in which they comfort themselves with rituals like planning their garden for the following year. And where conventional war blurred the line between combatants and non-combatants, unconventional war has dissolved it altogether: Holmes and his American counterpart, Commander Dwight Towers, are servicemen returned from a war they never saw, distinguished only by their uniforms from the millions of uncomprehending spectators. Given their plight, it is as though the characters are in the wrong novel; that is, of course, what makes them so right.

What the characters fear almost as much as death are 'scenes' disturbing their sedulously constructed illusions; echoing 'The Hollow Men', they 'grope together / And avoid speech'. When Holmes invites Towers to his home, he has misgivings: 'Northern hemisphere people seldom mixed well, now, with people of the southern hemisphere. Too much lay between them, too great a difference of experience. The intolerable sympathy made a barrier.' His assurances that Towers will be 'all right' don't impress Mary: 'That's what you thought about that RAF squadron leader. You know – I forget his name. The one who cried.'

In fact, a relationship blossoms between the straitlaced Towers and Mary's hard-drinking, plain-speaking friend Moira Davidson. But it remains unconsummated: Towers still feels the tug of the family he left in Connecticut. 'I suppose you think I'm nuts,' he explains. 'But that's the way I see it.' Moira joins in the charade: she looks forward to meeting his dead wife, offers gifts for his dead children, then sees him off to scuttle his submarine so it cannot be seized by a dead enemy.

The scientist Osborne is perhaps the most intriguing character, being Shute's characterisation of himself. He provides the most rational views – 'You've always known that you were going to die sometime. Well, now you know when' – and the least rational reaction. Shute raced his Jaguar at the newly constructed Phillip Island grand-prix circuit in order to research the scenes in which Osborne enters his Ferrari in a wild 300-car race. This lawless, heedless chase after no prize worth having, in which death has an eerie allure, is Shute's most sophisticated and extended allegory: humanity, harnessed to powerful machines that are also instruments of death, circling in crazed futility.

*

'Nevil Shute Wipes Out Human Race in Notable Novel.' With headlines like this in the *Chicago Tribune*, *On the Beach* was received, dissected and disputed. By no means was its reception entirely cordial. It was decried on the Republican right as communist sedition, its fatalism tantamount to treason: with its 'tiresome descriptions of vast atomic destruction', sighed a critic in the *National Review*, the book was clearly 'designed to destroy whatever is left of American faith in the military'. It also irked religious conservatives. 'If ever Mr Shute intended to show his utter poverty of spiritual values,' wrote Ronald Conway in the *Advocate*, the Catholic newspaper, 'he could not have displayed it better than in *On the Beach*.'

Others found *On the Beach* darkly stirring. In September 1957, it became a talking point during a party at the retreat of Lord Beaverbrook in the South of France, where Winston Churchill was overheard saying that he intended presenting a copy to Nikita Khrushchev of the Soviet Union. 'I think the earth will soon be destroyed by a cobalt bomb,' Churchill opined. 'I think if I were the almighty I would not recreate it...'

In the *New Republic*, Robert Estabrook described *On the Beach* as an 'evangelical' book in the tradition of *Uncle Tom's Cabin*. And Shute found an improbable admirer in Billy Graham, who on his crusades began brandishing a Bible in one hand and a copy of *On the Beach* in the other. 'If a minister got into the pulpit and said some of the things in the book, he would be considered a sensationalist,' he claimed. 'He would be accused of trying to frighten people. Yet this book has been a success and the film will be a success.' *On the Beach*, Graham proselytised, foretold the fate of humanity without God: 'The imagination of Mr Shute in *On the Beach* could become a reality in your generation.'

Shute kept his own counsel on this. Although one of the biggest beneficiaries in his will was St Thomas' Anglican Church at Langwarrin, he was not a regular churchgoer, and preaching wasn't his way: sixty years ago, the publication of a book was a cue for people to read it, not to interview the author. That has led to some divergent views. Shute's biographer, Julian Smith, deemed *On the Beach* 'a novel about suicide': every character chooses self-administered death over slow radiation poisoning. Profiling Shute in *Meanjin*, David Martin considered *On the Beach* 'a novel about immortality': every character continues planning for the future in spite of knowing their fate. Helen Caldicott interpreted the novel as about her: 'It described places I knew, devastated by nuclear catastrophe.'

Letters suggest that Shute nursed two serious grievances about the film adaptation. When Stanley Kramer had Dwight and Moira consummate their relationship, believing that the public would not accept Gregory Peck and Ava Gardner experiencing love without sex, Shute protested: he had made Dwight dutiful and Moira virtuous, he explained, precisely because nuclear war would not discriminate, killing the best as well as the worst. He also thought that Kramer had effectively substituted *eros* for *thanatos*.

The novel's characters weary, sicken and die. Finally, Moira watches the submarine *Scorpion* fade from view: 'Then she put the tablets in her mouth and swallowed them down with a mouthful of brandy, sitting behind the wheel of her big car.' The film sterilises the end of the world: Moira merely sees the *Scorpion* sail for the United States, like a war bride farewelling a sailor husband. Shute the conservative was more willing to confront his audience than Kramer the noted campaigner.

Since then, it sometimes seems, the world has turned topsy-turvy. It is conservatives who worship at the altar of progress, resistant to anything that would stand in its way, while liberals cheerfully make common cause with the forces of reaction, economic, technological and theocratic. Such is the tribalism of our politics that were *On the Beach* published today, Shute would probably be regarded as an apostate: a conservative and a believer in free enterprise dealing with concepts on which the left exert a monopoly. Not, mind you, that the Left would want him. In the United Kingdom, the Campaign for Nuclear Disarmament (CND) has marched a long way past Aldermaston, on which it famously advanced at Easter 1958: half a century later it was led by a Communist Party member who airily dismissed 'the supposed threats' of North Korea and Iran achieving their nuclear ambitions.

Yet it is not anomalous that *On the Beach* is a conservative novel; that, on the contrary, is the secret of its success. Where contemporary literature, film and theatre seeking political response is often shrill, prepared for the faithful rather than the ambivalent or the uncommitted, *On the Beach* works with the grain of a mass audience's hopes and fears. It inters humanity in a mausoleum of its follies and vanities, but it is not misanthropic. It warns against the heedless pursuit of technology and material pleasures, but it is not a jeremiad. It wears its politics lightly, free of boilerplate anti-Americanism. And it explicitly espouses non-proliferation rather than pacifism or disarmament. 'The trouble is, the damn things got too cheap,' explains Osborne. 'Every little pipsqueak country could have a stockpile of them...' Which, it turns out, is the nuclear dilemma besetting our own age. In his analysis of the 'nuclear poor', *The Atomic Bazaar* (2006), William Langewiesche explains:

> Simply put, large parts of the world are exposed once again to the universal appeal of atomic bombs – the fast-track, nation-equalising, don't-tread-on-me, flat-out awesome destructive power that independent arsenals can provide...Practically speaking...the poor, for a host of reasons, are more likely to use their nuclear weapons than the great powers have been since the summer of 1945.

*On the Beach* remains devastating, and that Shute could write a bestseller concerning what Paul Brians calls 'the most carefully avoided topic of general significance in the contemporary world' is an astounding achievement. In retrospect, 1957 was a hinge point in the Cold War, when passive resignation about nuclear arms began yielding to alarm and horror. It was the year that the CND was founded in Britain and the National Committee for a Sane Nuclear Policy was established in the United States; it was the year that the National Council of Churches warned that the arms race might 'lead directly to a war that will destroy civilization'. In 1955, fewer than one-fifth of Americans knew what fallout was; by 1958, seven in ten were saying they would favour a worldwide organisation to prohibit nuclear weapons.

How many people during that transition read J. B. Priestley's 'Russia, the Atom and the West' in the *New Statesman*? Or heard the Nobel-winning chemist Linus Pauling rail against nuclear arms? And how many read *On the Beach*? Nevil Shute's novel was the great popular work on the gravest matter besetting civilisation. If it doesn't meet the current taste in agitprop, or if Shute seems an awkward fit in the liberal pantheon, then perhaps the relevant criteria require review.

In his autobiography, *No Memory for Pain* (1970), Shute's friend Kingsley Norris recalled a premise for an unwritten book that for many years preoccupied the novelist:

> A paper plague was about to descend upon the world...all paper, all books, all records and archives would disintegrate and disappear. There still remained a short interval to decide what was worth preserving and to devise some means of doing so. Whenever I asked him how the idea

was working out, Nevil with his slight stammer would say, 'I am still not sure how I would go about it.'

If anyone does find a way, *On the Beach* should be among the first Australian books preserved.

# THE HISTORY BOY

## *Geoff Blainey's* The Tyranny of Distance (2016)

It was a hit almost before the public had read a word, remembers Brian Stonier. One evening in early 1966, Stonier, a founder of the new paperback imprint Sun Books, had the task of introducing historian Geoffrey Blainey to an audience in the library at Geelong College. He mentioned Blainey's seven previous works and publicised his next: 'We're hoping later this year to publish a new book, which we're thinking of calling *The Tyranny of Distance.*' The sixty schoolchildren burst into spontaneous applause. The book approaches its half-century as perhaps Australian history's biggest bestseller, having never been out of print, with about 180,000 copies sold.

Today Blainey is 86, weighed down with honours. Back then, he was a rather dashing reader in economic history at the University of Melbourne with a knack for reaching non-academic audiences: Monash University's Graeme Davison, who will present a birthday appreciation of *The Tyranny* this week on a platform with Blainey as part of Melbourne's Rare Book Week, believes him the first trained historian in Australia, and still one of very few, to live by his pen.

For the lay-reader, *The Tyranny* reads as vitally as ever, with, as Don Watson once noted, virtually a revelation a page. The pacing is flawless, the prose lean. Blainey is renowned for his fascination with mechanical ingenuity, and the book's components slot together with the ease of precision workmanship, like a ship captain's chronometer or a surveyor's theodolite. Aged fifty, it also invites appreciation as an historical artefact in its own right.

Born in 1930, Blainey was reared in a household with barely a word of Australian history on its bookshelves. Nor were there histories to be found in the library at the Ballarat Mechanics Institute when he joined it – he gorged instead on travel books. There is an autobiographical note when Blainey in *The Tyranny* describes Australians' staunch but oblivious Anglocentricity.

'Schoolchildren in Australia got it second-hand,' he wrote, 'and one of the curious effects of Australia's education system was that, as late as the late

1940s, most of those who left secondary school or university carried away the idea that Britain was still the leading power. One household item that had perhaps preserved the idea of the might of Britain and its empire was the map of the world. The splashes of deep red across the map seemed visual proof of Britain's power.'

There being few obvious entry points on a national story, Blainey first came at Australia from the obliquest of angles. Rather than being reabsorbed into academe after finishing his undergraduate degree at Melbourne University, he accepted a commission to write a history of the Mt Lyell Mining and Railway Company, which opened out into a stunningly original portrait of a landscape and way of life. His sojourn on Tasmania's west coast would also shape the thinking behind *The Tyranny*, not simply because of its isolation but because he subscribed to the roneoed newsletter of the Tasmanian Historical Association, which in 1952 published a remarkable, quixotic paper.

Ken Dallas was a shambling, ursine figure – an avowed socialist and an insouciant, self-educated, serially enthusiastic scholar. Delivered to the association's annual meeting, Dallas's 'The first settlement in Australia considered in relation to sea-power in world politics' dared depart from the script that the British had envisioned the antipodes simply as a penal sinkhole, pointing to its strategic significance in the southern seas and the potential of its commodities (flax and tall timber) to an empire sinewed by sail.

Blainey was captivated, perhaps above all by Dallas's heterodoxy. Later he would lure Dallas to Melbourne University as a guest lecturer. 'Students loved him,' says Blainey. Above all, in *The Tyranny*'s first chapter, Blainey would adapt and expand the idea of a mercantilist impetus to Australia's first settlement, then strongly defend it from criticism.

That lay ahead as Blainey refined his craft across the next decade in a succession of institutional histories: a bank, an engineering company, a university, a suburb, another mining company and, in 1963, the mining industry itself, then strangely neglected. The title, *The Rush That Never Ended*, further evinced Blainey's propensity for the ringing phrase, some of which have entered the vernacular ('black armband', 'nation of tribes'), others of which perhaps should have (such as 'the pale empire of ideas', Blainey's rendering of 'soft power' in 2000's *A Short History of the World*).

With his specialisation in economic history, Blainey had by then drifted back to his alma mater. He found it rather easeful: eight to 10 contact hours a week left ample writing time, and in 1964 he cheerfully accepted a commission from Stonier, who had established a local publishing list at Penguin's Australian outpost, to write a history of transportation in Australia.

Not, Blainey admits, that he was particularly well qualified; he simply liked the idea. 'I suppose I was getting more and more confident,' he says. 'Quite willing to jump into a subject of which I knew nothing.' He schooled himself partly by schooling his students. Some sections of *The Tyranny*, such as a salty and reeking chapter on whaling, were delivered first as lectures, and he regularly identified issues to elaborate from class questions. 'You often teach more interestingly if you're not sure where you're going,' he adds.

*The Tyranny* builds on certain core understandings with a quality of hindsight obviousness, such as that Australia cleaved to those commodities, wool and gold, that were easiest and most economical to move to markets. Wool was for men with capital, gold for men without it. Blainey also exhibited a capacity for reconsideration. He expected, for example, to add his voice to the age-old criticism of the builders of Australian railways, that they had short-sightedly relied on different gauges that finally proved impossible to link continentally. But on reading accounts of the uniting of railways connecting Melbourne and Sydney in 1884, he was struck by nobody seeming to think this was a big deal.

Well, yes, Blainey reflected – the laying of railways had begun a couple of generations earlier, to open interiors not served by waterways and to suit local terrains rather than to mobilise the minimal traffic between colonies already cheaply served by sea. Blainey encompassed the initially relaxed attitude to border changes of locomotives in a characteristic paragraph, concluding with a playful asperity.

> Men who were accustomed to travelling long distances in horse-drawn coaches liked to leave a train to stretch their legs. As trains had no dining cars passengers had to leave the train to buy a meal; at the border,

> moreover, their luggage had to be checked by customs officials, so that some delay was inevitable even if they did not want a pie and tea. Even the carrying of their personal luggage from the Victorian to the NSW train at Albury was not annoying, because most passengers were wealthy enough to hire a porter. The break of gauge lost its pleasures much later, when the customs inspection was abolished, when dining cars were coupled to passenger trains, the luggage porters' carts dwindled, the long train trip became a fast overnight journey ... and when we have all become lazier.

Such passages, occasionally almost sensual, lend *The Tyranny* its personality. Blainey is sometimes deemed a better historian of things than of people, but things in *The Tyranny* are imbued with rare character, whether whalebones on a beach at Port Fairy or Chilean flowers growing among discarded ballast on the Newcastle shoreline. Blainey evokes the soft pad of a night-time camel train, describes the greasy smell from the prior cargo of wool and tallow greeting immigrants descending into shipboard sleeping quarters. He sketches railway workers throwing together a temporary town, notes the changed urban order and odour when the internal combustion engine eclipsed the horse ('Horses were as detrimental to public health as the exhaust fumes which replaced them as the distinctive scent of cities').

Throughout, Blainey's is a strong authorial voice, measured and epigrammatic. Eschewing quotation and statistics for the purposes of narrative pace, he can be joltingly succinct, notably when he expresses race relations as a calculus: 'The coloured population which inhabited Australia before the white conquest was relatively sparse, and made sparser by the guns and diseases which Englishmen carried. The conflict between aboriginals and European invaders was costly for the aboriginals but not for the invaders.' Such unselfconscious use of 'conquest' and 'invaders' might today invite a reprimand from the *Daily Telegraph*. But in what he called his 'sort of history of Australia', Blainey arguably exhibited both the strengths and the limitations of the discipline of economic history.

Where Blainey succeeded, perhaps for all time, was in writing so invitingly, even excitingly. *The Tyranny* is concomitantly spacious, delighting in startling facts, unafraid of confident assertions – Australians' embrace of sport, for example, is baldly yet convincingly explained as a phenomenon of colonial gender imbalance, 'to be expected in a society dominated by young men'. Not for Blainey the tentative mode of many modern historians, content to 'pose questions'; he quested for answers by evidence and reasoning.

Despite this, the thesis came late. As Blainey explains, the book was written back-to-front, what was eventually the second half, called 'The Taming of Distance', came first. It was working his way backwards to James Cook's explorations that encouraged his seeing transportation through its challenges rather than its technologies.

It was the book's first half, actually written second, that originally was called 'The Tyranny of Distance', while the book's working title was *Distance and Destiny*. It was only just before the night at Geelong College that the titles of the first half of the book and of the book itself were transposed. Stonier credits the decision to a boozy lunch in Carlton. While not recalling it, Blainey agrees it's a story that should be true.

About the title, Blainey is modest. He is amused by its ubiquity – that it is the name of a cafe in Windsor, for example, and was quoted by Split Enz in *Six Months in a Leaky Boat* ("The tyranny of distance didn't stop the cavalier'). But he is surprised at its literal interpretation: 'It's a loose phrase. Something you'd put on a banner for a football team to run through.' No tyrant, he observes, ever went unresisted.

There is a curious link, meanwhile, between *The Tyranny* and two works of comparable stature and resonance preceding it: Robin Boyd's *The Australian Ugliness* (1960) and Donald Horne's *The Lucky Country* (1964). Boyd's and Horne's books were published by the newly expanded Australian outpost of Penguin yet severely aggravated tensions between the tweedy parent company and its confident young representatives Down Under – Stonier, Geoffrey Dutton and Max Harris. Penguin had refused to publish Boyd in Britain and agreed to take *The Lucky Country* only with misgivings and under the banal title *Australia in the Sixties*.

Stonier signed Blainey for Penguin, too, but by the time the manuscript was complete had walked out to establish Sun Books with Dutton and

Harris in June 1965. Blainey recalls: 'I said to Brian: "Well, I have to offer it to Penguin first". Brian said: "You must".' When Blainey received a terse rejection letter from Penguin – never explained – Stonier predictably was overjoyed. Sun matched Blainey in boldness. For a serious work of Australian history to be released first in paperback, and at $1.95 in the newfangled decimal currency to boot, was unheard of. A cool modernist cover by J. Walter Thompson art director Bryan Sadgrove tilted *The Tyranny* further toward a popular audience. 'I can say it was brilliant because I had no part in it,' says Blainey. Some disoriented historians marked it down as a 'quickie' on the basis of its bindings; most welcomed it warmly. 'Written in a delightfully lucid style, it will confound the severest critic of the present standard of Australian historiography,' the University of NSW's Frank Crowley wrote in *The Sydney Morning Herald*.

As well they might have: in some respects, *The Tyranny* represents the apotheosis of a certain kind of historical writing, ahead of a drift away from it. A readership, and a student body, were about to start talking back and among themselves. Blainey's instinctual generalism also would run counter to trends of specialisation in the humanities – to the writing, as Monash's Davison puts it, of more and more about less and less.

Yet, as Davison notes, *la longue duree* has made a subtle comeback in recent times, in the trend to indisciplinary 'big history' advocated by American history professors Jo Guldi and David Armitage in their monograph *The History Manifesto* (2014). In exploring the opening of new expanses of territory, *The Tyranny of Distance* also opened new vistas of history. That first burst of applause deserves renewal.

# 'I SAW THIS'

## *Goya's* Desastres (2020)

In *Homage to Catalonia,* George Orwell describes the arrival in Tarragona in Spain of his train, full of wounded, simultaneous with the departure for the front of another train of troops and artillery pieces. Those of his colleagues in the Workers' Party militia well enough to do so gather at the carriage windows to cheer and whistle; those in the other train, faces smiling, scarves fluttering, gallantly reciprocate the salutes as they draw away. 'It was like an allegorical picture of war,' Orwell recalls. 'The trainload of fresh men gliding proudly up the line, the maimed men sliding slowly down...reviving that pernicious feeling, so difficult to get rid of, that war is glorious after all.'

Orwell was a soldier; he had known men who had died; he had been wounded himself. Yet even this most scrupulously unillusioned of writers could not shake off the feeling he knew to be 'pernicious'. His own war, fleetingly dangerous, often uncomfortable but largely dull, had spared him direct horror; there remained, he was forced to admit, scope for fantasies of combat's nobility. It was Orwell who famously remarked on the 'constant struggle' to 'see what is in front of one's nose'. Further away than that, it seemed, and the seeing grew harder still. One had to look and look hard, insistently and unflinchingly. Which is what lends such force to the caption of Plate 44 in Goya's *Desastres:'Yo lo vi.'*

'I saw this': the words relate specifically to Goya's etching of a column of villagers retreating before the advance of the Peninsular War, which roved over the same countryside as Orwell's war 130 years later. But the assertion could frame the whole series, substantiating the claim for verisimilitude asserted in the work's full title: *Fatales Consequencias de la Sangrienta Guerra en Espana con Buonaparte. Y etros Caprichoes Enfaticos* ('Fatal Consequences of the Bloody War against Bonaparte in Spain. And other Emphatic Caprices'). From 'I saw this', of course, can be inferred qualification elsewhere. To claim eyewitness status in one instance is to imply its absence in others. It also conveys the difficulty of being an observer to the subject matter of *Desastres*, reinforced by the caption to Plate 26, where patriots, in anticipation of Goya's 'The Third of May 1808', crumple before a disembodied firing squad: 'One cannot look'.

How many of the events in *Desastres* that Goya actually 'saw' is the subject of considerable conjecture. It is known, for instance, that the Spanish commander Palafox invited Goya to tour Zargoza after the city's ruinous siege; the toll of the damage was the more meaningful for it being a locality with which Goya was familiar from his youth. For fifteen years or so, we also know, Goya had pioneered the habit of travelling with sketchbooks in which he recorded preliminary impressions; after a while, in the custom of English caricaturists such as James Gillray, he began adding terse, sometimes astringent captions. One caption, accompanying the sketch of a woman on trial for witchcraft in Zaragoza, rehearses the later claim in *Desastres*: 'I saw her.' Her grim fate became the subject of plates 23 ('Those specks of dust') and 24 ('Nothing could be done about it') in *Los Caprichos*.

But *Desastres* also contains scenes to which Goya can hardly have been in proximity. One can hardly conceive of him standing by, sketchbook in hand, recording the grisly work of the lynch mob in Plate 14 ('It's a hard step') and another firing squad in Plate 15 ('And there's no remedy'). Perhaps he read about, was told of or saw the aftermath of the events depicted; the implied caption is: 'I know this.' The female figure aiming the cannon from atop the pyramid of corpses in Plate 7 ('What courage!') is evidently inspired by the lone defiance of the Catalan heroine Agustina of Aragon in defending Zaragoza; the bodies, purportedly, included that of her lover. But how close his depiction hewed to reality is anyone's guess – it would have been Goya's guess also.

In one sense, of course, this is entirely by the way: in no sense does appreciation of *Desastres* depend on certification of Goya's presence and the faithfulness of his transcription. Nor need one know anything of the Peninsular War to share Goya's revulsion of the depravity depicted. Yet there's also no doubt that the plates in *Desastres* are enriched by their status as strivings for realism, works of reportage, of identification with real suffering, of testament to true horror. They were so confronting and unsparing, in fact, that they could not be published for decades after Goya's death; it matters, and Goya knows it, that 'I saw this', if not perhaps everything. He presents as getting out of truth's way, to offer us unimpeded access to the facts. 'With Goya we do not think of the studio or even of the artist at work,' noted Lord Clark. 'We think only of the event.' It is the most artful of deceptions. Robert Hughes called Goya 'the artist who invented a kind of illusion in the service of truth: the illusion of being there when dreadful things happen'.

*Desastres* is regularly described as anticipating, on the eve of the invention of photography, the realm of vivid, camera-can't-lie pictorial journalism. It anticipates this so successfully, I would argue, as also to dramatise this genre's dilemmas – those that arise out of simultaneously extracting authority from claims to authenticity and obtaining memorability from quality of image. Say it soft, but great photographers have never been averse to improving on nature: think of Arthur Rothstein carefully choreographing 'Fleeing a Dust Storm' for *Life*, Walker Evans moving the Alabama sharecroppers' furniture around their sparse cabins for *Let Us Now Praise Famous Men*. Truth being regarded as war's first casualty, there is a long tradition of interpretative scepticism about its photography. Were the cannon balls *really* like that when Roger Fenton found them in the Crimea? Did the marines *really* raise the flag the way Joe Rosenthal depicted them at Iwo Jima? Did Robert Capa's Spanish soldier *really* die? Every photograph from Gaza these days seems to run a conspiracist gauntlet. It caused the documentarian Errol Morris, in his *Believing Is Seeing* (2010), to wonder aloud: 'Why does moralising about 'posing' take precedence over moralising about the carnage of war?'

Even journalism of a non-pictorial nature faces such challenges. Journalists are only very seldom actual eyewitnesses to what they describe. Our business is imaginative reconstruction based on primary documentation, participant testimony and also a balance of probabilities – the 'ring of truth'. We take a lot on trust; we exaggerate the significance of what we know; we minimise and obscure what we do not; we rely, sometimes more than we care to admit, on prejudice. The English journalist Claud Cockburn once observed that the way people speak about 'facts', it was as though they lay around like nuggets in the Klondike, just waiting to be picked up. Nothing worth knowing comes the journalists' way so easily.

But war in particular presents almost insuperable obstacles to its first-hand reporting. The 'front line', reserved by definition for combatants, remains virtually out of reach. Reporting defaults to accenting the interludes of conflict, the befores and afters: soldiers in reserve awaiting deployment or on patrol preliminary to potential engagement; the aftermath of devastation; the chronicling of loss. Within these parameters, pictorial journalism has achieved powerful effects: Matthew Brady's body-strewn Civil War battlefields; Bernard Hoffman's images from the ruins of Hiroshima; Margaret Bourke-White's stark postlude of Buchenwald. But those celebrated images of actual conflict represent a vanishingly small proportion of the overall genre, not least because of their potentially propagandistic content. So emotive were certain images of the Vietnam War – such as Eddie Adams' 'Saigon Execution' and Nick Ut's 'Napalm Girl' – that warring nations have been on guard ever since to prevent their replication. The notorious 'Collateral Murder' video showing the slaying of a dozen people in Baghdad in July 2007 by two Apache helicopters only ever saw the light of day thanks to Wikileaks. The reporting of war, meanwhile, may be wrapped in romance, but it is also practical, and in its way sanitised for our consumption, summed up in the title of Edward Behr's classic memoir: *Anyone Here Been Raped and Speak English?* (1978).

Goya, whether he saw it, or heard it, or knew it, felt no such inhibitions, operated under no such constraints. He faithfully recorded his own forebodings in plate 1 ('Sad presentiments of what is to come'), which in its way is also a last warning to the viewer that what follows will be as pitiless as war itself – and so it is. The Peninsular War was notable for being waged, to a considerable degree, between Napoleon's Grand Armee and local militias who were the first to be known by the name *guerrilla* – the diminutive of *guerra,* Spanish for war. The result was unexampled civilian casualties, reprisals and atrocities; bodies twisted and bundled, as in plates 30 ('The ravages of war') and 60 ('the beds of death'); justice summarily meted out, as in plates 34 ('On account of a knife') and 36 ('Nor in this case); the defilement of bodies as an outlet for savagery and additional sentence on the already dead, as in plates 37 ('This is worse') and 39 ('A heroic feat!'). The tone is as urgent as the content is uncompromisingly explicit. Colour is absent, background minimal, stark effect repeated. And black and white being the traditional hues of war photography, comparison is unavoidable.

Sometimes the visions are so paradigmatic that they seem to prefigure certain canonical images since captured. Plate 15 ('And it cannot be helped') is echoed in Jahangir Razmi's 'Firing Squad in Iran'; Plate 60 ('There is no one to help them') can be felt in Dmitri Baltermants' 'Grief'. More often, however, Goya's scenes await a factual counterpart as compelling as they are. Women other than Agustina of Aragon found themselves involved in the resistance of Napoleon, and Goya was with them, paying tribute in plates 4 ('The women are courageous') and 5 ('And they are fierce'), counting the toll in plates 45 ('And this too') and 50 ('Unhappy mother'). Has there been a more tragic and affecting child in all of art than the bereft little girl in the last of these?

Certainly no photographer and arguably even reporter has so powerfully depicted rape in war as Goya in Plates 9 ('They Don't Want It'), 10 ('Nor do These') and 11 ('Nor those'). Only gradually have we come to an acknowledgement of sexual assault and violation as a battlefield weapon; historians and investigators have slowly identified and documented specially notorious campaigns, in Germany, in Bangladesh, in Bosnia, in Darfur. But the actuality of such horror has continued to elude us. One seemingly breakthrough image that purportedly showed Serbian soldiers raping an Albanian woman in Kosovo during the 1998–99 war was flourished last year by peace activist Flora Brovina – it quickly emerged as a fake downloaded from a pornographic website. In *Desastres*, Goya visualises the weaponising of lust as nobody since; indeed he accords it an importance that has until very recently eluded war's popular chroniclers. 'Truth has died,' Goya mourns over her prone figure in plate 79; she will always need reviving, which requires us to go on bearing witness, there or not, as best we can.

There remains something incomparably raw and rare about *Desastres*; perhaps we should not wonder why. In looking back on the Spanish Civil War, Orwell pointed to conflict's standard division of labour: 'It is the same in all wars; the soldiers do the fighting, the journalists do the shouting, and no true patriot ever gets near a front-line trench, except on the briefest of propaganda tours.' Goya goes on being perhaps the exception that proves this rule.

# THE TRUTH TELLER

## *Vasily Grossman's* Life and Fate *and* A Writer at War (2006)

When the KGB called on Vasily Grossman in February 1961, it was on a mission like no other. They were arresting a book: *Life and Fate*, Grossman's unpublished novel of World War II drawn from experiences as a battlefield correspondent, was to be confiscated; Grossman himself was to be left alone.

The secret police were extraordinarily thorough, taking into custody not only the typescript but also the carbon paper and typewriter ribbons. Yet the writer remained at large, to protest that he had merely written 'absolute truth' – a futile protest, for truth-telling was the essence of his transgression. At a pinch, Grossman was informed, the novel might be publishable in two to three hundred years.

Perhaps the KGB was right that in confining the book, they captured the man. Exhausted, destroyed, Grossman died three years later. Their triumph, nonetheless, was temporary. Two other copies of the manuscript that friends had exhorted Grossman to secrete were spirited to France a decade after his death. Now, a quarter of a century after its first publication in the West, *Life and Fate* has appeared in a splendid new edition, translated by Robert Chandler, and is coupled on the shelves with *A Writer at War: Vasily Grossman with the Red Army 1941–1945*, extracts from Grossman's diaries and frontline reports edited and translated by Antony Beevor and Luba Vinogradova. Like the country in the period they describe, Grossman's works have fought back from the brink of oblivion.

Grossman's oeuvre was itself an act of rescue. Much of *A Writer at War* was written in foxholes, tents, trenches and peasant huts. The eyewitness reports, the fearful descriptions, the interviews with soldiers and civilians of often unexpected depth and eloquence: these are the authentic sights and sounds of what Russians still call the Great Patriotic War that state propaganda, which Grossman mocked as recounting how 'Ivan Pupkin has killed five Germans with a spoon', strained to drown out.

As a journalist for *Red Star*, the Red Army's newspaper, Grossman's actions were more independent than his thoughts. Incomparably brave under fire, he was perhaps even more courageous in recording war's aftermath. Perhaps no writer in history has encountered devastation and suffering on such a scale. How, he wondered often, could he bear witness to these unendurable ordeals? 'Sometimes you are so shaken by what you've seen, blood rushes from your heart,' he reflected. 'And you know that the terrible sight that your eyes have just taken in will haunt you and lie heavy on your soul for the rest of your life. It is strange that when you sit down to write about it, you don't find enough room for it on paper.' His response was a martial sense of responsibility: 'It is the writer's duty to tell this terrible truth, and it is the civilian duty of the reader to learn it.' The prose is dense with detail, accreted to overpowering effect.

Grossman was the first war correspondent to document the horrors of the Shoah, yet his essay 'A Hell Called Treblinka' has hardly been improved on: a painstaking reconstruction that draws the reader through the camp's mechanics, leading them finally to the teeming mass graves:

> The earth is throwing out crushed bones, teeth, clothes, papers. It does not want to keep secrets. And the objects are climbing out from the earth, from its unhealing wounds. Here they are, half-ruined by decay, shirts of the murdered people, their trousers, shoes, cigarette cases which have grown green, little wheels from watches, penknives, shaving brushes, candleholders, a child's shoes with red pompoms, towels with Ukrainian embroidery, lace underwear, scissors, thimbles, corsets, bandages. And a little further on, heaps of plates and dishes have made their way to the surface. And further on – it is as if someone's hand is pushing them up to the light, from the bottomless bulging earth – emerge the things the Germans had tried to bury, Soviet passports, notebooks with Bulgarian writing in them, photographs of children from Warsaw and Vienna, letters scribbled by children, a book of poetry, a prayer copied on a yellowed piece of paper, food ration cards from Germany...A terrible smell of putrefaction hangs over everything, the smell that neither fire, nor sun, rains, snow and winds could dispel...We walk on across the

> bottomless unsteady land of Treblinka and suddenly we stop. Some yellow hair, wavy, fine and light, glowing like brass, is trampled into the earth, and blonde curls next to it, and then heavy black plaits on the light coloured sand, and then more and more. Apparently these are the contents of one – just one – sack of hair which hadn't been taken away. Everything is true. The last lunatic hope that everything was a dream is ruined...And one feels as if one's heart could stop right now, seized with such sorrow that a human being cannot possibly stand it.

Grossman's reportage is the more extraordinary for the fact that the Shoah was an early casualty of the Soviet victory. The war's official version contained no scope for a competing suffering; Stalin, in any case, was an anti-Semite scarcely less vicious than Hitler. *The Black Book of Soviet Jewry*, a documentary account of the Shoah in Russia and Poland on which Grossman worked for three years, was suppressed, then destroyed; Grossman was himself a signature or two from arrest when Stalin died. It was this, and the state's steady reversion to its pre-war brutality, that disillusioned and then radicalised him. He began to understand Stalingrad as a heroic resistance not merely of fascism, but also of the mind-forged manacles of communism.

*Life and Fate* is often catalogued as a war novel. More accurately, its chief protagonist, Viktor Shtrum, and all one hundred of its dramatis personae are responding to tyranny: as its resistors, its servants, its dupes, its victims. In the quarter-century between revolution and war, of course, Russia had been criss-crossed by waves of repression and murder, climaxing in the Great Terror, waged from 1937 against whomever stumbled into its path, taking hundreds of thousands of loyal, innocent and uncomprehending victims, many of whom as their last sentient action signed a confession or pleaded guilty under torture. The Terror's legacy pervades *Life and Fate*, not just in horror and trauma, but also in moral disorientation. 'Innocent people don't get arrested,' states Shtrum's wife, Lyudmila. 'People don't get arrested for nothing,' avers the general, Nyeudobnov. 'Why did they all confess?' wonders the veteran revolutionary, Krymov.

War, then, for all its terrors, is also clarifying, redemptive. Something is worth fighting: fascism. Something is worth dying for: Russia. Even the hero of 1917, Krymov, feels it: 'Sometimes it was as though he were in a kingdom where the party no longer existed; sometimes he felt he was breathing the air of the first days of the revolution.' Shtrum, Grossman's fictional alter ego, cannot believe what he is hearing: 'What power and clarity lies in the word! In the unfettered, carefree word! The word that is still spoken in spite of all one's fears.' Shtrum begins to doubt his friend Sokolov, fictional embodiment of the novelist-turned–Stalinist-hack Ilya Ehrenburg: 'He seemed to accept the anger of the State as other people accept the anger of Nature or the anger of God.'

The state remains a brooding presence, an invisible third party in every conversation, tinging the moments when people reveal their thoughts with danger. Yet the state is also, however momentarily, off balance, more spasmodic in its diligence: there is room to breathe, to think. The ludicrous excesses of Stalin's personality cult are almost occasion for laughter: 'It was as though Stalin himself ploughed fields, forged metal, fed babies in their cradles and handled a machine-gun – while the workers, students and scientists did nothing but pray to him.'

Victory then reveals a deeper horror: that one tyranny has been routed to perpetuate another. Shtrum's work as a physicist is denounced – idiotically, chillingly – for deviating from Lenin's theory of matter. The 'invisible force' of the state reasserts itself: 'He could feel quite tangibly the difference in weight between the fragile human body and the colossus of the state. He could feel the State's bright eyes gazing into his face; any moment now the State would crash down on him; there would be a crack, a squeal – and he would be gone.'

Stalin himself intervenes dramatically, rehabilitating Shtrum by a brief phone call, similar to the one in April 1941 that suborned Ehrenburg. But this entails another sentence; Shtrum's flirtation with freedom of thought ends when he consents, in an agony of self-disgust, to endorse a document condemning innocent colleagues, paralleling the letter Grossman signed in December 1952 supporting harsh punishment of suspects in the fabricated Doctor's Plot.

Krymov, meanwhile, provides the perspective of the falsely denounced. Arrested on trumped-up charges, he nonetheless suffers a 'chilling sense of irreparable guilt', which his cellmate Katsenelenbogen explains: 'The concept of personal innocence is a hangover from the Middle Ages. Pure superstition!...No one in the world is innocent!' So it proves. Krymov's file – 'a word or two about a book he had read, a comic toast he had made on someone's birthday, a three-minute telephone conversation, an angry note he had addressed to the platform at a conference' – sets at nought a lifetime's loyalty.

Again, it is not merely the huge tale that is Grossman's triumph in *Life and Fate*. It is the incidental detail that isn't so incidental, reducing stupendous horrors to human scale without minimising them. The insanities of bureaucracy are glimpsed in Yevgenia Nikolaevna's attempts to obtain a residence permit in Kuibyshev; the inconceivability of the Shoah's toll is understood through the accountant-turned-gravedigger Naum Rozenberg, who copes with his plight by counting the bodies. Grossman's characters, however brief their appearance or slight their apparent influence, never simply act out concepts, or mouth views; they are thrillingly, pulsatingly realised. As their multiple independent narratives subtly cross one another over, questioning and answering, echoing and challenging, the effect is like a whole nation in unconscious conversation. Sokolov's brother-in-law Madyarov thrills and terrifies his circle with a vision of a free press: 'Information! Can you imagine a newspaper like that? A newspaper that provides information!' But the unfree press, personified by the propagandist Sagaydak, isn't budging: 'He himself felt that his power, his skill and experience as an editor were revealed by his ability to bring to the consciousness of readers only those ideas that were necessary and of true educational benefit.'

Life can be barely distinguishable from death, as in the household of Shtrum's mother-in-law: 'All they ever spoke of was food and material things; the world they lived in had room only for objects. There were no human feelings in this world – nothing but boards, paint, millet, buckwheat, thirty-rouble notes.' Yet the brink of death lends life a phosphorescence. As Sofya Levinton, a doctor whose journey to a gas chamber is traced in painstaking detail, reflects: 'It was as though people now understood death, as though it had at last revealed how humdrum it was, how childishly simple.' Grossman himself observes: 'A man cannot believe that he is about to be destroyed. The optimism of people standing on the edge of the grave is astounding.'

Likewise, perhaps, the optimism of a reader on finishing *Life and Fate* – but it is palpable. For all its terrors and torments, its perishable hopes and endless sorrows, *Life and Fate* is a triumph of humanism; to delve so deeply into freedom, tyranny and moral corruption in these relentlessly trivial times is to be reminded of the transformative power of literature. Grossman held fast to hope: 'Man does not renounce freedom voluntarily.' He barely sampled that freedom; we should bless the day his novel did.

# THE TRUTH TELLER 2

## *Vasily Grossman's* Stalingrad (2019)

Among colleagues in the ranks of Soviet war correspondents, Vasily Grossman was known for narrow shaves and fortunate escapes. Once, a grenade landed between his feet and failed to explode; on another occasion, a shell punched a hole in a boat he was travelling on, and he used his greatcoat to plug the hole. Myopic and unathletic, he routinely stumbled past death, earning the nickname 'Lucky Grossman'.

The epithet might have applied more generally. Born in the year of Bloody Sunday and the October Manifesto, dying in the year Khruschev was deposed, surviving the bloodiest decades in human history despite the high-risk identity of Jewish Soviet intellectual, Grossman did well to live long enough to die of cancer in Moscow fifty-five years ago.

The toll was instead borne by his work, including three postwar fictions informed by his wartime experiences: *For a Just Cause* (1952) was execrated, suppressed and censored; *Life and Fate* (1961) was deemed unpublishable by the KGB; his last-gasp novella *Everything Flows* (1964) was left incomplete.

Twenty years ago, however, Grossman was introduced to a new, Western readership by the publication of Antony Beevor's bestselling account of the five-month battle for Stalingrad where Russian and German armies sustained two million deaths. Having scattered *Stalingrad* (1998) with selections from Grossman's incomparably vivid frontline despatches for *Red Star*, Beevor edited a collection, *A Writer at War* (2005), including his reportage of Nazi atrocities at Berdichev and Treblinka.

A still more ambitious project was even then underway: a series of stunning translations by the American husband-and-wife team of Robert and Elizabeth Chandler, beginning with *Life and Fate* (2006) – a book that in George Steiner's view eclipses 'almost all that passes for serious fiction in the west today'. *Everything Flows* followed (2011); between times the Chandlers also translated and collected some of Grossman's short stories in *The Road*

(2010) and travel writing in *Armenian Notebook* (2012). With this publication of the first English language edition of *For a Just Cause*, under Grossman's original title of *Stalingrad*, the scale of the Chandlers' achievement can be seen.

So extensively was the novel manhandled for ideological compliance that there is no single version of *Stalingrad*; the Chandlers have had to reconstruct it, often by recourse to Grossman's original notebooks and correspondence with publishers. The result is nothing short of a vindication of the power of literature even amid the worst of the twentieth century, during the clash of its most democidal ideologies. Might Grossman be the finest novelist of the twentieth century? The claim can finally be seriously examined.

Although it arrives now as a kind of prequel to *Life and Fate*, *Stalingrad* was originally the first volume of a dilogy featuring many of the same characters, chiefly the family Shaposhnikova, the ebullient physicist Viktor Shtrum and the austere commissar Nikolay Krymov. A useful appendix enumerates no fewer than 150 named participants.

What is *Stalingrad's* relation to *Life and Fate*? The novels form part of the same continuum; they are also clearly distinguishable, partly because of the politics prevailing during their creation. After his reports of the Shoah during World War II, Grossman was recruited to the cause of the Jewish Anti-Fascist Committee: a group of writers dedicated to documenting Jewish suffering on the eastern front. When a recrudescence of Soviet anti-semitism at war's end put paid to what had become *The Black Book of Soviet Jewry*, Grossman grew circumspect. To his later shame, he appended a self-preserving signature to a petition calling for draconian punishment of the innocent accused in the so-called Jewish Doctors' Plot – Stalin's final paranoid rage.

Written in the 1940s, then, *Stalingrad* falls in with the postwar climate of patriotic self-celebration: the imposed title was from a speech by Molotov. Characters were added to enhance its ideological purity, such as Shtrum's academician boss Chepyzhin, because a Jew could not enjoy too conspicuous an authority, and the invincible Donbass coal miner Novikov, who provides wholesome affirmation of the ennobling properties of labour.

Yet Grossman worked with this grain to remarkable, subtly coded, effect.

Chepyzhin, the Chandlers advise, seems to have been partly based on Lev Shtrum, a former university lecturer of Grossman's liquidated in the Great Terror. There is also a heart-stopping scene where Viktor Shtrum receives an account written by his mother of her last days in the Jewish ghetto of Berdichev prior to the infamous September 1941 massacre – which in real life numbered Grossman's mother among its 30,000 victims. It being impossible to write of the Shoah, Grossman made overt his not writing about it. Instead of relating the letter's contents, he has Shtrum slip it into his jacket pocket, and later occasionally touch it. It will be unfolded at last in *Life and Fate*.

*Stalingrad* also mimics the development of the eastern front in operating at ever decreasing distances. In the first half, the Germans sweep on relentlessly, the Russian front is in constant collapse. Shtrum is described preparing for a train journey to Moscow as though undertaking an expedition. Krymov is glimpsed changing his headquarters' ordnance survey maps almost daily. War, Grossman reports, pursued the fleeing Red Army like a 'dark shadow'.

> Those who retreated brought the war with them, close on their heels. The vast spaces to the east were a dangerous lure. The limitlessness of the Russian steppes was treacherous; it seemed to offer the possibility of escape, but this was an illusion.
>
> The retreating troops came to peaceful orchards and villages. The peace and quiet were a joy to them – but an hour or a day later the black dust, the flames and thunder of war would burst in after them. The troops were bound to the war by a heavy chain, and no retreat could snap this chain; the further they retreated, the heavier the chain grew and the more tightly it bound them.

Krymov is then seen, at a critical and allegorical moment, fighting his way to Stalingrad through a crossing teeming with retreating soldiers and desperate refugees: 'Here, on this bridge, Krymov at once sensed his own power – the power of a man going slowly and calmly west when everyone else is going east.' As the city of Stalingrad is at last besieged and bombarded, the action condenses to streets, corners, even rooms.

> The bombs reached the ground and plunged into the city. Buildings began to die, just as people die. Tall, thin houses toppled to one side, killed on the spot; stockier, sturdier houses trembled and swayed, their chests and bellies gashed open and exposing what had always been hidden from view: portrait on walls, cupboards, double beds, bedside tables, jars of millet, a half-peeled potato on a table covered with an ink-stained oilcloth.

Death stalks this suddenly alien landscape, but also life, in the soldiers Grossman knew from his journalism – dogged, earthy, fatalistic, unillusioned. Vavilov, Filyashkn, Shevdkov, Kovalyov: we come to know them all. 'What strength, what sadness,' Grossman writes. 'And what emptiness around these men.'

Grossman is concerned in *Stalingrad* chiefly to indict fascism, which he submits to ambitious study, even bringing us into the presence of Hitler, first lording it over Mussolini, later lecturing an obsequious Himmler. In a lengthy disquisition, Grossman summarises fascism as 'a rebellion against millennia of human history', in being 'a challenge to mankind's humanistic prejudices'. It was not open to Grossman, of course, to identify similar propensities in communism. *Stalingrad* is free of Gulags and devoid of secret police, while the desiccation of Soviet bureaucracy is only briefly embodied, in Lt Col Zvezdyukhin:

> 'We need documents. Nothing can be determined without documents.'
>
> He gave particular weight to word *documents*. Against the background of his habitual monotone the word sounded almost succulent.

The sole anti-regime voice is a drunken village peasant nostalgic for tsarism, who to the passing Krymov wants 'to speak freely…about everything that had been forbidden', and whose warning hangs heavily: 'There are young men who think the same as me, and there are old men who think the same as me. You're not going to be able to shoot all of us.' Again, the state will bulk more darkly in *Life and Fate*: Krymov will become a victim of the party he has so selflessly served, and Shtrum be forced into strike a devil's bargain like Grossman's during the Jewish Doctor's Plot.

Does this make *Stalingrad* a lesser achievement than *Life and Fate?* It is certainly narrower, less even, more inhibited. Grossman was clearly aching for the thaw on thought that the ascension of Khrushchev fleetingly promised. Grossman would snatch at it – in the instant, overeagerly. At the same time, *Stalingrad* has the breadth of humanity and depth of sympathy that the scale of Soviet sacrifice called for. Only after first attending to the Russian people could Grossman take up his quarrel with the ideology and institutions that had enslaved them. He was here less lucky than he had been on the battlefield. The luck instead is now ours.

# THE WAR LESS THOUGHT

## *A review of Les Carlyon's* The Great War *(2007)*

It was said of World War I that it was two wars in one: the war fought, and the war spoken. To this has since been added the war written. 'There are, of course, far too many books about the First World War,' wrote Niall Ferguson, at the beginning of his own, *The Pity of War* (1998) – a book actually rather more necessary than most. But the impulse is understandable: as a subject, World War I can dismay and inspire, horrify and excite. Such waste; such valour. Such dumb obedience; such nobility and sacrifice.

It is, in Australia, also History with a capital H: the good stuff, uplifting, nutritious. And history is, hereabouts, an increasingly politicised domain, so many of our great national debates being appeals to the past, both real and imagined. One suspects that Les Carlyon, arguably the outstanding Australian journalist cum writer of his generation, is a slightly uneasy conscript in these latter-day History Wars. His magisterial *Gallipoli* (2001), perhaps the best and certainly the most successful work of Australian history since Robert Hughes's *The Fatal Shore* (1987), has been seized upon by conservatives as an antidote to all that po-mo persiflage corrupting impressionable minds in our excuse for a university system. His new book, *The Great War,* was launched by the prime minister, who called it an 'epic work of Australian history', and hymned its 'beautiful style'.

That it certainly has, with hardly a page passing that is not distinguished by Carlyon's flair for either keen observation or the pungent putdown, whether he is seeing Field-Marshal Haig 'laced up so tightly that in all his photographs he seems to be holding his breath' or damning Kitchener as having 'failed to live up to the promise he had never shown'. It is characterised not only by immense, almost religious fidelity to its primary sources of letters, diaries and eyewitness accounts of devastation and courage, but also by temperate, fair-minded judgements. And yet. And yet. The sum of such parts should be a far greater whole.

The problems of *The Great War* begin there: with the title. For this is not the story of the Great War at all; it is the story of Australian involvement in the Western Front between 1916 and 1918. And this story does not shape itself: unlike Gallipoli, where the action was naturally condensed by time and geography, the Western Front was huge, sprawling; unstable one minute, uneventful the next; manned by the armies of many nations, answering to a host of faraway commanders, beholden themselves to crowned heads and cabinets. Any chronicler must define and contain their sphere of operations, and this Carlyon seems loath to do. If anything, the opposite is true: he regularly widens the focus to include glimpses of distant diplomatic salons and political putsches, from Lloyd George, Clemenceau, Wilson and Hughes through Foch, Petain, Ludendorff and Hindenburg to the likes of Lenin, Hitler, Ho Chi Minh, Goering, Macarthur, Patton and Truman, who bear hardly at all on the core narrative. These digressions are neither vivid nor weighty enough to justify their distorting effect: like Haig himself, Carlyon struggles to sustain activity across too long a front, bending his narrative out of shape so as to include observations that Truman cursed like a mule trader and that Lenin had a 'vaulting forehead and withering glare'.

This is anomalous, because Carlyon at other times makes the opposite case, and convincingly: that lines of communication were so articulated and prone to rupture in battle that men were often on their own, lost in the proverbial 'fog of war'. 'Misinformation flowed up this line and back down it,' he notes. 'Everyone in the chain of command wanted to give the impression that they actually knew what was happening behind the smoke some of them couldn't even see. None wanted to be thought timid.' To the quotidian life of the digger, then, what Haig thought, or what time he had breakfast, is of distinctly secondary importance, while the shape of Lenin's forehead is of no moment whatsoever. The logical corollary of this would be to ignore or circumscribe reference to as much of the macro history as possible. Instead, by telescoping back and forth so freely, from the fate of the liberal democracy to an Australian blowing up a pillbox, Carlyon fosters the illusion of direct connection, from which a false totality emerges.

The most stirring writing in *The Great War* is the work of the soldiers themselves, still stunning in its immediacy, and far more varied in content than might be imagined. It is breathtaking, for instance, to be able to read the scribbled thoughts of Corporal Arthur Thomas under bombardment at Pozières:

> For Christ's sake write a book on the life of an infantryman & by doing so you will quietly prevent these shocking tragedies...I have seen things here that will make the bloody Military aristocrats' name stink forever.
>
> [11am]...hundreds of shells from big 12-inch howitzers are being fired at us. God! It is cruel. What humans will stand is astonishing.
>
> [1.30pm]...I turned my head sharply right & saw a decapitated man – one of ours. It is bloody gruesome – ah well, it will soon end – this awful game. Plenty of lives – just gun fodder. Our casualties are very heavy... This is truly the Valley of the Shadows – God help us.

Likewise, it is bracing to encounter Private Jimmy Downing, blood and dander up, after Villers-Brettoneux:

> We were Beserk, every one of us...There was no quarter. I remember bayoneting one Hun, a square fair solid fellow, and one old score was paid off. The bayonet passed right through his heart with surprising ease... One came to a machine-gun post which kept firing at us till we were on it & then surrendered. It was no use, this man said: 'How many of you are there? Oh six. Then share that among you' and he dropped a bomb among them...'Now you've got your issue'...I saw Hun running away. I shot one Dead. The rest disappeared in the gloom. The killing went on. I was mad. There was blood all over my rifle & bayonet & hands and all...I wouldn't have missed it for anything. We settled many an old score.

To my mind, however, *The Great War* does not interrogate its primary material nearly enough. Since Bill Gammage used letters and journals to such impressive analytical effect in *The Broken Years* (1974), they have been the staff of life to scholars. Carlyon tends to let them speak for themselves: a laudable notion, but also reducing them to postcards in a travelogue, vivid but superficial.

Consider the questions that might arise from the foregoing. In Arthur Thomas's diary, bitter fury is mingled with religious resignation. Yet nowhere in *The Great War* is it acknowledged that Australia in 1916 was a religiously observant country, and fought on explicitly Christian principles backed by militarist churchmen. 'A good chaplain,' philosophised Haig, 'is as valuable as a good general.' Nor, of course, were the Australians on their own. Wittgenstein famously enlisted in the Austrian Army on the war's first day, believing it would make him a better man: 'Now I have a chance to be a decent human being, for I'm standing eye to eye with death...Perhaps the nearness to death will bring light into life. God enlighten me.'

What humans will stand, as Thomas observed, *is* astonishing. *The Great War* doesn't really postulate how the diggers did so, beyond that Australians were a hardy race, brought up with good, old-fashioned Victorian values: 'Stoicism was a virtue, so one pretended to enthusiasm even if trembling inside.' Jimmy Downing, among others, hints at a dimension of war that Carlyon leaves unacknowledged: the exhilarations of martial life, its opportunities for masculine validation and for individual freedom. He approvingly, if awkwardly, invokes Freud in the context of shellshock: 'The Victorian mind was suspicious of this condition. Sigmund Freud's *The Interpretation of Dreams* had only appeared sixteen years earlier.' But what of Freud's contention, in 'Thoughts for the Times on War and Death' (1915), that war reasserted 'the primal man', sweeping away the 'conventional treatment of death', revealing that 'our unconscious is just as...murderously minded towards the stranger, as divided or ambivalent towards the loved, as was man in earliest antiquity'? A similar argument has been made more recently by the Dutch-Israeli military historian Martin van Creveld; as he puts it in *Transformations of War* (1991): 'However unpalatable the fact, the real reason we have wars is that men like fighting.' After all, the canonical works of World War I include Rupert Brooke as well as Wilfred Owen, Ernst Jünger as well as Erich Maria Remarque.

The canon also contains, especially for Australians, Frederic Manning's *The Middle Parts of Fortune* (1929): Carlyon cites it appreciatively as 'one of the most stylish pieces of writing to come out of the war'. Yet Carlyon's book lacks the insight in Manning's title, a citation from *Hamlet* conveying how most soldiers felt most of the time: not great, not bad, not shooting or being shot at, but not completely safe either. In *The Great War,* battle follows battle, commanders bungle, soldiers die and valour is measured out in thickness of Victoria Crosses, which Carlyon acknowledges are inequitably distributed, but to which he remains in thrall, rather as movie buffs scoff at the Oscars but can't help cheering. It's magnificent – to borrow from Marshal Bosquet in another context – but it's not war, for the Australian soldier revealed as much about himself in repose as in conflict.

At the end, too, Carlyon rather squibs the verdict, even where Haig is concerned: having been depicted mostly as a blimp and a dunce, he is finally credited with a 'profound sense of duty'. Arguments about the point of the war are then dismissed rather airily: 'It is fashionable to argue that the Allies, particularly Britain and her dominions, fought the Great War for nothing of value. If they had not fought…human progress would have been turned back to the absolutism of pre-Enlightenment times.' These arguments – made, incidentally, by Niall Ferguson – that war was avoidable, futile and 'the great error of modern history', deserve better than the blithe and rather prime ministerial backhander 'fashionable'. It smacks uncomfortably of intellectual timidity, incongruous in a writer of Carlyon's generally unflagging humanity. Perhaps, in Australia, we now need a fourth war: in addition to the wars fought, spoken and written, a war thoroughly thought.

# THE GENERATION GAME

## *Saving the National Archives* (2021)

The novelist and critic Alexis Wright, celebrated for her panoramic narratives of indigenous life in the far north, recently had a remarkable encounter.

For years she had known of a Chinese great grandfather who had arrived in the Territory late in the nineteenth century and married into the Waanyi people; then one day, miraculously digitised by the National Archives of Australia, she saw him. A full-face photo, a side profile, a hand print, along with biographical information gleaned by a long-forgotten bureaucrat. It was, she says, 'an enormously important gift to our family'.

It's one reason why Wright last week was among more than 150 signatories of an open letter drafted by Graeme Davison, emeritus professor of history at Monash University, calling for a better deal for the National Archives of Australia, which since 2015 has suffered an annual appropriation decrease of nearly $9 million and shed approximately a fifth of its staff. The self-styled 'memory of the nation' is at risk of subsiding into dementia.

The provocation for the campaign was an appearance at senate estimates by assistant Attorney-General Amanda Stoker on 27 May. 'Time marches on,' Stoker said airily, deprecating reports of decaying records as 'part of the ageing process', studiously indifferent to projections that nearly all the NAA's holdings of film and magnetic tape will be irretrievably damaged by 2025.

NAA was already a byword among historians for collapsing standards of service, swingeing copying costs, atrocious delays, and a worseningly opaque secrecy, manifest in last year's pointless and expensive fight to prevent the Palace Letters becoming public. Now its minister was dismissing the loss of records from entirely avoidable lack of care as 'business as usual'.

So Davison and I started seeking supporters. No luvvies. No Twitter windsocks. Only individuals with a substantial commitment to the written word, printed document and institutional memory, and reflecting all shades of politics and belief. These included two Nobel laureates (Peter Doherty,

J. M. Coetzee), three Australians of the Year (Doherty, Sir Gustav Nossal, Fiona Stanley), winners of the Windham-Campbell for non-fiction (Helen Garner, Maria Tumarkin), of the Booker Prize (Tom Keneally) and the Miles Franklin for fiction (Wright, Tim Winton, Tara June Winch), not to mention a score of winners of the Prime Minister's own awards.

They were joined by the last two director-generals of NAA (Ross Gibbs and George Nichols), the previous director-general of the National Library (Jan Fullerton) and a patron of Victoria's Public Records Office who also happens to have been a Liberal premier (Ted Baillieu). Likewise compelled were a former NSW Chief Justice (Jim Spigelman), two former justices of Victoria's Supreme Court (Stephen Charles and David Harper). Academic ranks were swelled by the Australian-born Regius Professors of History at Cambridge and Oxford (Sir Christopher Clark and Lyndal Roper); there are Australian educators at universities in the UK, Europe, the US and China, plus official historians of the Vietnam War (Peter Edwards) and ASIO (David Horner).

Biographers of Alfred Deakin, Malcolm Fraser and Sir John Gorton mingle on the list with biographers of Gough Whitlam, John Curtin and Paul Keating. Stan Grant and Henry Reynolds are shoulder-to-shoulder with John Carroll and Paul Santamaria; Jenny Hocking is at one with Troy Bramson. Archives have never been a partisan issue in Australia. What they have required has been imagination and initiative.

In June 1920, on the site of the projected Capitol of the mooted capital at the foot of Kurrajong Hill, the Prince of Wales laid a polished granite commemoration stone for a structure in which would be 'enshrined the records of Australian achievement and the archives of the nation'. It was reported that the ceremony's legacy would be 'preserved in history for future generations of Australians'.

It wasn't. The building never materialised; the stone disappeared; for another four decades, Commonwealth record keeping was, haphazardly, the domain of the Parliamentary Library. Only sixty years ago was the Commonwealth Archive Office, NAA's forerunner, finally peeled away, forming part of the great Menzian legacy of collecting institutions, bracketed by the National Library and the National Gallery.

Archives had a innate appeal to Menzies, who argued that those ignorant of history could have 'no sense of proportion' and 'no benefit of experience in dealing with new problems as they arise'; records offered a guide to 'what errors were made and should be avoided' in future.

Archives, in fact, are paradoxically forward-looking institutions. Their creation gestures to confidence in a country's future – a prediction that there will be great things worth recording and bad things worth pondering, even if these may initially be difficult to distinguish. For it is impossible to foresee all the ways a record may become relevant. As Davison put it in his letter, NAA's 'most important users are not yet born'.

Consider NAA: SP605/7, 1951/2058, which is the seventy-year-old butt of a certificate of exemption from the provisions of the Immigration Act, number 512058, for an officially 'stateless' seven-year-old girl, Erika Strausz. It was on this condition of 'statelessness' that Erika's son, treasurer Josh Frydenberg, relied last year when his eligibility to sit in parliament was challenged in the Federal Court. He could find the relevant document with a few keystrokes, like I did.

Yet in his recent budget, Frydenberg did no more than continue NAA on the short rations of the preceding decade, during which it has fallen ever further behind its mission, despite recommendations of not one but two recent reports. Presented in February 2019, the Inquiry into Canberra's National Institutions deemed NAA fundamental to 'conserving, interpreting and facilitating engagement with Australia's history, culture and national identity', and among its recommendations acknowledged 'the need for the digitisation of analogue audio-visual items in the collections of the institutions, to ensure that all such material is digitally preserved by 2025'. So that's gone well.

For the last eighteen months the government has also been sitting on the Functional and Efficiency Review of NAA, which it disgorged only after repeated FOI requests from Senator Rex Patrick – perhaps because its author, respected former finance secretary David Tune, did not give them what they wanted.

In Tune's searching review, enriched by more than 100 submissions, words recur like 'struggle', 'limited', 'long response times' and 'resources are needed'. To 'stay contemporary in the digital age', Tune concluded, would require substantial investment. He stressed the urgency of a seven-year program for the digitisation of at-risk records, at the additional cost of $67 million albeit spread over seven years – in budgetary terms barely a rounding error.

But where the government is lavishing $500 million on superceding a celebrated twenty-year-old building at the Australian War Memorial, NAA has been reduced to rolling out a half-baked membership programme so far raising a meagre $30,000. For this 'new way', seemingly a stalking horse for an ideological drive to fund NAA by philanthropy, Stoker professed great enthusiasm: 'It's about public engagement. It's about active citizenship, by participating and understanding what the archives do.'

It's not and she doesn't. NAA is not a gallery, museum or concert hall, which lend themselves readily to corporate largesse; it is not a prime ministerial photo opportunity or a marginal seat winner. It is, in the first instance, a backstop of government, a promotor of good governance, and nowadays a pillar of cyber-security, whose function only then is to 'encourage, facilitate, publicise and sponsor the use of archival material'.

Tune draws attention in his review to conclusions of the Royal Commission into Institutional Responses to Child Sexual Abuse that poor record-keeping and information sharing was a factor in failing to thwart offenders. That is precisely why NAA falls into Stoker's bailiwick rather than being part of the arts portfolio; that is why NAA has an advisory council chaired by a 76-year-old Queensland Liberal Party retainer with a fondness for family history, Denver Beanland, rather than a board with top-end-of-town connections.

Stoker is right to suggest that the subsidising of a public good by private interests would represent 'an enormous transformation of the way we do archives in this country'. It would also be an extremely bad transformation, a stealth privatisation of the national story, not to mention almost certainly unfeasible: Tune has already concluded that such course 'would not yield significant income', and involve the expenditure of almost as much as was made.

Let's be clear. To wilfully let irreplaceable archival records decay is not a passive response to 'the ageing process'. It is an unpersoning; it is, if you like, a cancellation. It is, arrogantly, to stand in for posterity, to say that this or that will never matter to anyone for any reason. To invest in archives, by contrast, is to honour our historic endowments, to make a gift to our descendants, and to have sufficient faith in our own bona fides that we are prepared to abide their judgement. We took forty years to commit to Australian archives and sixty years to nurture them. On present trends, this government will undermine them irrevocably in the next five.

NB: A few weeks after the publication of this j'accuse, the federal government picked up the gauntlet our campaign had thrown down by committing $67.7 million in emergency funding to the National Archives of Australia. It's at least a start on repairing the damage wrought by a decade of neglect.

# TOTALLY WIRED

## *Wire's* Object 47 (2008)

*Live at the Roxy London WC2 (Jan–Apr 77)*, one of punk's indispensable curios, begins much as you'd expect, with three tracks of phlegm-flecked mindlessness from Slaughter & The Dogs and The Unwanted – bands as boneheaded as their names. Then there's a drawling voice, gentle but insistent: 'Pay attention...we're Wire.' The tone is of advice rather than demand, and rather fails to register. The band lurch into the low-fi drone of 'Lowdown', restarting every time they seem about to stop: 'Another cigarette / Another day / From A to B / Again avoiding C, D and E.' Finally, they grind to a halt, almost arbitrarily, amid uncomprehending silence. No applause. No cheers. Somewhere, a bottle can be heard smashing.

The attention has been a long time coming. Last month, 150 bands strutted seven stages over two days in Hainault Forest, near London, during the sprawling Offset Festival, a showcase mainly for young hipsters like The Maccabees and The Young Knives. Top of the bill were Wire, with a new album to spruik, *Object 47*. Covered over the years by performers from REM and Henry Rollins to fIREHOSE and the New Bomb Turks, they now find themselves being name-checked by bands whose members were not even born at Wire's 1985 reunion, let alone their 1977 inception. For long-term fans, it's a slightly odd feeling, like being a lifelong lover of quilting, then learning that Paris Hilton is to base a reality-television show on her new besottedness with appliqué.

*Object 47*, so named for being the forty-seventh item in Wire's catalogue, is disarmingly smooth and fluid; a compact, melodic, egg-headed 35 minutes, with lyrics full of bleak, dry humour. Which invites a musing: how many bands 31 years after their first recordings are bothering with new material, new directions, and so obviously aiming primarily to satisfy themselves in the process? For unlike the host of 1970s bands revived by their members for superannuation purposes, Wire still play like they mean you to pay attention.

The night I saw Wire on a flying visit to Melbourne's Corner Hotel, a few years ago, started wretchedly. I arrived with a friend during the performance of a support band so self-consciously apathetic that I couldn't be bothered learning their names – lucky for them. Wire then took the stage, somewhat inauspiciously, the four members in their fifties and looking it. Vocalist Colin Newman could have been an academic from a Malcolm Bradbury novel; guitarist Bruce Gilbert so resembled the English tourist of imagination that he should have been wearing one of those zip-up moneybags around his waist. To be sure, you'd have avoided burly bass player Graham Lewis if you'd glimpsed him on the Tube, imagining him on the way to manning a door at a nightclub; but drummer Robert Grey (AKA Robert Gotobed) would have looked more at home pottering round his vegetable garden. So, there they were: Wire. If they'd turned up for karaoke, you'd have been embarrassed for them.

The night remains one of the most cherished memories of my music-going life. Wire burst into tracks from their latest release, *Send* (2003), whose power-packed rhythms took the band's sound to the brink of techno, and absolutely nailed them. Newman commanded the stage with a kind of owlish charisma; the sonic wallop of Gilbert's guitar reverberated off the walls. After three songs, my friend and I exchanged excited glances. They were good. They were *so* good. In the second half of the set, Wire started picking at random from their first three albums, *Pink Flag*, *Chairs Missing* and *154*. Nor were these easy-listening singalongs for the fans, but big, beaty, pumped-up and punked-up, as though the songs had been written the week before, not during the Queen's Silver Jubilee. It was only as the band members sloped off the stage that they looked a little senior for all this excitement, ready for bed and a Horlicks. The mood in the audience was not just ecstatic but validated. I bought a T-shirt, which when it quickly disintegrated was converted by an artful girlfriend into a toiletries bag. Not everyone can say they think about Wire every time they shave.

Wire's story, in fact, is also partly that of its fans. *Pink Flag* remains Wire's masterpiece and manifesto. Here, the 35 minutes were jammed with 21 songs, some as short as jingles, all pared back to the essentials. Wire were grouped with punk because of their minimalism, but it was a minimalism of deliberate austerity rather than self-conscious crudity. Arts students in Watford, the band members tackled their songs as art projects: the title track is an attempt to rewrite 'Johnny B Goode' using one chord; '106 Beats That' is an effort to write a 100-syllable lyric. At the time, in the way of these things, *Pink Flag* achieved neither commercial success nor critical acclaim. But if you bought it, you played it incessantly, and today no album from 1977 sounds so starkly, uncompromisingly modern.

*Chairs Missing* (1978) and *154* (1979) smoothed off some of Wire's rougher edges: the lyrics to 'Outdoor Miner' were inspired by a wildlife documentary about a burrowing insect, but its gleaming pop surface conveyed it to the lower reaches of the charts. It wasn't to last. When their next release centred on one 15-minute song and featured solo-performance art pieces by each band member, their label sent them packing with the timeless censure: 'EMI is not the Arts Council.'

Which left the fans, often quite oblivious to one another's existence and the more ardent for it. Wire were taken up, improbably, by the hardcore 'straight edge' movement, disinclined to artistic flourishes, but similarly minimal in their methods: in *Our Band Could Be Your Life* (2001), Michael Azerrad describes an early Minor Threat gig at which all seven bands on the bill performed a Wire song. Wire became the choice, too, of indie connoisseurs: in 1987 alone, REM performed 'Strange' on *Document*, Big Black issued a thunderous 'Heartbeat' on *Headache*, and the Rollins Band (as Henrietta Collins & The Wifebeating Childhaters) amped up 'Ex-Lion Tamer' on *Drive By Shooting*. These were, moreover, covers as genuine tributes, quite moving – at least to other Wire aficionados – in their sincerity and fidelity.

Wire's members had by now resumed collaborating in a series of projects that brought them into the general vicinity of industrial music, albeit that songs as arch as 'Kidney Bingos' and 'Eardrum Buzz' were funnier and cleverer than anything perpetrated by Coil or Nine Inch Nails. From this regeneration came more fans, and the impetus for the compilation *Whore* (1996), on which 21 performers covered a favoured Wire cut, including My Bloody Valentine's living, loving take on 'Map Ref 41°N 93°W'.

Curiously, though, Wire seems to have come even more firmly into its own over the last little while, having outlived the era of all-powerful major labels and a slavishly fashion-conscious music press, and into one where distribution is chiefly electronic and fan bases are connected as never before. I've bought the live album *The Scottish Play* (2004), *Read & Burn 03* (2007) and *Object 47* from the band's website, www.pinkflag.com, which also directs visitors to an email newsletter, a MySpace page and an online forum. When a band with the loyal following of a Wire seeks attention today, it has a host of ways of keeping it.

# THE PURSUIT OF USEABLE BEAUTY

## *A profile of Damien Wright* (2009)

Every so often, Damien Wright will down tools to work on his computer, answer emails, update files. It's okay. He can do it. For a day, anyway – maybe two. Then his back will begin to ache, his eyes to tire, and he will get ever-so-slightly nervous. He struggles to explain how he became, without a minute's formal training behind him, perhaps Australia's most successful solo woodworker: 'I just figured it out, really. Turned out I could do it.' But he understands why he perseveres: 'Emotionally I need it. It answers a need in me...to make.'

Wright is speaking in his workshop in Northcote, and proving difficult to interview. Not because he is inarticulate – on the contrary, he speaks with unfaltering adamance. But he is visibly restless. He drops into a rocking chair. He moves to his office. He ascends a ladder. He orbits three giant slabs of walnut on his bench, appraising it with eye and hand, thinking aloud about the trend in craft to separation of design and manufacture. 'I can't make that separation – which commercially is to my detriment,' he explains. 'I design as I make and I make as I design, and I think if you separate them then you stop adapting to the timber, which you learn to read in the way you learn to read anything.' He pauses, peering into the walnut, with a half-smile: 'I see stuff in this that's just wicked.'

On 2 February 2009, one of Wright's most ambitious projects entered the service of another ambitious project: a bar table for the new Koori County Court in Morwell. Around it will be tried indigenous offenders, in consultation with aboriginal community and family members – a model that has successfully slashed recidivism rates in the Magistrates Court, although untested elsewhere in Australia in a court of this seniority. The Victorian country town is a world away from justice's highest counsels, the courtroom's picture window framing the eight smoke stacks of Hazelwood power station. Yet at the inauguration last November, the table was the show-stopper:

simple from a distance, intricate up close, caressed by guests with furtive delight. 'People walked in, and just went: "Wow",' says County Court CEO Evi Kadar. A DVD showing scenes from its making was watched in quiet obedience. So *that* was how they did it?

This is how.

*

It was a chance commission. Four years ago, Kadar's predecessor Neil Twist, walking Plenty Road with his partner, stopped at a window to admire a vase. It was the window of a factory front behind which Wright then had his workshop. Twist and Wright got to talking: Twist was looking for a bed; Wright offered his services, and crafted a frame of laminated sassafras and silverwood.

In September 2006, Rozenes and Andrew Jackamos of the Department of Justice's indigenous affairs unit convened a conference at the Koori Heritage Trust at which judges, corrections officers and tribal elders considered a Koori County Court. Rozenes argued that the idea needed some sort of physical form; Twist offered Wright's name. As it happened, an example of Wright's craftsmanship was readily to hand: four years earlier, he had made a new lectern for Courtroom 1 of the Federal Court.

The lectern was of a unique wood: ancient redgum, from the Murray of 10,000 years ago. This provenance had appealed to Chief Justice Michael Black, who explained at its first silking ceremony: 'It is symbolic of the ancient land that we share and it is also symbolic of the excellence to which we all aspire in our respective callings.' Exactly, concurred his fellow judge. 'You walk into the Koori courts at magistrates level, and the bar tables are inconspicuous,' says Kadar. 'Here, the table was in the budget from the beginning. Although we weren't sure what, we wanted something really special.'

Still, the commission almost did not proceed. By the time Wright came to meet the project manager and architect a month later, the deal had somehow changed. Neither was interested, nor really understood, the ancient redgum. They wanted a straightforward table of American oak, a plantation wood favoured for its connotations of sustainability. Wright sighed: 'I said, "Look, this isn't for me. I can direct you to a good joiner, but this isn't what I'm interested in.'" He rang Twist to extricate himself from the project. Twist wouldn't let him.

> Neil says: 'OK, what would you do?' And because I'd been thinking about it, I came out with it straight away. I said: 'I'd make a 4.5m ancient redgum table. Jet black. So that everyone who came into the court had to acknowledge what it was: 10,000 years old. So that a place that's all about protocol and precedent contains an object 8000 years before the idea of common law. That acknowledges this is an ancient place, but also one that needs to be rearticulated, and to defer to the hierarchies of the court.' Neil says: 'That's exactly what we want. Let's start again.'

*

Wright is fond of saying that he 'lets the wood do the talking' – this wood had a lot to say. The simple designation 'gum' harks back to April 1770, when Cook named 'Botany Bay' in recognition of 'the great quantity of plants' visible from the *Endeavour,* including trees exuding a 'reddish gum'. 'Most of the trees were gum trees,' noted Joseph Banks after returning from Thirsty Sound three weeks later, fusing the words forever.

The redgum *eucalyptus camaldulensis* embodies the confusion of European templates laid across the unknown land. The genus eucalyptus was compounded of the Greek *eu* (well) and *klyptus* (covered) by Charles Louis l'Heritier de Brutelle, French magistrate and amateur botanist; the species *camadulensis* lining the Murray was first described by Frederick Dernhardt, chief of the Naples Botanic Gardens, and named for the private estate of Tuscany's thousand-year-old Camaldoli monastery.

The particular redgum exercising Damien Wright had a tale both more ancient and more recent. In 1990, samples of a mysterious dark, damp and fibrous wood posted to the Museum of Victoria landed on the desk of geology professor Jim Bowler. For years, great quantities had been set aside and burned at CSR Readymix's Wodonga quarry, where it was regarded as a nuisance.

Bowler is best known for discovering, nearly forty years ago, Australia's oldest human remains, near Lake Mungo in south-western New South Wales; a richly imaginative scientist, he lists his recreation in *Who's Who* as 'contemplating the mysteries of the cosmos and my place in it'. Now he contemplated the mysteries of this wood. Microscopic examination of thin sections revealed its redgum structure; radio-carbon dating placed its age between 5000 and 10,000 years old, consistent with having been felled at the end of the last Ice Age. Sea levels then were far lower, the Murray far more seasonal. At summer's end it barely flowed at all; during the spring thaw, it roared with snow melt, three or four times the volume of today, sweeping along gravel shed by the mountainsides. The water's acid content preserved fallen trees entombed in this gravel by preventing build up of decaying bacteria. Instead, the accreting iron and silica ebonised the redgum, bringing it to a stage preliminary to fossilisation, although it remained recognisably wood when disinterred and ignited: despite being up to ninety-eight per cent water, it smoulders smokily, like peat.

Having opened another window on Australia's prehistory, Bowler was keen to pull something through it, proposing that the museum gift shop craft objects of ancient redgum. 'It is that concept of touching something so full of the memories of the most important and iconic of our rivers,' he says. 'The wood speaks to you of its own extraordinary history.' But Bowler picked a bad moment in his state's life cycle – after the VEDC, after Tricontinental, Victoria was getting out of businesses rather than into them and his attempts to go it alone were abortive. Until he met Kelvin Barton.

*

Kelvin Barton's family have farmed cattle on about 400 hectares near Wodonga for seven generations; his father, eighty-eight but still spry enough for six hours in the saddle, lives next door; a first grandchild is on the way. Barton himself is fifty-eight, although a spade-like white beard makes him seem older, and first impressions are of a dour, taciturn man. In fact, he is a serial enthusiast for manual labours of all kinds. At twenty, for instance, he paid $200 for a Land Rover with a broken gear box. Despite having no mechanical training, he repaired it by following a manual, then drove round Australia. He essayed photography and built his own dark room; he tackled leatherwork and travelled the country in search of the dwindling community of whip-plaiters. Each old whip-plaiter thought he was the last – they would hastily cover their work when Barton visited. Gradually, however, he earned their trust, and assembled Australia's largest private collection of stockwhips. Each has a story. A 'whips wanted' advertisement in the *Weekly Times* thirty years ago led him to a Geelong octagenarian whose grandfather had brought back two whips from Sturt's expedition. He bought a prized Porter Bros whip from Johnny Brady, Australia's only professional whip cracker, and sometime Hollywood stuntman. In May 1992 he helped found the Australian Whipcrackers and Plaiters Association, which now oversees a national championship.

Even then Barton was running headlong into his next enthusiasm. He wished to craft some redgum kitchen benchtops from sleepers on the disused Wodonga-Kariong railway. Despite not owning a single handtool, the expense of having the timber milled convinced him he could do the job more cheaply. Barton strikes you as having all the time in the world, yet doesn't dither when he decides. He began accumulating secondhand machinery: a jointer in Bacchus Marsh, a thicknesser in Swan Hill...Modern joiners wanted gear with computers; Barton was happy with winding handles and big old-fashioned bearings – stuff going for a song. To dry timber, he bought an insulated shipping container from Wreckair, installed an air conditioning unit, circulating fans, a dehumidifier and a tray on rails. Unimpressed by quotes for laying the concrete slab for his workshop, he paid $500 for a clapped-out tip truck and gouged the gravel from the river himself; the slab is now snug beneath an eiderdown of sawdust.

Barton started gathering timber – and hasn't stopped. 'That's the trouble,' he says. 'I've probably got enough to last me a lifetime, but I like it so much I keep buying more.' He patrols the region like an arboreal vigilante. Trees going under the axe; trees felled in storms; trees hit by out-of-control cars; brigalow, gidgee, beefwood, stringybark, peppermint, yellowbox, applebox, redbox, and above all redgum, whose resilience, density and range of shades he hymns endlessly. About pressing a tree into something usable, there is also an epic quality. To enter Barton's showroom, one must walk beneath two towering, twenty-five tonne redgum slabs; they were once part of 40m trees wrested by excavator from the Mitta River flats. When Barton taught himself joinery, began making tables and chairs, and put on a couple of apprentices, he felt a little like those ageing whip-plaiters, preserving a lost skill. 'The kids at TAFEs these days know nothing about wood,' he says. 'They'll use MDF for cabinets, laminex or granite for benchtops: there's a whole generation of cabinet makers growing up with no contact with wood.'

The ancient redgum to which Jim Bowler introduced Barton, through mutual friends Ken and Jenny Gorman, was very much to his taste. With his ersatz kiln, he was already equipped to undertake the delicate task of reducing its water content from supersaturation to about 10 per cent without inducing undue cracking; he had even worked out a way to ascertain the wood's equilibrium by cooking chips at intervals in an ordinary microwave oven until they weighed as much before as after, indicating stability. And gradually, it began paying off. What started as an indulgence became Barton Timbers, a business that not only allows him to eke out a subsistence income on a property that has had five years of drought, but links him to a network of loyal clients who have become friends, like Damien Wright. Barton speaks of him with affection, and deep regard. 'Damien?' he says with emphasis. 'Damien is a *true craftsman*.'

*

Growing up, Damien Wright became conscious of a galling cultural divide. 'Clever' children read books; the rest were expected to work with their hands. Except that this didn't square with home life. Father George was one of eleven, whose own father and all seven of his brothers worked at Mackay's Farley Sugar Mills. George was the 'black sheep', becoming a schoolteacher, but loved making and repairing things. 'I wasn't particularly good,' he says. 'But I liked having a go.' His mechanical rite of passage paralleled Kelvin Barton's. One day, George found himself beneath a secondhand Land Rover attacking a broken axle, having prepared for the task by reading a manual.

He mused momentarily: 'I'm about to start something that I have no idea whether I can finish.' But he did.

Damien struggled at school, until his last two years when he suddenly discovered reading, with a preference for the pith of Hemingway and Steinbeck. Abruptly deemed 'clever', he segued into a double major in history and politics at Melbourne University. But his chief pleasure was football, which he played for Port Melbourne, and on graduating he took laboring and gardening jobs with the Education Department – at least, until premier Jeff Kennett's top-to-bottom restructuring left him suddenly out of work.

By now what to do hardly mattered; it simply had to be something. While surfing at Morgan's Beach, he and his girlfriend Clare had begun collecting driftwood, which Damien had a knack for turning into simple tables and boxes. Now, he started buying old tools in flea markets and op shops, and executing commissions for friends in recycled timber: two beds for writer Tony Birch, a sock box for actress Alice Garner. 'It wasn't serious,' says Clare. 'Just a way of keeping off the streets.' When the couple set off round Australia fifteen years ago, however, they met a number of furniture makers, including Glen Holst at Bridgetown on the Margaret River. 'He had this big workshop with his kids running round,' recalls Clare. 'As we talked to him, Damien started to get excited because he could see there was a future in this.'

Who would teach him to be a craftsman? Seeking role models while traveling on the west coast of the US after their marriage, Wright was inspired by the examples of Sam Maloof, whose famous chairs have rocked presidents Carter and Reagan, and James Krenov, founder of the College of the Redwoods woodworking school. But he and Clare also wanted to come home to have children – Wright would just have to teach himself. When they rented in West Brunswick, Damien obtained the shed behind next door's newsagency as a workshop. And when he broke his hand while captaining North Ringwood in the Essendon District Football League, that was it – no more football. Figuratively and literally, his life was in his hands.

*

It sounds routine: a man in a shed making furniture. But at the degrees of quality Wright has achieved in the last decade, which have included commissions for the National Gallery of Victoria, the Immigration Museum and scores of private clients, it makes him a veritable freak. In an arts and crafts establishment jangling with MAs and PhDs, he has had not a minute of formal training; a thick-set 85kg, he looks more like a tradesman than a sensitive aesthete. In fact, in six years on the board of Craft Victoria, his direct manner and instinctive suspicion of the high-falutin' offended milder souls. 'Damien speaks like a bloke,' says his friend Kevin Murray, then the chief executive. 'He doesn't talk about new baroque or post photography. That makes him a very rare voice in a feminised culture. He likes to get everything out on the table and discuss it. It's like someone has just walked in off the street, and wants to start an argument.'

The bluntness, the Puritanism remains. For instance, Wright detests the self-marginalising definition of 'fringe': 'I won't define myself as on the fringe; I won't be a fringe player. I want to be right in the guts.' He disapproves of the Australian Centre for Contemporary Art: 'Something like the ACCA screams indifference to the community. It's like this spaceship that just landed here. It's the most uninviting place on earth – you can't even find the door. The grafitti is the most interesting thing about it.' He was irked by the art-for-art's-sake apologetics of the Henson Affair; he is uneasy about the mechanics of self-promotion. He has never quite got round to a website. He is a slapdash businessman, hopelessly behind in his book-keeping. There is just his wood, his hands, and a long list of taboos: only organic finishes, only homemade veneers; no computers for design, no hardware for convenience.

> There's a whole stream of joinery completely dependent on what I'd call 'techy' stuff. From screws to mechanical drawer sliders to cam lock-fixing devices. It's about the industrialisation and standardisation of cabinet making. It has its place. But I'm making handmade things, so my solutions are handmade.
>
> I know makers who are excited by it, love a new gizmo. I just don't. I don't like touching metal. I don't trust the fittings in the long term.

> It doesn't suit the way I problem solve, or my designs. I think the 'techy' approach ends up dictating the design. Computers do the same. They allow designers to conceive things that have a cartoon relationship to something as trivial as gravity. That can be liberating but it just gives me the shits. To me, it's all about how it feels to use. I like the way a solid wooden drawer works – the feel of it, the sound.

'You watch people talking to Damien and they get this look,' notes Clare. 'You can see them wondering: "Which century is this guy from?"' And to be sure, the definition 'craftsman' today is both anachronistic and timeless; against the grain of a mass production/mass consumption culture, while also somehow connecting us to a set of identifiable and pleasing pre-modern values. We revel in abundance, but still also in uniqueness. As the economist Thorstein Veblen noted a century ago, 'the visible imperfections of handwrought goods...are accounted marks of superiority, or serviceability, or both'. For modern elites, argues David Brooks, 'roughness connotes authenticity and virtue'; surrounded by 'rootsy stuff, the reactionary and the archaic', they can be 'egalitarian and pretentious at the same time'.

The rise of industrial society tugged 'craft' in opposite directions. Those aspiring to exquisite one-off objects began seeking the validation of 'art': at a contemporary craft exhibition, one is assailed by pretentious and prolix 'artist's statements', ostensibly to explicate but essentially to impress. Those who craved commercial success were drawn to the fashionable and affluent world of 'design', which governments in Australia also liked the sound of. 'In the 1990s, there arose a very widespread belief that craft was outmoded,' says Kevin Murray. 'That design was 'the new craft', that the future in Australia was in designing things, that manufacture was something done in the Third World. And that kind of fits with a platonic hierarchy, that ideas are what matters, that execution is purely supplementary. That became an elixir for governments, because they can talk about "innovation".'

When the Australia Council was founded thirty-five years ago, the Crafts Board, representing still strong state craft bodies, was one constituent. But about twenty years ago, the Crafts Board was merged into the Visual Arts

Board, thence into the Media Arts Board, so the Council now provides no funding for craft, while state craft bodies have been buried beneath layers of jargon: in Western Australia, for example, FORM purports to be 'an independent cultural organization that works to enhance Western Australia's competitiveness and creativity through creative, cultural and social capacity building projects'.

Now and again, someone sets to challenging the orthodoxies, albeit never for long. At the 2020 Summit, the prime minister decried 'this false divide between the arts and science, between the arts and industry, between the arts and the economy'. This inspired Dr Terry Cutler, chair of the Review into the National Innovation System, in a speech last year entitled 'Creativity, the Arts and Innovation, to delineate the 'craft of innovation': 'The other great cultural divide is between the realm of the conceptual, the intellectual, and the artisan and craftsman. The role of crafts and trades in innovation has been massively neglected, particularly in the important areas of continuing incremental innovation in the workplace, whether that be a workshop, a factory floor, office, or farmyard.' Fine-sounding sentiments – yet nothing remotely similar found its way into the final draft of *Venturous Australia – building strength in innovation*.

American craft, an industry valued at $US30 billion, forms a vibrant contrast. Thirty-five million Americans sew regularly, and the Stitch'n'Bitch Café has made a multimillionaire entrepreneur of founder Elissa Meyrich. Knitting, too, has a hip young face: comely 'crafty gRRRL' Vickie Howell of television's *Knitty Gritty*. Filmmaker Faythe Levine traversed 30,000km to assemble her forthcoming feature film *Handmade Nation: The Rise of DIY Art, Craft and Design*. But while American craft has always had a dimension of patriotic expression, the default left politics of craft producers in Australia has over time inclined them against overt national pride. 'This isn't the 1930s when the Boyds were adding kookaburras to Murrumbeena pottery,' notes Murray. 'And that's because there is a mindset now that it is not the business of non-indigenous people to talk about the land. We're part of a globalised, urbanised culture that doesn't have an authentic relationship to nature.'

Which is where Wright comes in. Instead of trying to straddle the worlds of 'art' and 'design', he seeks useable beauty. He sheers away from the purely decorative: 'Craft threw up its hands a long time ago and said: "We can't do that. We can't work collaboratively." But craft can't be this radically individualistic experience creating objects that everyone feels grouse about but which don't work.' He views craft as in part an act of citizenship. A common criticism of Australian colonial woodworkers is that they barely used native timbers at all, deeming them fit only for firewood, fences and sleepers. Australian hardwood, born of a land of poor soil, meagre rainfall and constant fire, was unlike anything encountered: the frustrations of pioneers has been passed down in colloquial names for timbers, like ironbark and axebreaker. 'Damien turns that all around,' observes Murray. 'He brings out the value of these indigenous timbers – the ones we didn't want, because it was easier to work in teak and pine. There's a wonder to it; it's like alchemy.'

*

Wright's task in the Koori County Court was reconciling two cultures with ample reason for misunderstanding: indigenous society and the justice system. He was helped spanning them by two women doing the same.

County Court CEO Evi Kadar has had twenty-five years in 'corrections' – that polite bureaucratic euphemism for prisons. It is all she ever wanted to do after discovering a 1962 English children's book, *The Probation Officer,* in the Genazano Convent School library. She has run a women's prison, a juvenile justice centre and a victims support agency. She planned Pentridge's closure, and Victoria's response to the *Royal Commission into Aboriginal Deaths in Custody* – in that time, indeed, nothing has seemed to Kadar so desperate as the plight of young indigenous offenders. 'The cycle is so routine,' he says. 'One community service order will become several, then prison – then there's no way back.'

Koori County Court project manager Rosie Smith, meanwhile, is an aboriginal woman much of her time: Tasmania's third indigenous law graduate, she worked as a judge's associate then in senior clerkships with the Aboriginal Legal Service, before coming to the mainland when Victoria launched its first Aboriginal Justice Agreement in June 2000. The Koori

Magistrates Courts she has been involved with have reduced reoffence rates from as high as seventy per cent to twenty-five per cent.

In Koori courts, judge, court officials, prosecution, defence, defendant, family and elders sit round one table. The judge directs proceedings, but solicits contributions from each in turn – a disarmingly effective protocol. It is a recognition that conventional courtroom environments are often experienced by indigenous people like the airless Townsville chamber in which much of Chloe Hooper's *The Tall Man* is set: 'a grand wooden box with ultramarine carpet' hung with a 'relief featuring a British lion and unicorn'. Hooper describes the reception accorded the Palm Island women who attended the trial of Chris Hurley: 'All of them were mothers with lost sons: sons in custody, sons who'd died in custody, sons who claimed to have been beaten by the police. To enter the courtroom they had to show ID, before being electronically wanded, then patted down.'

Koori courts still have many detractors. Andrew Bolt decries them as 'apartheid justice', because they 'enshrine racism'. In fact, when it comes to arraignment and sentencing, Koori courts are no different to ordinary courts; and, as Smith points out, the procedure can be a more rather a less confronting option.

> Courts can be a formal and an alienating environment for an aboriginal person, but they can also hide behind their solicitor, and might end up saying very little. In a Koori Court, they don't get away with that. They are sitting with their family, who they might have brought shame on, and across from elders, to whose questions they must respond out of respect. They are actually much more accountable. At the same time, the elders know the offender rather than only the offending behaviour, and the defendants are able, often for the first time in their life, to talk about themselves and be listened to.

Kadar and Smith met Wright for the first time at his workshop last July. Kadar felt an unlikely kinship immediately. She and her partner of twenty years, another corrections veteran in the 'major offenders unit', collect wood and wooden objects – some crafted, most not. She heard Wright evoke the meanings of the ancient redgum; she noted the delicacy with which he held it. 'Wow,' she thought. 'This is our man.' Smith then took Wright to Morwell to learn about the court, study the courtroom itself, and meet members of the Koori County Court reference group and elders of the Kurnai people.

The Kurnai have inhabitated Gippsland more than 15,000 years. They were probably the first Victorian aborigines to see evidence of Europeans, watching the *Endeavour* sail by in 1770, and the shipwrecked crew of the *Sydney Cove* struggle overland twenty-seven years later. They were nearly annihilated by first contact. By the middle of the nineteenth century, barely thirty Kurnai remained, although more is known of their customs and structures than of most indigenous peoples, for they fascinated the peripatetic explorer Alfred Howitt. They became the subject of his *The Kurnai: Their Customs in Peace and War* (1880), the first significant ethnography of an aboriginal community. Howitt was an unsentimental observer, assuming his subjects foredoomed: 'In this memoir of the Kurnai, I have occasionally used the present tense in speaking of their customs, when the past would have been more correct.' Yet he was also among the first white observers to touch on the ritual significance of handmade objects in indigenous society, in a detailed appendix about the turndun, a bull-roarer carved from native cherry and swung on the sinew of a kangaroo: 'The awe with which this *turndun* is even now regarded by the surviving Kurnai is so strong, that when, on lately meeting two of them, I spoke of the *turndun,* they first looked cautiously round them to see that no-one else was near and then answered me in undertones.'

Indeed, the Kurnai elders grasped the table's significance quickly. 'Hand craft is central to aboriginal culture,' observes Smith. 'The Kurnai still make shell jewellery in the traditional way. They understand beautiful objects made with care.' The ancient redgum was potentially a source of tension, being from Yorta Yorta rather than Kurnai country. But after consultation with Kurnai elder Lloyd Hood and Yorta Yorta elder Carl Walker, it was agreed that the migration was not unnatural: relations between the people had generally been friendly. To capture the idea of authority meeting consultation and old meeting new, Wright also abandoned his initial plan for a formal rectangle, and settled on an ellipse 4.55m long, 1.45m at its widest, with a central strip of stainless steel concealing an inset array of electric sockets and phone lines adapted to the court's existing wiring footprint.

Normally, Wright would have spent some time with Barton evaluating wood options. On this occasion, the only ancient redgum slabs suitable declared themselves by size: Barton, en route to a cattle muster in Queensland, trucked them to Preston himself. Even then, they weren't quite the required length – a problem Wright solved by ingeniously assimilating a Kurnai motif. Happening on a painting of a long, thin Kurnai shield by local woman Eileen Harrison, he noticed that each end was bound as it tapered to a point. In imitation, he decided to add sections to each end of the table with the grain at right angles to the rest. Then he lowered his studio's Roll-A-Door and went to work.

*

When his father George retired from teaching ten years ago, Wright encouraged him to put some part-time hours in at the workshop. Previously their only collaboration had been a fence to keep a dog from running away; it has since evolved into a curious partnership, father as apprentice to son, although George's influence manifests itself in different ways. The son's belief in Australian wood for Australian projects, echoes the father's belief that the family should honour its country.

> I was very resistent to that notion that the real world is Europe or England home. I impressed on the kids that we should see Australia at every opportunity. Madeline [his wife] did want to go to Europe, but I always said: 'Australia is where we live. We ought to know about it'...I didn't like it when characters on British television shows talked about how they would 'go to Australia'. I used to rail at this idea that Australians ran Australia for the purposes of somebody else, that Australia was a place where you went to get timber, wheat and wool.

It's hard to imagine George railing about anything: he is a man of unfailing politeness, which rather suits working with his son. 'He's a great talker, isn't he?' George observes. 'Some of the time I don't have to do anything at work except listen. He'll discuss and discuss and discuss, and my job is just to be sounding board.' Exactly what he means can be seen in films that the pair began making of their collaborations five years ago. The first shows their making a table from brigalow, a desert timber. The setting is unmistakably Australian. The cricket is on the radio, the air is full of sawdust, and Wright's boys Bernie and Noah gambol through the workshop while dad and granddad work patiently. Wright can be heard griping about the lack of craft in *Master and Commander*: 'Instead you have to put up with Russell Crowe's psychological predicament. Everyone has to be Woody Allen.' George listens. Most of the time, he's a step behind his son, checking and tidying fastidiously. 'It's a place I like being,' he says. 'I try not to do anything to upset that.' It's the voice of parental letting-go: 'Eventually I won't be there, and he'll have to figure out some things on his own.'

Nonetheless, the bar table reflects George in one particular. 'Strictly speaking we didn't have to make a perfect ellipse,' he explains. 'Oval tables are seldom exactly elliptical. But I said: "Why not?" It's an exercise in conic sections I used to teach in mathematics: the formula $x2/a2 + y2/b2 = 1$, where a is the semi-major axis, half the total length of the table; and b is the semi-minor axis, half the total width of the table.' Father and son traced the ellipse with a string from two points on the centre line, then drew a quadrant of the same shape in MDF that acted as a guide for their router. With each day and each treatment, the wood was peeled from its ancient state, coated and polished to a velvety matt black, then docked with the mandated componentry.

Kadar wondered privately if, after all the consultation, she had enough time to finish the project. Wright made time; although he never let on, indigenous justice has, for him, an individual dimension. Fifteen years ago, his uncle, Dermot Tiernan, publican of the Australian Hotel in the Queensland township of Murgon, was roused by the noise of police attempting an arrest. The aboriginal teenager was wild, throwing punches indiscriminately; one collected fifty-two-year-old Tiernan, as he held open a divvy van's door, and killed him. Wright moved north to help his family pick up the pieces, and spent four months pulling beers – some nights in the lounge, generally reserved for whites, others in the bare and bleak front bar, the preserve of local aborigines.

For Murgon is an old frontier in black-white relations: nearby Cherbourg is the reserve to which the decimated aboriginal community of Fraser Island was removed a hundred years ago. In considering the youth's appeal against his manslaughter conviction, Justice Tony Fitzgerald adumbrated his 'all-too-common life experience', as 'poorly educated, unemployed, angry, aggressive and sometimes violent, especially when intoxicated'.

> Cherbourg is an unattractive town, and young people living there have virtually no cultural, recreational or employment opportunities; many are bored, and gravitate to Murgon, which is about five kilometres away, where they drink in the hotel and, often, fight; fighting between young aborigines and white persons is common, and frequently leads to the police charging the youthful offenders, who quickly build up a criminal record, and thus are initiated into a lifestyle which often ends in tragedy, both for the aborigines and the victims of their violence, which frequently is associated with the excessive consumption of alcohol.

Wright isn't silent about his uncle, but nor is he talkative. He didn't share the story with his collaborators; we had been in touch several months before he mentioned it to me, and then indirectly, seemingly anxious that a personal story not overshadow the principles incarnate in the Koori County Court. It was a commitment difficult not to respect. One day on the road back from Morwell, he permitted himself some stories of his uncle: his kindness, his whimsy, his very Irish gregariousness. Then he trailed off. 'We're all in this together,' he said presently. 'We've got no choice.'

*

The week Wright finished the table was the week all thirty-five members of the Koori County Court reference group were convening in Traralgon for a training session in the nitty gritty of procedural management: judges and lawyers, elders and indigenous bureaucrats ranged from how to address offenders to how much time to allocate participants. One night, they adjourned to watch *First Australians* on SBS, the episode featuring the story of Doug Nicholls, Fitzroy footballer, South Australian governor. By coincidence, they had in their number Nicholls' daughter Pam Pederson, an elder of the Koori Children's Court. When the show finished, colleagues prevailed on 'Auntie Pam' to describe her improbably privileged childhood: the weird whitefella food she had to eat, the quaint gubernatorial restrictions on her playtime. Pederson, a natural story-teller, had her audiences in stitches then in tears.

Next day the group attended the court complex in Morwell, where Wright's table was being assembled. Again, the process was filmed: there's a low and deferential murmur as the parts slot soundlessly together, bursts of appreciative pleasure as hands are run along its surface. For a project of this nature, there was a strikingly celebratory air to the court's official launch a few weeks later. Aboriginal dancers danced. Kutcha Edwards sang. Aunties and uncles circulated sunnily. A traditional smoking ceremony was held, with laughter as it predictably activated the fire alarms. The communal mixed with the personal when Wright himself spoke. He thanked his indigenous and non-indigenous collaborators, his family and finally his father, at which he faltered, eyes prickling with tears; behind sunglasses, George also choked back tears. Many stories will be told across this table in its active life; it already contains quite a few.

# THE DISAPPEARING WOMAN

## *An interview with Fiona Wright* (2016)

On the courtyard fence of the Newtown cafe in Sydney's inner west where I'm to meet Fiona Wright is hanging a small but cheerful wooden sign. This place, Wright has advised, is one of her preferred haunts. Yet my eyes keep darting to the three red letters, to which has been added an explanatory spoon: 'EAT'.

It's a year since Wright, now 33, a poet and critic, published *Small Acts of Disappearance*, a suitably slim and compact collection of 'essays on hunger' reflecting on an eating disorder that has lasted nearly half her life. Widely acclaimed, recently awarded the Kibble and shortlisted for the Stella, it frames the world, through an anorexic's eyes, as an unpredictably frightening landscape in which an injunction to eat may be heard as a plea, a demand, a threat or a lament.

I'm pondering this when Wright arrives, smaller and frailer than on the cover of *Small Acts*, where she resembles a Botticelli angel. My hand, not big, feels like it is engulfing hers. But when I mention the sign, she's amused, chuckles wryly. No, she hasn't noticed it before. The cafe is one of several to which she comes to write as a break from her office at home. 'It's nice to be out in the world,' she says. 'Not quite with people but around people. I enjoy watching and listening.' Is that subtly homologous with *Small Acts*, which puts Wright in public, albeit at a writer's remove? 'Yes, people either instinctively get that or they don't,' she says. 'And that bit about seeing and hearing stuff and filing it away.' She pauses. 'I hear there are people who don't do that.' She laughs again.

She laughs a lot, in fact, and with a happily symphonic range. Listening back to a recording, I hear sniggers and chortles, snorts and guffaws – all to scale, but ringing genuinely, and somehow delightfully. Written across four years of equivocal recovery, *Small Acts* is an unsparing book. There are floods of tears, cascades of vomit. It is also seriously clever in its meditations on the motifs of hunger and addiction in the works of Christina Stead, Tim Winton, Carmel Bird and John Berryman, with the 'shock of recognition' they occasion. But Wright in person is disarmingly warm, a broad symmetrical smile breaking regularly across her face.

How would she describe herself now? 'I like to say better but far from well,' she says patiently. 'I've got a long way to go yet. That's OK.' There have been, she adds, many surprises along the way. 'Hormones. Those things are a bitch.' A real horse laugh here.

Wright's disease remains an enigma, too. She was reared in a loving family in Menai in southern Sydney, was a geekily clever girl at St George Girls High School, a selective school in Kogarah. She was never overweight or even thought she was.

At university, self-conscious about seemingly assured peers, she flirted for the first time with dieting, because 'all of a sudden, being a smart kid didn't quite cut it'. But her developing eating problems were initially diagnosed as rumination – a little-understood physical and psychosomatic condition in which a contraction of muscles around the abdomen causes involuntary vomiting. And they were not to intensify until 10 years ago, when she undertook a placement in Sri Lanka in the newsroom of English-language weekly newspaper *The Nation* – an experience that was the subject of the opening essay in *Small Acts*, 'In Colombo'.

Wright's consciousness of her physical collapse dawned on the flight home, 22 hours via Singapore. She could not get comfortable. She recalls how the thin padding of the seat was unforgiving of her protruding hardnesses, and this time the laughter is rueful. She remembers her parents' shock when they collected her from the airport: 'Their faces collapsed.' Yet as intractable as the illness remained, Wright refused to believe in it. 'I can genuinely say I didn't entertain the slightest sliver of doubt that it was a purely physical condition,' she says. 'It's amazing to me now how deep that denial was. But people took me at my word, I was so convinced. I guess they thought: "Diabetic Auntie Betty avoids this and this. Maybe this isn't so different."' During the next couple of years, Wright emerged as a poet of considerable promise, with a signature pared-back expression and love of the minute. But the blurb of her debut collection *Knuckled* (2011), describing the poems as 'bony and assertive, stripped down to the detail, which appeals in its physical quality... as much as in its compression of feeling', now seems almost as descriptive of the author. And as dedicated as Wright was to her craft, her work also involved a practical accommodation with her disease: 'Poetry's a great form when your concentration is intense but limited.' Much of the time, she recalls, she was in thrall to 'the nagging voice that's telling you what you can and cannot do'.

When at last a psychologist persuaded Wright to enter an eating disorders program, she was terrified, not just about her weight but her work. A theme *Small Acts* fathoms deeply is the relationship between the instincts to starve and to write – their origination in the urge to order, to control and to craft. Three spells as a hospital day-patient, in regimes Wright sometimes found punitive and infantilising, proved to be of limited help. Not until she consulted a special psychologist independently did she make still anxious but discernible progress, which in turn made possible longer meditations, deeper insights.

'You can't write long form from the middle of the disease,' says Wright. 'Because you can't concentrate long enough...As I recovered, my writing time took longer blocks than it ever had before. I could think an idea the whole way through.' Her writing took on a different relationship to her disease – it enabled her to see it in perspective.

A revelation came in her studying the neuroscience of eating disorders, how they alter brain chemistry and structure. 'I found that very freeing,' she says. 'I had always known these things were ridiculous, yet couldn't stop doing them. Now I understood it was because my brain had changed. It does away with a lot of the blame. That was exhilarating – and makes sense of why it's so hard to change.' Wright was further surprised to find how effective 'putting words down' was in shedding her of encumbrances. 'That was what I didn't expect. I didn't expect to feel...' She laughs.

Errr, purged?

'...lighter.' More laughter. 'It felt like I'd leeched my ideas of their poison. I hadn't realised how ashamed I was. It's a difficult thing to write through shame. It's so easy to hesitate.' Wright felt most like hesitating before she first read in public about her condition, at a Sydney Writers Festival event at Bankstown Arts Centre in May 2012. 'I've always enjoyed reading to audiences,' she recalls. 'But I was sitting backstage beforehand and thinking, "I don't know about this. I'm not sure about this at all." Then when I got out there it was an amazing feeling – speaking the piece rather than simply writing it felt so powerful. The audience was silent. I remember looking out at one stage and thinking, "I've got you guys."' One of those guys was the publisher of *Knuckled*, Giramondo's Ivor Indyk, who first envisioned the book *Small Acts* became.

Wright is resigned now to being an object of curiosity, not least among fellow sufferers. It's one of the reasons for a small act of editing in *Small Acts of Disappearance* – she never divulges her varying weights. 'Anorexics are crazy competitive,' she says. 'The minute you put a number to your weight, people will say, "I can do better than that" or "I never got that sick".' But she's also utterly frank about her struggles even in the present: 'I'd love spontaneity around food. Eating out is still difficult for me. I'd love to be able to do that with ease. That would be pretty great.' Breakfasting with a friend recently, she was struck by his salivating excitement on reading the menu: 'I thought, "Imagine that." Because when I get a menu I start going, "No–no–no–hell no–well, maybe", but probably just the thing I get all the time. Other times people will say, "I feel like a sweet breakfast this morning." I think, "How do you tell? How do you know what you feel like?" The only time I ever know what I feel like is when I feel really hung-over. Which is kind of joyful.' Another laugh.

Wright is newly in a relationship. Does this involve 'R', I ask, about whom she wrote last year in a piece for Seizure, 'What She Could Not Tell Him' – a kind of postscript to *Small Acts*.

'No...Noooooo. Heh, heh, heh. That's over. Learned a lot that way. No, this is new. I don't know. It's hard for me to ask him for help when I need it. I struggle with that a lot, being honest about what's going on. The vulnerability terrifies.' It's a paradox of anorexia, Wright says, that at their physically weakest, sufferers feel psychically strong, fortified, autonomous.

'You feel invulnerable because nobody can make you do anything you don't want to, because nobody can get through to you either. If you don't need anything from anyone, then you win.' Would she say, then, that recovery involves a kind of gracious acceptance of defeat? 'Yes,' answers Wright. 'It's terrible.' She laughs one last time.

'That was fun,' she says, as we pass the 'EAT' sign on our way out. And it was.

# SHIT LIT

## *The rise of the koob* (2004)

Almost a hundred new books are published in Australia every week. And when you walk into a bookshop these days, it feels like it.

Harry P! Bridget J! Di! Hef! Chick lit to the left. TV tie-ins to the right. Tables groan beneath the collective weight of Dan Browns and Tom Clancys. Piled high, the latest bulletins from Discworld and Dune. Cookbooks are propped, incongruously, beside diet guides. Advice on how to make money competes with advice on how to spend it. Renovate your house. Renovate yourself. And, when I visited the local Borders superstore last week, no fewer than fifteen shelves allocated to editions of Tolkein, even as a *Lord of the Rings* DVD played on an endless loop.

The impression is a powerful one: that here are hundreds upon thousands of books waiting not to be read but simply to be sold. For Borders was also festooned with images of what appeared to be its model customer: everywhere one looked was the same poster, featuring a comely twentysomething peering archly over the cover of her book.

Mysteriously, the volume appeared to be a *Handbook of Psychiatry* – either this was the only title to hand, or it is required reading among the chain's best brains. Oddest of all, the poster girl's ears were plugged with the headphones of a portable CD player. The implication was arresting: that the book was here simply one among the host of leisure devices. Perhaps there are other images in which readers read while jogging or flinging a Frisbee.

In the bookshop of yore, the emphasis was on the *book;* now it is on the *shop.* But this is merely a window on the publishing trade itself, which submits literature to the same market forces and reflects the same homogenised values as movies, television, DVDs and /or video games. In her artful new collection of essays, *Thank You For Not Reading* (2004), Dubravka Ugresic defines an emergent distinction. 'The concept of literature is disappearing,' she argues, 'and its place is increasingly being taken by books.'

Ugresic, an *emigre* Croatian now resident in the United States, describes her discovery that she hadn't moved nearly so far as she thought when she came to the west. The home of the brave (author) and land of free (market) looked suspiciously like the old eastern bloc: 'Contemporary market literature is realistic, optimistic, joyful, sexy, explicitly or implicitly didactic, and intended for the broad reading masses.' It was as though the old Soviet genre of socialist realism has been reborn: 'The old communist utopia, in which art is created and consumed by everyone, has been transformed by the modern market into a possible reality.' Stalin, Ugresic reminds us, ran a stern literary school: 'Stalinism made writers into professionals, who would surely be rampaging through the international literary market now, if only they'd lived.' But the modern writer for the mass market would fit right in: 'If Stephen King had found himself in Stalinist Russia, he would undoubtedly have gotten the Stalin Prize.'

For all its tranquil and faintly unworldly air, a sizeable proportion of book world has always been involved in reifying literature into a market commodity. In his 'Detached Thoughts on Books and Reading' in *Last Essays of Elia* (1833), Charles Lamb minted the phrase *biblia abiblia* – 'books which are no books' – to describe those works that infiltrated people's homes because they looked good, because they were 'volumes which "no gentleman's library should be without"'. He lamented: 'I confess that it moves my spleen to see these things in books' clothing perched upon shelves, like false saints, usurpers of true shrines, intruders into the sanctuary, thrusting out the legitimate occupants.'

Thanks to the spread of mass literacy and the rise of the circulating library, however, books were even then undergoing their own industrial revolution – with all that this entailed. George Gissing's great masterpiece of *biblia abiblia, New Grub Street* (1891), centres on the exploits of two producers of it, Edwin Reardon and Jasper Milvain. Earnest Reardon has nonetheless sold himself into slavery, churning out the popular genre of three-decker novels at 4000 words a day, albeit with the deepest chagrin. 'It's good enough for the market; that satisfies them,' he laments bitterly of his peers. 'And perhaps they are justified'. Cooler Milvain, one of those peers, produces 'rubbish, but rubbish of a very special kind, of fine quality'. He concentrates on obtaining the maximum effect from the minimum effort, and excels at self-promotion. 'If a man can't hit upon any other way of attracting attention, let him dance on his head in the middle of the street,' he philosophises. 'After that he may hope to get consideration for his volume of poems.' It is Milvain, inevitably, who inherits the earth.

In more recent times, the distinguished Canadian publisher James McClelland evolved the expression *koob* – book spelled backwards – to describe those works filling a commercial rather than a creative or cultural need: 'book-shaped objects that were not in fact books'. One of his great discoveries at McClelland & Stewart, Margaret Atwood, then developed the idea of the *schlovel*: 'self-help books designed as fiction'. Speaking at the award of Canada's Arts Club Medal for Literature in 1997, she warned: 'Just as the hero of Ionesco's play wakes up one day to find that everyone else is turning into a rhinoceros, we may wake up one day to find that most of the books have turned into *koobs*, and most of the novels into *schlovels*.'

Publishers, of course, have traditionally justified *biblia abiblia, koobs* and *schlovels* on grounds that these endow worthier projects: the dividend of a successful gift book of cat pictures might, for instance, permit half a dozen homegrown novels. Such cross-subsidy has been integral to what is, by its nature, a high-risk, low-margin business. This is no longer the case. Our big publishers, all multinationals, ears cocked for the gay strains of any passing bandwagon, have channelled their energies into risk reduction and margin enhancement. Most return unsolicited manuscripts unread. Few publish anything not immediately and obviously sellable (there were only 124 Australian novels published last year out of more than 4500 non-educational titles, for instance, while Australian poetry has disappeared from the lists of big publishers altogether). Non-fiction seems at an even lower ebb. Biographies have been marginalised by popular life stories and onanistic memoirs from actors, athletes and media personalities; history, if it does not involve sunburned ANZACs, is bunk. The purpose of *biblia abiblia* today? To beget more *biblia abiblia*.

What sells here is what sells everywhere. Were it not for the presences of Bryce Courtenay, and to a lesser degree Tim Winton and Peter Carey, our lists of bestselling fiction would be indistinguishable from lists in the US or the UK. Far and away the biggest local non-fiction author, meanwhile, is Bradley Taylor Grieve, whose slender illustrated volumes of life-affirming dreck read like desk calendars without dates.

Quality has always struggled to make itself known in the mass market. After all, nobody reads a book *before* buying it. An unknowable but sizeable proportion of books, furthermore, are not read by their purchaser: they are bought as gift objects, for the effect occasioned by their unwrapping ('You've bought me *Happy Days With The Naked Chef*? You know, you really shouldn't have!') But where these used to be regarded as unfortunate realities to be resisted where possible, they are now treated as factors to be exploited by marketing externalities: covers, design, titles, blurbs, promotions, author tours – anything to make the buyable more buyable still.

These epiphenomena are not, moreover, to stimulate browsers with the thought of anything new. They promise instead a lulling repetition of something already experienced: 'The long-awaited sequel to…'; 'By the bestselling author of…', 'In the tradition of…'; 'If you liked that, you will love this'; 'If you saw the film/watched the series/played the video game, you are bound to want…'. If you find a successful formula in this age, you stick to it like a veritable Gwyn Barry. In Martin Amis' *The Information* (1995), if you recall, Barry writes a memoir, *Summertown*, that fares modestly, then an execrable fantasy, *Amelior*, that sells by the truckload. 'Jesus Christ,' thinks his fellow Oxonian Richard Tull when finally he chances on Barry's new title. 'Gwyn's third novel is called *Amelior Regained*. Not *Summertown Regained*, you notice. Oh no. *Amelior Regained*. And why did they need to regain it? They never even lost it.'

How has publishing evolved this way? Most point to the absorption of the industry's leaders into huge, faceless, characterless conglomerates – News Corporation Bertlesmann, Holtzbrinck, Viacom, Pearson – that demand a bang for their buck. But the situation also happens to suit very well those whom it principally benefits. In this order of things, the author is not less important but more, if not for their prose, certainly for their profile, and their ability to hustle.

Some recent novels, like Amis' *The Information*, Percival Everett's *Erasure* (2003) and William Kotzwinkle's *The Bear Went Over The Mountain* (1997) have made merry of this trend. The chief protagonist of Everett's novel, the erudite but seldom-read black American writer Monk Ellison, decides to craft a story in ghetto patois, only to find *Fuck* by Stagg R. Leigh taking on a life of its own. Kotzwinkle's fantasia involves a black bear which, emerging from the woods of Maine carrying a manuscript by an aspiring romance novelist that it has found buried, winds up with a contract. Tell us about yourself, the publishers ask. You like hunting? And fishing? Perfect: the new Hemingway. 'Sportsman, adventurer, larger than life, the man of action who can tell a love story...We'll play on your love of the outdoors, but I'd like to put an environmental slant on it, the sacredness of nature, how you respect it...I don't mind if you've killed any cute little animals but some people might.'

Yet the laughter is rueful – even for publishers. Under present circumstances, it is the big-name, best-selling authors who hold the whip hand. In a fascinating series of lectures at the New York Public Library collected as *Book Business* (2002), Jason Epstein, co-founder of the *New York Review of Books*, pointed out that the Kings, Clancys, Crichtons and Grishams 'no more need publishers to edit and publicise their books than Nabisco needs Julia Child to improve and publicise Oreos'.

'To retain these powerful authors, publishers already forgo much of their normal profit, or incur severe losses, by paying royalty guarantees far greater than can be recouped from sales,' Epstein said. 'In effect, name-brand authors are already their own publishers, while their nominal publishers are a vestigial, nonessential convenience, beneficiaries (or victims) of inertia on the part of agents reluctant to forgo the security of a publishers' guarantee.'

Neurotic about keeping their big names, he said, publishers were becoming increasingly indifferent to their less commercial authors – the ones traditionally who never sold out on the day of release, but who used to be relied on to turn over steadily. As resources were concentrated on 'front lists', 'back lists' had been radically pruned. 'When this phenomenon first became apparent some thirty years ago, the industry joke was that the shelf life of a book had fallen somewhere between that of milk and yoghurt,' recalled

Epstein. 'Since then the situation has worsened and the joke is no longer heard.'

And what aesthetic criteria will develop in a world where so much attention and avidity falls on the big, the popular, the hip, the hyped, the *biblia abiblia*? Has the old-fashioned non-book mutated into a more malign anti-book, that soothes the mind, dulls the senses, and purports to give a 'reading experience', while preventing us being waylaid by uneven, unpredictable, uncompromising literature? In Ugresic's essay 'Alchemy', she recalls the exclamation of a friend, a European university literature teacher: 'I know perfectly well that the book is shit. But I loooove it!' There is, she concludes, 'something in the very nature of shit that makes it so loooved... its availability'.

'Shit is accessible to everyone,' Ugresic writes. 'Shit is what unites us, we can stumble across shit at every moment, step in it, slip in it, shits follows us wherever we go, shit waits patiently on our doorstep.' And now you can find it all over your bookstore.

## AND YOU CAN TOO

### *The rise of subtitles* (2008)

The mass of books lead lives of quiet desperation. Compared to the dowdy shops of yesteryear, the modern bookstore is a place of gaiety, even exuberance. But with essentially three months to make their mark before returning from whence they came under Australia's self-devouring sale-or-return system, books must dress to impress. While they've got you – that is, while you're looking at them, perhaps fondling or flicking through their pages for a tactile acquaintance – they strain for the maximum impact. Everyone, of course, is after that dazzling image, that killer title; less obvious, perhaps, is the irresistible spread of the expository subtitle, now so subtly pervasive that non-fiction books going without seem perfectly underwhelming.

Lately subtitles have begun sprawling so lavishly as to collapse under their own weight. For *Charlie Wilson's War*, George Crile just gets away with *The Extraordinary Story of How the Wildest Man in Congress and a Rogue CIA Agent Changed the History of Our Times*. But Christopher Booker and Richard North have had to disaggregate *Scared to Death: From BSE To Global Warming: Why Scares Are Costing Us The Earth*; likewise Tim Baker with *High Surf: The World's Most Inspiring Surfers, Waveriding as a Way of Life, the Ocean as Teacher*. So much ozone does Lawrence Solomon deplete in naming his climate change screed *The Deniers: The World Renowned Scientists Who Stood Up Against Global Warming Hysteria, Political Persecution, and Fraud*, that he needs another breath before a footnote adding *And Those Who Are Too Fearful To Do So*.

The objective is two-fold. One is to dress the book in a brief authority, to make it appear not just more important than it actually is, but more popular. It was Norman Mailer who commented that Americans were incapable of approaching a book that was not already a success, and the essence of marketing in publishing today is gilding titles with the aura of bestseller before they have achieved, or even approximated, such status. The effect of browsing in a bookshop, as a result, has become like speed-dating a string of garrulous drunks. Psst. Wanna know *The Inside Story of how Jack Welch Talked General Electric Into Becoming the Greatest Company in the World?* Yep, that's me: *Jacked Up*. Let's get it on, babe.

The subtitle also operates as a trailer to a motion picture – albeit that just as some trailers leave you with the feeling of having already seen the film, so some subtitles induce a distinct déjà vu. Let's check the American politics section out, shall we? Richard Savage's *Takeover: The Return of the Imperial Presidency and the Subversion of American Democracy*. (Hmmm). Kevin Phillips' *American Dynasty: Aristocracy, Fortune and the Politics of Deceit in the House of Bush* (Wait a minute). Frank Rich's *The Greatest Story Ever Sold: The Decline and Fall of Truth – The Real History of the Bush Administration* (What's going on?). Craig Unger's *The Fall of the House of Bush: The Untold Story of How a Band of True Believers Seized the Executive Branch, Started the Iraq War and Still Imperils America's Future*. (Haven't I just read this?) Michael Moore's *Stupid White Men...And Other Sorry Excuses for the State of the Nation, New Edition with Added Extras, Completely Updated, New Foreword, the Number One Bestseller*. (Ah, now I get it). Harriet Lamb's *Fighting the Banana Wars and Other Fair Trade Battles: How We Took On The Corporate Giants to Change the World*. (Next!) At its worst, the effect is a gobful of sententious clichés. For Al Gore's assault on prose, *The Assault on Reason* amply suffices: nothing is added by *How the Politics of Fear, Secrecy and Blind Faith Subvert Wise Decision-Making, Degrade Democracy and Imperil America and the World* except the sense of a Nobel Prize fashionably squandered.

Once, of course, books had no need of such otiose elaboration. To stick with American politics, there once existed the cultural literacy that made possible titles like *Nixon Agonistes*, with its echo of Milton, or *All the President's Men*, with its revision of Robert Penn Warren. Critics vouchsafed standalone titles of such solemn grandeur as *The Death of Tragedy*, *A Gathering of Fugitives*, *The Evening Colonnade* and *Under The Sign of Saturn*. Historians bandied around bald provocations like *The Decline of the West*, *The Revolt of the Masses*, *The Making of the English Working Class* and *Anti-Intellectualism in American Life*.

Now it's easier to have a few goes, and hope that one somehow makes an impression. Actually, there is a parlour game in the making imagining what modern marketing might have made of canonical classics; say Kant's *The Critique of Pure Reason: Why Space and Time are a priori intuitions, Why we cannot meaningfully conceive of an object that exists outside of time and has no spatial components, Why we are prohibited from absolute knowledge of the thing-in-itself...and 101 ways to Save the World* (nobody will read long enough to learn that the last part is bogus); or maybe Plato's *Republic: The Seven Habits of Highly Successful City States* (always use 'seven': it's publishing magic). T. E. Lawrence was obviously ahead of the curve with *The Seven Pillars of Wisdom,* but would surely have savoured greater success with *How I Rallied Arab Irregulars, Tied Down the Ottoman Empire, Masterminded the Capture of Aqaba and Damascus...and You Can Too.*

Or maybe not. It takes courage to stand or fall on a single line – and pulling it off has a certain brio. Many of our most noteworthy Australian titles are the more memorable for their lack of exposition. *The Female Eunuch, The Lucky Country* and *The Australian Ugliness* are unimproveable, any addition to *The Tyranny of Distance, The Fatal Shore* or *Dancing With Strangers* unimaginable. Perhaps one day there will be a version of Manning Clark's *History of Australia* amplified by *Phar Lap Wins Twice: Better Than The Real Thing!* But not yet.

It's also worth noting some of the books that have recently scorned further explanation, exhibiting their one-punch title almost as a badge of publishing potency. Richard Dawkins denounces *The God Delusion* and Tamas Pataki is *Against Religion* – nothing more nor less. Don Watson keeps it simple with *American Journeys;* ditto Les Carlyon with *The Great War.* Geoffrey Blainey offers *A Short History of the World;* Bill Bryson furnishes *A Short History of Nearly Everything.* Recent reprints of Paul Kelly's *The Hawke Ascendancy and The End of Certainty* have shorn them of former elucidations. For some authors, concision marks their graduation as a brand name. Neil Strauss had to bolster *The Game,* his book on sexual hustlers, with *Penetrating the Secret Society of Pick-Up Artists;* now in a position to assert that size doesn't matter, he plonks down *Rules of The Game* for the sequel. For others, it is a risky, but calculated, gesture of beguilement. A personal favourite of recent times has been Anna Funder's *Stasiland*: confronting but mysterious, foreign but familiar, and capable of being sung to the tune of the Richmond Football Club song.

Just to confuse matters further, some novels are drawing titles from what seem like subtitles shaken loose, such as *Salmon Fishing in the Yemen, A Short History of Tractors in Ukrainian, Everyman's Rules for Scientific Living* and *An Arsonist's Guide to Writers' Homes in New England*. But perhaps this is a sign of the subtitle's increasing obsolescence, that it is now so worn out from overuse as to be readily amenable to parody. After all, a little economy can go a long way. One night after he had won America's National Book Award for his mighty saga of East European Jewry in the US, *World Of Our Fathers*, Irving Howe was bailed up by querulous female reader. Why, she upbraided him, had he chosen a title so obviously sexist? Far fairer would have been *World Of Our Fathers and Mothers*. 'Madam,' Howe replied mildly, '*World Of Our Fathers* is a title. *World Of Our Fathers and Mothers* is a speech.'

# THE COMMANDING HEIGHTS

## *Australia's first skyscraper* (2016)

In a land boasting more skyscrapers per capita than any other, Australians today would be pardoned for missing their first, a quarter the height of what's now the tallest. Yet no building has exerted such influence on Australian cityscapes as Orica House on Melbourne's Eastern Hill – its everyday inconspicuousness attests the ubiquity of the form it pioneered.

Stand closer to what was originally ICI House and the view changes. 'I tell people I'm showing round that this was the iPhone of Australian architecture,' says Tim Leslie, a studio director at Bates Smart McCutcheon (BSM), which not only designed the building but, in a form of architectural ancestor worship, have since made it their headquarters. 'It was so different to everything that had gone before.'

As Graeme Davison, author of *City Dreamers* (2016), a new history of the Australian urban imagination, puts it: 'In one bold leap, Melbourne threw off its Victorian dowdiness and became the most self-consciously modern Australian city.' In the spirit of the 1956 Olympic Games and the advent of television, the International Style of ICI House married the cosmopolitan and the technological in exciting and optimistic proportions. Yet death and disaster also intruded. And not all the changes the building presaged were welcome. Aesthetic returns diminished swiftly: within a decade of ICI House's slim, glassy elegance, the Gas & Fuel Corporation had inflicted on Melbourne not one but two hunched brown brick towers with tiny aluminium windows, proverbial in their monotony – the so-called 'ugly sisters'.

And by his death in 1983, ICI House's architect, Sir Osborn McCutcheon, had lost a good deal of his faith in industrial civilisation, and architecture's place in it. 'What would Os think of us today?' asks his son Andrew. 'He would be aghast that property development has become such a major force in individual wealth creation. He saw planning land use as a stewardship of the land in the community interest...We seem to have to reinvent the wheel in every generation. History is not all a story of progress.'

At Andrew McCutcheon's breakfast table in St Kilda poring over his father's early sketches, recently discovered in BSM's archives, we're a world away from the turbocapitalism of modern development. There was no degree course when Osborn McCutcheon felt drawn to architecture – one designed one's own. His family was not rich but comfortable, part of the tight circle of respectable Methodist Melbourne – he would later marry his first cousin. He worked in practices in San Francisco and London, and the immaculate line drawings of cathedrals and cottages, wells and windows, were the fruits of a year's wandering in Europe in 1925. For his first few years at the firm Bates & Peebles, where he had earlier been articled, McCutcheon had a negative income, subsisting on borrowings.

That may partly explain the eventual panache of ICI House, its pent-up fullness with ideas. What with Depression and War, there were more bad years than good in McCutcheon's first two decades' practice. He designed a number of celebrated Melbourne buildings, including the striped classical AMP Society headquarters (1932), the vivacious Jazz-Moderne Buckley & Nunn men's store (1933), and the Moderne–classical Second Church of Christ, Scientist, in Camberwell (1937). But much of his work was domestic – commissions for houses from Melbourne's well-to-do. More formative were probably two and a half hectic years spent with the American military.

When the US Army Corps of Engineers (Southwest Pacific Area) was established in February 1942, McCutcheon was recruited to head an architectural section which churned out hundreds of designs for military buildings – huts and warehouses, hangars and hospitals. Major McCutcheon, as he was, nearly came unstuck in New Guinea, bringing home malaria that turned him a vivid yellow, but also a strong faith in dry construction and prefabrication, which he would loudly defend to a sceptical profession ('I have no time for the view that such an approach to architecture inevitably lowers our standards.'). ICI House – hugely simplified, for example, by its identical and interchangeable 3ft by 5ft enamelled glass panes – is in a way its monument.

Architecture in Australia was muted in the first postwar decade by a shortage of materials and of capital, but not by a dearth of ideas. Practitioners looked on enviously but excitedly at developments overseas – signature projects in New York like Wallace Harrison's United Nations Secretariat in New York (1948–1952) and Gordon Bunshaft's Lever House (1950–52). McCutcheon himself toured Scandinavia in 1948, borrowing ideas from its state-of-the-art hospital designs for his Footscray & District Hospital (1953). But he signified his embrace of modernism mainly by living in it, completing an ingenious 'passive solar house' for his family in Mt Eliza, a rural enclave 30 miles from the city, at Christmas 1950.

'Kackeraboite', named after the local creek, was a long slim rectangle the width of a single room, north wall sheathed in glass, with huge sliding doors and banks of operable glass louvres split by a breezeway, sitting on an asphalted concrete slab that acted as a heat bank. Sun that penetrated to the back wall in winter did not hit the slab in summer, regulating internal temperatures. When McCutcheon's contemporaries Robin Boyd, Frederick Romberg and Roy Grounds hosted Walter Gropius in May 1954, Kackeraboite was the venue of the reception – the Bauhaus sage wandered fascinated in the surrounding bushland, looking for koalas.

By that stage, McCutcheon had been drawn into one of Australia's most rancorous aesthetic controversies, architecture's counterpart of William Dobell's 'Mr Joshua Smith' winning the Archibald Prize. In January 1952, fire had gutted the great Gothic Revival pile of Wilson Hall at Melbourne University. Opinion was starkly divided about how to replace it.

The university council initially agreed to an exact rebuilding. But when it baulked at the expense, McCutcheon proposed a far cheaper modern alternative: a concrete-encased, steel-framed rectangular box with glass curtain walls and brick in-fill, and an interior of Swedish birch incorporating an intricate stained-glass screen designed by Douglas Annand and a chancellor's throne fashioned by Grant Featherston.

The professoriat rebelled. But for a young colleague, Robert Dunster, it evinced McCutcheon's leadership and urbanity. 'Wilson Hall was the first building in Melbourne for decades that wasn't simple or mundane, a house or a factory,' says Dunster. 'And McCutcheon wanted perfection. He wanted a building to stand for a couple of hundred years. And he was able to inspire colleagues, the university and building workers with that idea.'

McCutcheon scorned flamboyance, but exuded a certain flair. The hour's morning commute from Kackeraboite to BSM's St Kilda Road studio was spent planning: by the time he arrived, trailing butter paper and cigarette smoke, he had laid out his daily objectives. Dunster recalls an afternoon standing at his boss's desk awaiting attention. At length, McCutcheon looked up and said: 'Three and a half minutes.' Then he resumed his activities for exactly that time before engaging again.

When not filling notebook after notebook with emphatic scrawlings, McCutcheon would be rotating his pencil in his mouth. The tell-tale mark of pencil lead between his two front teeth was a firm in-joke. He abstained from alcohol – the sherry decanter on the sideboard at Kackeraboite was for the pleasure of visitors. But he was a peerless networker, especially over luncheon tables at Melbourne's elite Savage Club, connected among politicians and planners, councillors and builders alike. In the 1930s, for example, he had designed the Ivanhoe mansions of the brothers Ernie and Frank Watts, who ran the city's biggest construction company. In some respects, their partnership in ICI House was foreordained.

That, but maybe not much else. A walk round Melbourne's central business district 60 years ago would have revealed a riot of bluestone, sandstone, brick and stucco, with the occasional flash of marble and granite – and, compared with today, very much more light. That was because Melbourne, like every Australian city bar Perth, and the vast majority of the world's bigger metropolises, observed a height limit.

Melbourne's, set in 1916, was 132 feet; Sydney allowed 150 feet. These horizontal slashes across Australian skies irked local architects, who argued that their various rationales, about fire safety and urban congestion, were outdated. But by some standards, the allowances were quite generous: London had only just begun tinkering with its 100-foot limit, while Paris (despite the Eiffel Tower) had ruled itself off at 65 feet. Nor did ICI Australia and New Zealand (ICIANZ), the antipodean arm of Britain's sprawling

Imperial Chemical Industries, seem a prime candidate to scour the sky.

ICIANZ straggled over eight sites in Melbourne, including a termite-ridden archive in an old chemical plant in Yarraville presided over by an aged ex-serviceman with a wooden leg; it had only just retired a logo featuring Britannia staring wistfully out to sea. Its parent, meanwhile, was a waddling, paternalistic bureaucracy, whose own London headquarters was a neoclassical low-rise faced in Portland stone and festooned with sculptures: Millbank was known among chafing middle managers as 'Millstone'. ICI's chairman, Sir Alexander Fleck, was a childless widower whose passions were hill climbing, tree felling and the Venerable Bede.

Something at ICIANZ, however, had recently shifted. A generational change in management had placed two younger men at the top: 50-year-old Ken Begg as chairman and 40-year-old Archibald Glenn as managing director, who wished to signify their ambitions with a new headquarters. In March 1952, the company had acquired a 2,340-square metre site at one of Melbourne's highest points, Eastern Hill, where Lonsdale Street protrudes beyond the Hoddle Grid. Aligned with Parliament House and the Treasury Building, it seemed to cry out for a bold, proud building. And McCutcheon was eager to provide it.

McCutcheon's first innovation was a cunning way to meet the spirit of the height limit while defying its letter, proposing a rectangular 'tower-type building' of 203 feet that would occupy only 41% of the block at ground level; the rest of the block would be allotted to a courtyard garden featuring public artwork of the kind with which he had enriched Wilson Hall. McCutcheon soothed the anxieties of the State Building Regulations Committee by persuading them that approval for ICI House need not prelude rampant development: section 214 of the *Uniform Planning Regulations* entitled the committee to modify rules without amending them. But nobody missed the implications when *The Herald* foreshadowed the plans in May 1955: 'New Skyline for City?' read the headline.

The Metropolitan Fire Brigade was anxious. Not only was the height limit calibrated by the reach of their ladders and water jets, but the 360-degree view of Melbourne they enjoyed from their watchtower, only 200 yards from the site of ICI House, would be disrupted. To placate them, McCutcheon incorporated into his building elaborate fire protection measures, including a pioneering sprinkler system above the fifth floor. Others were also discomfited. The Eastern Hill block was not only home to the Salvation Army, but also several brothels. Not so much could be done in design terms here.

Fortunately, the atmosphere was one of excitement. Melbourne was about to sample something hitherto confined to the get-ahead United States. Robin Boyd, not only an adventurous architect but a popular arbiter of architectural taste, used his bully pulpit in *The Herald* to welcome the slashing of 'the red tape which restricted Melbourne'. In the lineage from the Tower of Babel to the Eiffel Tower, here was a skyscraper worth the name: 'This is a clean, precipitous tower in the best tradition. Elbow room is the first essential for effective skyscraping, and the ICI has that.' ICI had actually obtained even more elbow room than bargained for: having applied for permission to erect to 203 feet, it was approved to build to 230 feet thanks to the transposition of the '3' and the '0' by a Melbourne City Council typist.

Yet height was only the most obvious feature of McCutcheon's design. Externally and internally, it was absolutely *au courant*. Without, McCutcheon clad ICI House in gleaming glass curtain walls to north and south that would flood the interior with natural light – a homage to New York's UN Building and Lever House. Within, he offered vistas of uninterrupted space, a pioneering open plan, by quarantining the building's services, such as lifts, plumbing and air conditioning, in a discrete 275-foot service tower, initially behind the core tower, then at right angles – a solution adopted in Chicago's Inland Steel headquarters (1957) and San Francisco's Crown Zellerbach Building (1959), classic glass curtain wall skyscrapers whose construction was concurrent with ICI House.

Perhaps the cleverest feature, meanwhile, was something the public never saw. Drawing on his experiences with the US Army, McCutcheon made extensive use of prefabrication and dry construction: floor units, beam encasements, concrete spandrels, panels of the west and east walls and the synthetic granite panels enclosing the service tower were all fabricated off site.

This, then, was a bold experiment. To be on the safe side, McCutcheon trialled several features, including the curtain wall detailing, service tower and reliance on prefabrication, in another smaller building in William Street, a headquarters for brickmaker Humes, whose construction was proceeding just in advance of ICI House. But it would be an underestimate to see Australia's first skyscraper as a triumph of technology. It was a testament to McCutcheon's personality, his calm authority, that Begg and Glenn bought into his vision so comprehensively. 'It wasn't ICI telling McCutcheon it wanted a glass box for its headquarters,' observes heritage architect Peter Lovell. 'It was the other way around.'

The activity, moreover, formed part of a general building boom, unmatched in Australia since the 1880s. 'It wasn't simply about modernism,' says Philip Goad, deputy dean of architecture at Melbourne University and author of the history *Bates Smart* (2004). 'It was about modernisation, a sense that the country now had to get its act together.' After two fallow decades, more than a score of tall office buildings would be completed in Melbourne between 1955 and 1960. It excited rivalry too. The final unveiling of plans in April 1956 was front page news in the *Sydney Morning Herald*, beneath the shocked headline: 'Melbourne to have tallest building.' In due course height limits would stand no chance against the urges of oneupmanship.

BSM benefited: the firm was commissioned to design a second ICI House (1957), at ten storeys, on Circular Quay, and handsome headquarters for Mutual Life and Citizens Assurance (1957–1960) in Sydney, Adelaide, Perth, Brisbane and Hobart. But Melbourne was the place to be. As EA Watts Pty Ltd began to manoeuvre the steel skeleton into place in May 1957, ICI had to erect a viewing platform for the benefit of 'pavement superintendents' – the crowds, sometimes running into hundreds, who gathered round the site each day, including one man who would come every single morning, without exception, for nearly two years.

Watts' workforce was itself a cross-section of the new postwar Australia: Australians and Englishmen alongside Italians, Greeks, Dutchmen, Americans, Yugoslavs, Poles and Egyptians, building their futures by making up to £50 a week. They worked speedily and harmoniously, completing the framing by Christmas, and the flooring systems within six further months. They paid a price too: three workers died, two in falls from height. Struan Gilfillan, then the most junior architect on the BSM team assisting McCutcheon, and today the last survivor, recalls the headlong rush: 'Towards the end I was doing much of my work on the site. You'd design something one day, it would be built the next day, and you'd be inspecting it the day after.'

Though ICIANZ's Begg and Glenn were interested clients, BSM exerted a control over the project that by modern lights seems quite extraordinary, even designing the custom-made furniture, manufactured by Collingwood's Hunt Son & Oliver, with contributions from Grant Featherston. For browsing architectural eyes, there was much to see. The pilotis harked back to the Villa Savoye (1928) in Pouissy – the prototype modernist dwelling, designed by Le Corbusier. The landscaped courtyard garden, with its fountain sculpture by Gerald Lewers, was patterned by John Stevens on a similar feature of the Ministry of Education and Health (1936) in Rio – the original International Style office building, designed by Lucio Costa and Oscar Niemeyer under Le Corbusier's sway.

The entranceway steps, which subtly slow the visitor's transition from outside to inside, are a Japanese motif. The interior reliance on wood – warm and easy on the eye – shows Scandinavian influences. All of it encased in a characteristically American building typology for a British multinational client...and in an Australian city.

Height's allure could be baneful also. On 6 November 1958, fifty-eight-year-old PMG technician Ben Edwards had not been himself for some days. Since starting a course of blood pressure tablets, he had been forgetting things, feeling panicked. Could he be going out of his mind? His GP assured him otherwise, but he hesitated to go to work in Flinders Lane that morning, before deciding he must.

At 1.45pm, having drawn his pay, he asked leave from his superior to sort out some money orders. Two hours later, he became the site's fourth death, plummeting to the pavement of Albert Street from the roof of the nearly complete ICI House, falling past two window cleaners, who took him for a large bag. The next week his wife received two money orders, although no note, and the coroner returned an open verdict. (The twenty-five-year-old investigating constable who deemed there 'no suspicious circumstances' also played back pocket for St Kilda. Allan Jeans went on to be a sainted name in Australian rules – in Melbourne, you are never far from football).

When ICI House was opened a fortnight from Christmas, the fascination it exerted was more obviously wholesome. In his speech to assembled dignatories, British chairman Fleck spoke of 'an Australian landmark', 'a Commonwealth occasion', and of the duty borne by companies 'to see that the buildings they commission shall be not only appropriate to their needs and efficient, but also aesthetically satisfying'. McCutcheon's speech notes, dashed off at typical speed on the back of a memo, capitalised the word 'DIGNITY' next to a lower case 'efficiency'. And it is fair to say that of the 20,000 citizens who took the opportunity to tour ICI House during the ensuing Open Week, very few were enticed by its efficiency. On the contrary, the building seemed the last word in worker comfort, from its 100-seat ground floor theatre and Wales banking chamber, to its top floor 400-seat cafeteria with uninterrupted views for 70 miles in each direction and gleaming Gaggia coffee machine.

By day the air conditioning system and sealed windows, maintaining a constant 20C and 50% humidity, were a revelatory relief from summer swelter. Then there were the pampering indulgences like the roof garden, sub-basement recreation rooms and 12th-floor staff lending library. By night, with 5,500 electric lights, ICI House blazed like a Chinese lantern. 'Probably no other building project since...the Exhibition Buildings in 1879 has captured Melbourne's imagination as much as this glass-house giant,' reported *The Herald*, whose cartoonist 'Weg' (William Ellis Green) depicted ICI House as a vitreous mountain menaced by three mischievous cricket-playing boys. 'Please! Kids!' exclaimed a suited businessman. 'Don't play here!'

Such critics as had existed were disarmed. The ageing artist Norman Lindsay had denounced the glass box as 'a final triumph to modernistic art, with its cry of death to all beauty'. As if to head the charge off, ICIANZ began amassing what became Australia's most extensive corporate art collection, including works by Arthur Boyd, Arthur Streeton, John Brack, Sidney Nolan and…Norman Lindsay. The collection complemented a building that was itself a kind of art object.

A 20-minute ICI movie, *Skyscraper Story*, painted its headquarters in heroic hues. Soaring towards the clouds reflected in its glass, ICI House was the perfect subject for the cool, functionalist, objective photography of Wolfgang Sievers. Arising like a mirage beyond the foliage of Parliament Gardens or contrasted with the antique Lonsdale Street, ICI House appealed to the alert and discriminating urban eye of Mark Strizic.

Particularly reveling in the attention was the company's public relations manager, Peter Ryan – later, at Melbourne University Press, one of Australia's most distinguished publishers. For him, the building was an 'unimaginable boon', redefining what had been a rather dour and inscrutable enterprise: 'For a time, editors and journalists from all over Australia would do almost anything to be invited on a personal tour of inspection, accompanied by lunch in the splendid private dining room.' Through Ryan, Geoffrey Blainey was employed to write a company history of ICIANZ, on which he worked in ICI House for a year. 'It was very handsome from the outside,' he recalls. 'In the low skyline of that era it stood out like a glass trophy.' Like many a worker since he was less enamoured of the open plan, which affirmed a personal preference: 'I like rooms with walls.'

Another significant and sincere admirer also withheld a little of his approbation. Robin Boyd was then embarked on his seminal modernist critique of *The Australian Ugliness* (1960), with its denunciation of the local taste for busy and obtrusive 'featurism'. He welcomed ICI House, relieved that 'even in a frantically featurist society a non-featurist building can be a success'. Here was 'as good a representative of the crystallised mid-century style as can be found anywhere in the world', particularly ingenious in its 'clever separation of service and office areas', which were 'nicely complementary to each other in strength and proportion, like male and female'. At the same time, part of him shrank from its implications: in future corporate design suites, he speculated in *The Puzzle of Architecture* (1962), there might be 'no seat…for the architect, let alone a throne'.

'Boyd saw that office building could become a formularised system,' says Melbourne University's Goad. 'With the standardisation of work spaces, the exterior mattered little in the long run, and architectural aesthetics were unnecessary, which worried him greatly – because at the other end of the spectrum were the Eero Saarinens and Jørn Utzons, one-off gymnastic performers. In an architecture of extremes, how do you teach beauty? How do you judge whether the Opera House is spectacular, or just an ugly spiky thing? So although he admired ICI House, it also caused him grief.'

By then, too, grief had come McCutcheon's way, and more directly. At first, the only problems with ICI House were minor, even amusing. It was found, for example, that the building swayed ever so slightly – at the top, about ¾ of an inch in a 80mph gale. The only place this was perceptible was in the fish tank on the executive floor, where the water lapped gently from side to side – BSM's solution was a thick black line round the top of the tank.

Then, just before Christmas 1960, one of the glass panes shattered into tiny fragments. It was such a shock that, at first, a sniper was suspected. But then another shattered, and another. 'Everyone hoped that it wasn't anything major,' recalls Struan Gilfillan. 'You always accept a few breakages. But pretty soon they seemed to start falling like confetti.' Altogether, 71 panes of the Pan-O-Glass from Belgium's Société Belge d'Exploitations Verrières would shatter, and it would be more than a year before any explanation emerged. In the hiatus, timber canopies had to be erected over nearby footpaths.

BSM smarted. 'Oh, we were shocked and horrified,' remembers Gilfillan. 'The criticism from architects at other firms was endless. "Oh, you're from Bates Smart? You did *that* building, did you? Well, fancy that." We were very relieved when the scientific analysis was done.' Research by ER Ballantyne of the CSIRO's Building Research Division sheeted the blame to the manufacturer, explaining how the Pan-O-Glass was fatally weakened by nickel sulphide impurities, particles smaller than the head of the pin, as they expanded and contracted in Australian temperatures. That Ballantyne's paper, 'Fracture of Toughened Glass Wall Cladding, ICI House, Melbourne' (1961), was another world first was little consolation. ICIANZ's announcement that it was replacing all the panes on the west wall at a cost in excess of £50,000 made for an unwelcome front-page headline in *The Herald* in March 1962.

Glass curtain walls would prove problematic in other ways too. ICI House was an expensive building to operate, air conditioning absorbing nearly 40% of the building's running costs. Others experienced difficulties still more pronounced. In January 1962, Sydney clawed back the mantle of the location of Australia's tallest building, opening a 25-storey tower at Sydney Cove. But when the sun got the better of the AMP Tower's unsheltered northern curtain wall, it became virtually uninhabitable. When its architects, Peddle Thorp, were sought to design a headquarters for Custom Credit on St Kilda Road, the commission specifically referred to 'a dignified building...not a flimsy glass box...something to reflect the stability of the credit system'. The glass curtain wall lost Australian favour, and was scorned for decades afterwards.

In the end, ICI House's chief legacy became its size, on lists of which it steadily slipped down. Developers, whose ambitions increasingly defined city skylines, used their emancipation from height limits not for aesthetic enrichment but steeper rents; much as Boyd had prophesied, the architect's role was diminished. Corporate image-making was likewise refined, visible in the contrast between ICI House and BHP House (1972), the definitive headquarters of the next generation. The former looked as stylish as James Bond's cigarette lighter; the latter, designed by the mighty American corporate practice Skidmore Owings & Merrill, was as darkly cool as a presidential limousine.

As it transformed city streets into dark and windy canyons, sucked energy, crammed people and flattened textures, the tall office building also began courting a critical eye. 'So here we are,' sighed the *Sydney Morning Herald's* arch sceptic George Molnar. 'Our boxes are not economical. They are functional in a restricted sense only. They fail in the aesthetics they profess. What made us build them? It is an old story. Unnecessary centralisation in the city through real-estate speculation. They are jungle creatures, rising to the sky for light...It is not just a question of style. We should aim for a saner conception of our cities.' And one who would have nodded approval Osborn McCutcheon.

If he never regretted ICI House, McCutcheon grew to share Boyd's ambivalence about its unintended legacy. Knighted in 1966 and increasingly required to act as a grand old man of architecture, he enjoined audiences to design more humanely. 'We act for communities; for private and public bodies; and not as creators of monuments to directors or to ourselves,' he warned. 'The test of a building is the human responses it evokes, not its size or glamour.' McCutcheon was strongly influenced by The Club of Rome's sobering world prospectus *The Predicament of Mankind* (1968), Paul Ehrlich's Malthusian prophecies in *The Population Bomb* (1968), and Ian McHarg's hopes of ecological redemption in *Design with Nature* (1969). Some of his writings assumed almost a mystical air: 'The simple man, the quiet man, is moved and has deep satisfaction from earthy smells, the sky, wind, tree; by the storm and night murmurings, by the friendship and companionship of birds and animal life, and the power to plant and tend growing things and to human relationships.'

Seventy-year-old McCutcheon then founded, as a joint venture between BSM and engineering firm Rankine & Hill, a unique multi-disciplinary planning consultancy to provide more holistic solutions to what were commonly typed building problems. Urban Design and Planning Associates was led by his son Andrew, who had qualified as an architect, sheered away to become a Methodist minister, then studied social planning in the UK on a Churchill Scholarship. UDPA rose and fell, at one with the planning propensities of Whitlamism, at odds with the intellectual apathy of the Fraser years – although by standing between rapacious developers and recalcitrant protesters in the 1970s, it did much to save what remains today of Sydney's Rocks.

By the 1980s, ICI House itself looked in peril. Grandiose head offices fell from fashion – some argued that they were no longer necessary, tied up capital and induced bureaucratic torpor. Some of ICI House's luxuries, like the lofty cafeteria and roof garden, were sacrificed to economy. When ICIANZ was granted independence by its restructuring parent company in July 1997, the great art collection was dispersed, and the building itself sold to Macquarie Bank. ICIANZ's descendant, Orica, now occupies only five levels; the building's top floor is rented by British engineering consultancy Arup.

Fifteen years ago, however, a new tenant looped Orica House back to its origins: BSM, architectural credits now including the likes of Melbourne's Crown Casino and Federation Square and Sydney's Mid City and Police Headquarters, moved into the sixth floor of its most significant building. Observing the new fashion for post-industrial bareness, but also as if to admire its original handiwork, it stripped the suspended ceiling system to reveal the prefabricated concrete flooring so revolutionary in its time. And while the face of the city has changed, the tall building of today being the soaring apartment tower, the thrill of gazing on it from elevation abides. 'Many big buildings these days are very fat for economic reasons, which is why you end up with big windowless areas,' says Melbourne University's Goad. 'So while there are some inefficiencies in the slab plan, the amenity advantages are huge – potential for cross ventilation, visual connection etc. Not only can you see out both sides of Orica House, but the views are...well, they're to die for.'

Multiple overlapping heritage protections, and nomination as one of eight buildings on the World Register of Significant Twentieth Century Australian Architecture, have further secured that outlook. Sensing that a touch of *Mad Men* chic might enhance its rental appeal, current owner Charter Hall has recently begun refurbishing its eight lifts, inspired by the original BSM design fished from a microfiche in the firm's archives, with Aalto-esque curved timber ceilings that roll gently into the rear wall.

What once seemed to dwarf human scale today seems tactfully restrained – refraining from gobbling its whole block, making good on the ground its imposition on the sky. And what once was a vision of Melbourne's future now offers a powerful sense of communion with the architectural and social past.

# DOWN ON THE STREET

## *Weegee and Winogrand* (2018)

In an era when everyone with a phone is potentially a street photographer, the genre, famously associated with Arbus and Atget, Maier and Meyerowitz, seems almost too diffuse to grasp. On Google Street View, whole cities unfold for our delectation, the 'decisive moment' decreed by Mountain View, California. What price the precious instant against such consuming relentlessness?

A first full-length biography of Weegee and a handsome monograph of Garry Winogrand are radically different but pleasingly complementary contributions to an understanding of that quixotic figure of the photographic flaneur. Both are best known for prowling New York, Weegee by night, Winogrand by day, thirty years apart – working, as it were, opposite sides of the same streets.

Weegee was in headlong pursuit of event: murder, fire, confluence, confrontation. Winogrand was the master of the non-event that somehow gained significance through his recording of it. Weegee longed to step out from behind his camera, to achieve notoriety, to be a subject. Winogrand as he went on seemed almost to merge with his camera, photographing so ceaselessly that a substantial portion of his oeuvre has never even been processed. Both their careers were angled obliquely to the times.

As Christopher Bonanos notes in *Flash*, Weegee tackled news photography when its practitioners were almost entirely anonymous. He cites a huge 1935 Knopf anthology of new pictures called *The Breathless Moment*: 'In its roughly two hundred pages, not one photographer is named, and the introduction doesn't bother to apologize or explain.' Yet New York was simultaneously becoming a bastion of the pictorial press. There were nine daily newspapers, notably the *Daily News*, a pioneering tabloid which at its peak sold nearly five million copies, and which advertised its commitment to the visual with a masthead incorporating a Grafflex Speed Graphic – the same camera

Weegee would brandish as his permission to go anywhere.

Born Usher Fellig into a family of Galician Jews in 1899, Weegee landed at Ellis Island aged ten, and grew up in same Lower East Side streets he later photographed. Yet he sloughed that identity off almost entirely: his boastful and wisecracking autobiography *Weegee by Weegee* (1961), Bonanos notes, is materially unreliable, even about his number of siblings.

Fellig became the definition of a self-made man, composed, as it were, of the photographs he started taking in his teens, in and around work as a printer in newspapers darkrooms – in which, permanently impoverished, he sometimes slept when park benches were unavailable or doss houses unaffordable.

New York in the 1930s was raw, rackety, dense and dangerous. Bonanos has poured stupendous effort into pinning down the provenance of some of Weegee's most famous images – the blood-stained corpses, the perp walks, the jagged juxtapositions, the slices of tenement life. On some, such as cornered, battered 'Mad Dog' Esposito and femme fatale Norma Parker, whole novels could be written. On others, Weegee even had a go himself, adding punchy titles. The rubbernecking crowds of 'Their First Murder' and 'Balcony Seats at a Murder' bely Weegee's dismissive remark: 'I have no time for messages…That's for Western Union and the Salvation Army.'

What he loved adding most was a rubber stamp on the back demanding credit for at first 'A. Fellig', then 'Arthur (Weegee) Fellig', and finally 'Weegee the Famous'. Bonanos describes how sedulously Weegee marketed himself and his working methods with images of his half-room over a gun dealer's shop in Little Italy with a single chair, typewriter, newsprint wallpaper and bookshelf containing copies of *Live Alone and Like It* and *The Sex Life of the Unmarried Adult*.

Weegee's nickname was a photographic brand *avant le lettre*, allegedly derived from Ouija board – a reference to a supernatural talent for finding his way to crime scenes, which owed more to assiduous surveillance of police short wave traffic. In this way, Bonanos argues, Weegee became an archetype, popular culture reserving a place for 'the squat guy in a rumpled suit and crumpled fedora, carrying a big press camera with a flashgun mounted on its side, a stinky cigar clamped in the corner of his mouth', with the result that 'people who have never heard of Weegee can describe him'.

It's a provocative claim and, unfortunately, Bonanos doesn't convincingly elaborate on it. Just when you're ready to tour the depiction of photographers in cinema and/or an exposition of how Weegee's use of single light sources influenced noir aesthetics, the author's interest flags. We get Weegee's role in providing the look and title of Mark Hellinger's *The Naked City* (1948), but not the inspiration he supplied to more recent movies such as *Two Evil Eyes* (1990), *The Public Eye* (1992), and *Nightcrawler* (2014), which actually started as a biopic.

A by-product of Weegee's relentless self-mythologising, too, is that the reliable biographical material is thin, which Bonanos can do little to disguise. For an approximate date of the dissolution of Weegee's short marriage, for example, he has to rely on a pawnbroker's ticket for $3 for what may or may not have been his wedding ring. More material concerns Weegee's later life, when his work was far less even, and he became bizarrely obsessed with distorting lenses, enthusiasm for which he could not believe was not more widely shared. 'You're missing the boat,' he complained to a sceptical editor. 'These broads with five tits are gonna be a sensation.' By the second half of the 1950s, observes Bonanos dryly, 'Weegee had become an oldies act, and the distortion shots were the new album that nobody wanted to hear.'

By then, Winogrand was at work, turning his lens on a New York of calmer, more prosperous postwar streets, and in an arts environment more indulgent of photography: he benefited by three Guggenheim Fellowships. He too enjoyed a productive peak, in the 1960s, from which more than half the one hundred photographs in essayist Geoff Dyer's *The Street Philosophy of Gary Winogrand* are drawn. But Dyer has chosen with a free hand, inspired by personal affinities and creative responses, and the result is more than the sum of its parts, which were considerable anyway.

Where Weegee seductively normalised the shock value of his content, Winogrand was fascinated by the challenge of making a photograph 'more interesting than what actually happened', in a country of surface orderliness was now merely edged with unease. Dyer, whose *The Ongoing Moment*

(2005) was an invigorating romp through a selection of classic photographs, relishes sifting for the allusions and self-quotations in images populated not by individuals 'so much as highly individualised instances of character types'.

Four men gathered round an open bonnet evoke 'the capacity of a car engine to swallow up all the philosophical depth of which men are capable'; a man and a woman in distracted conversation at an airport explore 'talk as a way of killing time that is already dead'; a tiny figure sauntering past a blank bank wall 'looks like a sequence from a thriller as it might have been directed by Antonioni'. As Dyer observes: 'If you spend enough time on the streets you will come across everything.' Technology's instant totalities, then, will still not quite suffice to do them justice.

# THE GOOD DOCTOR 1

## *A profile of John Cade* (2007)

In the slim, synoptic history of twentieth-century psychiatry that he wrote after retiring as superintendent of Melbourne's Royal Park hospital twenty-eight years ago, Dr John Cade devoted a short chapter to lithium: the 'simple inorganic substance' that to this day, and for reasons only dimly understood, is astoundingly effective in counteracting the horrendous affliction known as bipolar disorder.

Like the rest of *Mending The Mind*, the chapter is discursive, clear and elegant, with a few characteristic flourishes. Cade, a scourge of Freudians, permitted himself a dig at 'the utter uselessness of psychotherapy based on psychopathological theories'; a devout Catholic, he digressed for a page and a half to muse on whether Pope Urban VI might have been a manic depressive. The chapter omits only one material fact: that he was lithium's discoverer.

One of the most revolutionary papers in medical history, published fifty-six years ago, ran to only three pages under the unprepossessing title 'Lithium Salts in the Treatment of Psychotic Excitement'. But when the *Medical Journal of Australia* surveyed the history of its contents six months ago, no contribution had been cited so often: 888 occasions. There have recently been other signs that Cade will receive belated due. In 2001, he was the subject of a bioplay, *Doctor Cade*, by Neil Cole, a former Victorian shadow attorney-general whose bipolar disorder was brought under control by lithium; an excellent documentary about lithium, *Troubled Minds*, directed by Dennis Smith, was aired on SBS in October 2004; medical historian Ann Westmore is planning a biography. But his significance is best conveyed by the title of his own book: *Mending The Mind*. When Cade became a psychiatrist, treatment of the mentally ill had barely changed since Hippocrates: patients were to be sequestered and subdued. Cade was among the first to conjecture that the mind could be 'mended'; lithium prefigured a revolution in psychopharmacology that has made life more liveable for millions, and virtually emptied the institutions that once teemed with apparently intractable manias, depressions and anxieties. He did it, moreover, in circumstances so extraordinary that some have thought it simply a great mistake; in the context of his life, in fact, they make complete sense.

Cade was born in Murtoa, in Victoria's Wimmera, on 18 January 1912. His father David, a general practitioner, served with the Army Medical Corps in France and won the Distinguished Service Order, but buckled beneath the strain of resuming practice amid the post-war flu pandemic, and accepted a less strenuous position as a medical officer in what was then called the Mental Hygiene Service – the very name attests the prevailing view of mental illness as a stain or contamination. The first mental patients that John Cade met were his father's at the Beechworth and Sunbury Asylums, and the encounters impressed him forcefully; at twenty-four, he joined the service himself.

The old jest holds that those choosing psychiatry first wish to understand themselves. Cade doesn't fit it. A slight figure with prematurely receding hair, seldom photographed without a tie, he was a man of pacific temper and quiet good humour, capable of disagreement without rancour and discipline without anger. Of modest means, he developed modest tastes to match. When he married a Royal Women's Hospital nurse, Jean Charles, who had seen him through a severe bout of bilateral pneumococcal pneumonia, he could afford neither an engagement ring nor guests at their wedding.

Cade's only disproportion was in his curiosity, insatiable and incurable. He was a close reader and a minute observer, who relished his garden and the bush. The Cades once took Mogens Schou – a Danish psychiatrist who Cade honoured as lithium's 'devoted foster father' – on a picnic to Healesville Sanctuary on Melbourne's outskirts. No sooner had they arrived than, without explanation, Cade picked up his sandwiches and disappeared into the woods. When Schou, embarrassed, finally asked if he had somehow offended his hosts, Jean reassured him: her husband was simply checking the animal droppings, which he was expert at distinguishing.

It was on his first posting to Beechworth that Cade emerged as a decidedly unorthodox clinician, startling colleagues by expressing an eagerness for ward rounds; he was thought stranger still when he began identifying, in the undifferentiated mass of the 'mad', patients whose problems were primarily medical rather than mental. Cade's son Jack recalls: 'He'd see some poor old duck with a rash and he'd say: "This woman has pellagra." He'd see someone whose teeth were falling out and say: "This person has scurvy." Or he'd find some freezing cold person wrapped up in a blanket and tell the staff: "Thyroid dysfunction." Mixed with the patients were a lot of people who were totally curable. I think it was where my father developed his belief that good psychiatry should be founded on good medicine.'

War interrupted these insights, then perhaps deepened them. In 1940, Cade was commissioned in the 2/9th Field Ambulance, Eighth Division, and posted to Singapore. He proved to be an excellent officer, uncannily calm even amid the chaos of the fortress's invasion. One night, in an ambulance in search of wounded, Cade and his driver found themselves flanked by columns of soldiers. 'I don't think we'll make it tonight,' Cade said at last. 'Let's head back to barracks.' Later he asked the driver: 'Did you notice anything about those soldiers?' When the driver admitted he had not, Cade said: 'They were Japanese.'

'Why didn't you tell me?' the driver complained.

'If I'd told you,' Cade replied, 'you might've panicked.'

During his three years in the infamous Changi prison camp, Cade did not merely continue his medical duties, but acted as the camp's secret information officer: he was delegated to commit the nightly BBC broadcast on the camp's hidden radio to memory for repetition to fellow POWs. Incarceration reduced Cade, like many others, to a 'walking skeleton' of 40kg; yet, the playwright Cole believes, it also crystallised his thoughts: 'If ever there was a place where you would have thought depression was widespread and reactive, it was Changi. But it wasn't the case. And it confirmed his own impression that there was depression "within" people irrespective of circumstance.' When Cade returned to work at Bundoora Repatriation Mental Hospital, he indulged his curiosity in a series of experiments so speculative that they seem closer to alchemy than medicine.

John Cade's *bete noir* was psychoanalysis. 'Dad thought Freud had really set back the cause of psychiatry,' says Jack Cade. 'Not that the mind did not exist, but that, as a method of understanding mental illness, it was totally sterile.

The brain was an organ. Like every organ, it was subject to injury; it was thus amenable to treatment.' Cade's objective was to find a chemical dimension to mental distress. In a wooden shed in the hospital grounds that he equipped as a laboratory, Cade began injecting fresh human urine into guinea pigs. The most toxic was the urine of patients with manic depression, the wild and debilitating fluctuation between euphoria and despair that afflicts about one per cent of the population, which Cade ascribed to concentrations of urea.

When he fortuitously used lithium urate to test how the concentration of uric acid affected the toxicity of urea, however, he was surprised to find that it seemed to have a protective effect; during a follow-up test using lithium carbonate, the animals lay contentedly on their backs for some hours before returning to normal. Was it safe? Cade answered that question, to his wife's dismay, by trialling lithium carbonate on himself. When it had no ill effects, he selected nineteen patients for a clinical trial: ten with manic depression, six with schizophrenia, three with melancholia.

Jack Cade and his younger brother David were bemused eyewitnesses. With their father's encouragement, they treated the hospital as a play area. 'Of course, when we were growing up, our schoolfriends would say: "You live in the loony bin!",' recalls Jack. 'But we learned such a lot about the patients: these lovely people whose brains had gone. At Bundoora, they were, of course, old diggers, including some from World War I. Lovely old guys, some a bit strange, some a lot strange, mostly completely lost; the hospital was their home.' David Cade points out, however, that his father's lithium brainstorm was decidedly out of the ordinary: 'I find it astonishing that Dad at that time thought it likely there was something to be found which would lead to real treatment of psychiatrically-disturbed patients. Because there was no evidence to lead him to believe that. It was pure intuition.' As David comments, his father's audacity, by modern standards, was also breathtaking: 'Even if he had been able to do that sort of work today, it would never have been accepted, because it wasn't done under a conventional research protocol; nor would it have passed any test of the Therapeutic Goods Administration here or the Food and Drug Administration in the US.'

Cade's research was essentially of his era, one in which the doctor omnipotent reigned; in mental health especially, clinicians enjoyed startling discretion. 'As a medical superintendent in the 1940s,' Westmore says, 'you could basically give your patients what you wanted. There were no ethics committees, no-one looking over your shoulder. You were the boss. Unlike a big general hospital, psychiatric hospitals were isolated from the mainstream.' Nonetheless, disciplines were no less binding for their self-imposition. Cade's decision to submit himself to lithium before administering it to patients recalls the military nostrum that no commander should issue an order involving risk he would not take himself. 'The military aspect of his [Cade's] life was a strong one,' agrees Westmore. 'Cade himself had been in the Melbourne University Regiment before the war, which his father was very keen on. He didn't love the army experience, but I think he did absorb some of its ethos.'

Cade's case notes of his first subject, fifty-four-year-old William Brand, known universally as 'Monkey', are now in Melbourne University's Medical History Museum. An itinerant labourer discharged from the Australian Light Horse due to 'dementia', Brand had been admitted by police almost five years earlier. Cade found him to be 'so lacking even momentary attention that questions usually fail to interrupt his flight of ideas'; his manic energies were most conspicuously applied to frantic lawn mowing. Yet within days of his first doses of lithium citrate on 29 March 1948, Brand was clearly calmer.

'Monkey' was a favourite of the Cade boys, whom he favoured with humbugs. 'We probably saw more of him than Dad,' says Jack. David recalls his father's questions: 'When he started the treatments, because he knew that we were good friends with Monkey, Dad started asking us: "Have you seen Monkey recently? How is he?" And we told him we'd found him remarkably normal: the change was very noticeable.' Within four weeks, Cade was noting in his small but tidy and legible hand: 'He now appears to be quite normal. A diffident, pleasant, energetic little man.' Eight weeks later, Brand was discharged, and returned to his old job. The results from the other nine bipolar patients were little less dramatic – the 'garrulous, euphoric, restless, unkempt' became the 'quiet, tidy, rational' – while as expected the others enjoyed no relief.

When Cade was almost finished writing up his researches, however, he received a demoralising shock. 'Monkey' was readmitted, wilder than ever. Cade was devastated: 'It was the most bitter disappointment of my life.' Then Brand's brother confided that 'Monkey' had grown 'blasé' and ceased taking his medication; the relapse attested lithium's efficacy rather than challenging it. Cade's efforts to restabilise 'Monkey's condition were ultimately unsuccessful – Brand died in May 1950 – but lithium was by then in the public sphere.

Here the tales of Cade and his wonder drug part, their only similarity being that both had long periods to wait before recognition. Lithium had to surmount three obstacles. As Cade expected, his own obscurity told against the discovery: an unknown psychiatrist, working alone in a small chronic hospital with no research training, primitive techniques and negligible equipment was hardly likely to be compellingly persuasive, especially in the US. Worse still, even as Cade's paper appeared, there were American reports of fatalities from lithium toxicity following its reckless prescription as a salt substitute. It was precisely the worst time to be recommending lithium's use for anything medicinal; not until October 1968 did the *American Journal of Psychiatry* publish details of clinical trials. Finally, there were economic realities. No-one can patent an element. Pharmaceutical companies, reliant on healthy margins to fund their research and development, scorned lithium until Pfizer and Rowell Laboratories made it available on a philanthropic basis from 1970. Then its results were immediate; it remains, in fact, an astoundingly powerful treatment, used in about a third of bipolar cases, alongside more recent drugs like carbamazepine and valproate.

Ten years ago, *Science* magazine estimated lithium's value to the American economy alone as $US145 billion. But it has proven to be more than a drug. As the first psychotropic (mood-altering) medication – preceding by four years the discovery of the anti-psychotic neuroleptic drug chlorpromazine – it was the vanguard of a whole new approach to the treatment of mental illness. That is to say, it was an actual 'treatment' in which the patient 'got better', rather than remaining confined to preserve the greater 'mental hygiene'.

Cade himself, meanwhile, all but abandoned lithium, content to leave its development to others better equipped, like Schou, who was spurred by the personal pain of a brother with bipolar disorder, and biochemist Edward Trautner, who in *Man and Medicine*, a 1955 publication by his Melbourne University, was even erroneously credited with its discovery.

Cade's indifference surprised many; even, David Cade recalls, Jean: 'Mum was disapproving that my father published his lithium research the way he did, after such a short time, and also that he didn't follow it through, because he was the expert in the field. But my father felt three things: first, that it was obviously very effective, and that the sooner the news was released, the better for patients; second, that he had reached the limits of what he could do, for he had no real research facilities, and many people were better equipped to do the developmental work; and thirdly, he had other objects in mind already.'

For Cade had embarked on new, often idiosyncratic, adventures. One long-term project was mapping demographic patterns of mental illness across Victoria: he came to suspect, for instance, that the relative sanity of the Goulburn Valley's inhabitants was associated with their consumption of stone fruits. Use of himself as a test tube also continued: he once said drolly that it 'saved a lot of trouble with coroners'. Once, Cade even took strontium. 'He nearly died,' recalls David Cade. 'For about a week, he looked shocking. Slate grey...Mum was terribly cross.' He joked towards the end of his life of having eaten his way through the periodic table.

It is Cade's cheerful amateurism that has led some to dismiss his discovery as chiefly accidental, yet lithium's properties could only really have intrigued such a happy wanderer of research. If anything, Cade's experimentation can be seen as conterminous with the main project in his life: his patients' welfare. As superintendent of Royal Park Psychiatric Hospital between 1952 and 1977, he was endlessly solicitous of their needs, and never, despite administrative pressures, absolved himself of daily ward rounds. In his retirement speech, he reserved his most heartfelt thanks for those he had treated: 'They taught me so much.'

As lithium came of age, Cade accepted recognition by his peers with characteristically little fuss: when he and Schou shared psychiatry's prestigious Kittay Prize in April 1974, he left for New York with a briefcase that contained only a clean shirt and a toothbrush. A journalist who visited him at the time found him at Royal Park in 'a rather Spartan little office, very public service décor, with green imitation leather chairs, drab carpets and grey metal filing cabinets'. Obeisance to departmental bureaucracy, in fact, never interested him; he lost himself only in cases. 'He was always thinking,' says David Cade. 'He commonly saw things that others didn't. It was a forte of his.'

Numerous stories concern Cade's lateral approach to diagnosis. One morning, for example, he encountered in an isolation cell a noisy and incomprehensible man brought in the night before by police, and asked for the patient's clothes. 'This man isn't sick,' Cade announced. 'Look at this paint. It hasn't even dried. I suspect he's a house painter, and that he was at work hours before he was arrested.' When Cade asked the Health Department to send a senior public servant with a command of Greek, the reality emerged. The patient was a migrant fresh from the boat and working for the painter brother-in-law with whom he was staying; celebrating his first week of work at the pub, he had become disoriented, then angry that he could not remember where he lived. Cade himself drove the man around the streets of Brunswick, the Melbourne suburb with the greatest concentration of Greek migrants, until a familiar landmark guided them to the bosom of an anxious family.

Cade's own family grew to four boys, all of them following him into medicine. Jack remains head of intensive care at Royal Melbourne Hospital, a role David filled at St Vincent's; born after the war, Peter became a surgeon, Richard a laboratory technician. They speak of their father with an affection and respect that is deep rather than effusive – rather like the man himself. Only once is he recalled as being moved to tears; and, despite a life in which he was exposed to some of the ghastliest human torments and tortures, its cause was a simple domestic drama, when the family daschund broke into the woodshed ate some strynchine baits, and began to writhe in pain, wracked by *grand mal* epileptic fits of increasing severity. Calmly, practically, John Cade took his shotgun, and ended the animal's agonies with a bullet in the back of the head. Then, to general surprise, he wept. For John Cade, this was perhaps the acutest suffering: a sense of being helpless to alleviate the suffering of others.

# THE GOOD DOCTOR 2

## *A profile of Bronwyn King* (2016)

On Good Friday this year, Dr Bronwyn King and her husband were staying with her parents in the quiet Victorian coastal town of Torquay. They started watching a movie – although Bronwyn, as she often is, was only half-there, busily pecking at her laptop.

'AXA – news…' said the subject line of the email from a French insurance executive. 'In confidentiality,' it read: 'we have decided to divest tobacco…If you can, let's discuss further. Thanks for your help.' Bronwyn felt momentarily giddy. It was six years since she had sent the first of tens of thousands of hopeful, courteous but determined emails with such ends in mind. She had already persuaded thirty-five superannuation funds controlling nearly half Australia's total funds under management to shun tobacco. This, perhaps, was her greatest success yet. But she eschewed a celebratory glass of wine: there was work to do, about the structure and timing of the announcement. When her family turned in, they left Bronwyn, as they are used to, at her laptop.

Two months later at Geneva's plush Beau Rivage Hotel, Bronwyn looked out over a sea of faces, mostly delegates to the forthcoming World Health Assembly, and introduced her 'new best friend', AXA boss Thomas Buberl. AXA, he said, would forthwith sell €200 million of tobacco stocks: there was applause. It would also, he added, run off €1.6 billion of tobacco corporate bonds. There was a hush. Had he just said billion?

In an old war, a new front had opened – perhaps belatedly. Tobacco kills six million people a year: the McKinsey Global Institute deems it humankind's greatest self-generated social burden, ahead even of armed violence, war and terrorism. Yet as an issue, observes Bronwyn's offsider Clare Payne, it has receded in public consciousness: 'There's this tendency for people to think: "Oh we're done with tobacco, aren't we? Everyone knows. It's a just a choice thing for people now." When we're actually in an epidemic – history's first epidemic of a non-communicable disease.'

To again make it the stuff of headlines, then, is no mean feat. 'She's a star,' says Cary Adams, CEO of the Union for International Cancer Control, who just over a year ago put Bronwyn in charge of the Global Task Force for Tobacco Divestment. It's not a mantle that rests easily with her. All the forty-one-year-old oncologist at Melbourne's Epworth Heathcare feels she's done is take to heart her Hippocratic Oath, especially the injunction to 'do no harm'.

*

Into her mid-twenties, Bronwyn King's career had seemed mapped out. At Fintona Girls' School in Balwyn, she had been a star junior swimmer, thriving on the daily pre-dawn starts and unrelenting competition, climaxing in medals at national championships and a victory in the Pier-to-Pub. On completing medical studies in 1999, she became an Australian swimming team doctor, and weighed up specialising in sports medicine and paediatrics.

In February 2001, however, Bronwyn began three months as a radiation oncology resident in the lung cancer unit of Peter MacCallum Cancer Hospital. She was, she confesses, a reluctant conscript. Radiation oncology, which uses giant linear accelarators to beat back advancing cancers, is a technically and emotionally challenging field of medicine, undertaken underground for the containment of its X-ray emissions, dedicated chiefly to the very sick. And sickest of all are smokers.

For Bronwyn it was an education. The five-year survival rate for lung cancer is 15 per cent: her job was largely to alleviate suffering from a brutal disease of unsung morbidity. Most people have an image of lung cancer sufferers propped in bed subsiding gently, maybe with a bit of a cough, possibly on oxygen. The reality is very different. In a fifth of cases, for example, lung cancer metastasizes to the brain, inducing paralysis and loss of cognitive function: the patient, literally, loses their mind. Death can come violently too. One morning Bronwyn arrived to find the corner of a ward absent not only its bedclothes but its curtains and furnishings. The night before a patient had essentially drowned in her own blood from a burst vessel, drenching staff in her death throes. In the room were three other terrified patients who had heard the whole thing.

Almost every interaction bore witness in some way to tobacco's toll. Taking a history from a new female patient one day, Bronwyn asked her age. 'I'm forty-three,' the woman replied. 'I'm getting quite old.' It transpired that her whole immediate family had died in their forties from cancers related to smoking. 'I had this overwhelming sense of the impact of tobacco,' Bronwyn recalls. 'The public did not know what was going on. They didn't know because I was a doctor and *I* hadn't known. Until I worked there. I started to wish I had a television camera with me, so people could see what I was seeing.'

But so much was out of sight for a reason – to which Bronwyn was first introduced by an older patient who beckoned her from his bed, looked around furtively, and whispered: 'This is because of the smoking, isn't it?' When she said it probably was, he nodded and looked away. Here were lung cancer's little-acknowledged secondary symptoms of disgrace and shame. Where families could be relied on to rally around sufferers from breast and prostate cancer, tension surrounded those with tobacco-related illness, perceived as having *brought cancer on themselves*. This has been an unforseen impact of the public health campaign to scare smokers straight: in a recent survey, thirty per cent of Australians agreed with the sentiment that lung cancer patients were less deserving of sympathy than other cancer patients. 'Lung cancer has become the syphilis of the 21st century,' says the head of Peter MacCallum's lung cancer unit, Professor David Ball. 'Patients are regarded as victims of their own lack of self-control. Whereas they're actually victims of a concerted and successful campaign by the tobacco industry to turn them into addicts.'

It was Professor Ball, a fixture at Peter Mac since 1973, who became Bronwyn's lodestar. Amid the unpromising circumstances, he instilled an environment of kindness and hope. For young doctors, says Professor Ball, it can be too much: 'I've had people in training in this specialty who've eventually been reduced to tears, saying they can't go on. They want all their patients to get better. Life's not like that.' He encourages them to think differently:

> For a doctor, lung cancer sufferers are tremendously rewarding to work with. They don't come in saying: 'Why me? I'm pissed off. Why aren't you working harder to find a cure?' They come in feeling ashamed. When

> you reassure them that you want to make their life as good as it can be, they're immensely grateful. Because they tend to stay long periods, you get to know them as people too. And you're at that very serious time of life, where the questions are deep and philosophical, and existential concerns come to the fore.

Those deep questions resonated with Bronwyn. 'People say that if you don't know what you want to do before you work with David, you will afterwards,' she says. 'He was the first doctor I really wanted to be – a great teacher, a great colleague, interested in everyone and everything. In that three months, I got to know patients, I got to know families, I worked with an inspiring medical team, I felt so privileged, and it changed me forever.' She dug in for what became the seven-year haul towards adding FRANZCR – Fellow of the Royal Australian and New Zealand College of Radiologists – to her postnominals. After a couple of years she was joined in this pursuit, and in her life, by Dr Mark Shaw, a quietly-spoken New Zealander whom she met at Geelong's Andrew Love Cancer Centre and married. Yet her lifechange remained incomplete until she and her husband emerged from their high-stakes, high-stress discipline to do something of utmost normality – buy a house.

*

Bronwyn calls it 'the story'; maybe it should be 'The Story'. It's how she prefaces most presentations – if ever time precludes it, she feels regretful. 'It explains everything, really,' she says. 'Sometimes I apologise to audiences for having told it so often. But people always come up afterwards and say: "I *love* that story".'

The scenario, a conversation about her finances with a consultant from Health Super in the Peter MacCallum cafeteria in March 2010, could hardly have been more prosaic. In fact, Bronwyn was standing to leave when a final question crossed her mind: was she meant to specify how she wanted her money invested? No need, said the consultant: her money, as it is with seventy-five per cent of Australians, was in the 'default option'.

Unaware there were alternatives, Bronwyn asked about them. Oh, came the reply, there was a 'greenie option', involving no investment in mining, alcohol or tobacco. The answer brought her up short. 'Does that mean I'm *currently* investing in tobacco?' she asked. Well yes, the consultant replied: '*Everyone is.*' Bronwyn sat back down.

It was worse. Two weeks later the consultant confirmed that four of the five biggest holdings in the international component of Health Super's default option were tobacco-related: British American Tobacco, Imperial Tobacco, Philip Morris and Swedish Match. Bronwyn shared this exposure with the overwhelming majority of Peter Mac's 2500 staff members. 'We're a dedicated cancer hospital,' she recalls. 'There was nowhere else this could have mattered more. The idea that all of us, the doctors, the nurses, the occupational therapists, the speech pathologists, were invested in tobacco companies...well, it had to be fixed.' Bronwyn's concerns were immediately shared by Peter Mac's CEO, Craig Bennett, who accompanied her to a meeting with members of Health Super's executive and investment team.

The response was cordial but bemused. 'It was strange for a financial institution to be approached by members about these issues,' Bronwyn recalls. 'Mainly they were surprised.' A 'good-natured' discussion ensued. Maybe tobacco stocks *were* a little objectionable, but wouldn't that 'greenie option' salve her conscience? Bronwyn shook her head; Bennett agreed.

Other factors then conspired to relegate tobacco to a back burner: Health Super commenced a merger with Sydney-based First State Super. In the hiatus, Bronwyn started educating herself. Australian super funds had only between 0.5 and 1.3 per cent of their assets in tobacco. But in a $2 trillion pool, that was still in the region of $10 billion. The seven biggest funds with health professionals as members all offered 'greenie' opt-outs, designated 'sustainable', ethical' or 'socially responsible'. But four of these actually *had money in tobacco.*

After a year's to-and-fro with Health Super, Bronwyn finally got in front of its board, flanked by Craig Bennett and David Ball, punctuating her PowerPoint presentation with knockout statistics: that someone in the world dies from tobacco use every eight seconds; that these include 15,000 Australians a year; that no substance takes a steeper toll of lives and years lost.

Bronwyn was nervous and exhilarated: 'I was presenting to all these people from a world I knew nothing about sitting next to the man who knows everything [Ball].' She was also shortly to take maternity leave: 'I thought: "If this doesn't work, it's probably going nowhere".' But the response was gratifying: 'I could also tell by the end of that meeting we had a lot of friends.' The impression deepened at the first instance of what would be a recurrent experience, when a director trailed her to the lift. 'Just so you know,' the director said, 'my mother died of lung cancer. Thank you for doing this.'

About to fold, Health Super's board bequeathed the issue to its new parent. First State Super CEO Michael Dwyer is an unusual boss – inspired by visiting Timor Leste in 2000, he co-founded Australia for UNHCR, which raises funds for the United Nations High Commissioner for Refugees. He sensed a problem it might be prudent to get ahead of: a group with 40 per cent of its members in health services that had $170 million invested in tobacco was bound to hear more about it, from members and media.

Like other super funds, First State Super was required to observe the *Superannuation Industry (Supervision) Act*, binding trustees at all times to act in members' best interests, which has tended to be interpreted by law in a narrowly financial sense. But at this point, another statute made its presence felt: tobacco share prices were hit by, among other things, the proclamation of Australia's *Tobacco Plain Packaging Act*. 'I could tell the board that these were stocks whose product was being condemned and restricted by every government round the country,' says Dwyer. 'They had no redeeming feature. As Bronwyn says: "There's no such thing as a safe cigarette."' In July 2012, CEO and doctor put their names to a press release declaring First State Super the first Australian superannuation fund to renounce tobacco; six months later HESTA, whom Bronwyn had also courted, followed suit. And though the process had taken two years, she was used to long hauls. 'I started thinking,' she says, 'if they could do it, why not others?'

*

Superannuation conferences can be dry affairs. So when Dwyer started dropping Bronwyn into programmes through 2013 and 2014, her presence and message quickly gained a following. Grabbing audiences with The Story, she did not let go. 'I've never seen anyone network like Bronwyn,' says Michael Baldwin, CEO of the Funds Executive Association, an industry group whose conference she addressed in June 2013. 'It's a skill I wish I had. People love dealing with her.' She distributed a business card bearing the rubric Tobacco Free Portfolios, featuring a logo designed online for $300 transfiguring the ribbon that is a cancer remembrance's best-known symbol into a cigarette. She piled up cards she collected and studiously emailed the addressees, politely petitioning to meet directors, trustees and investment managers – even just to 'have a coffee'.

Those meetings regularly begat further meetings, and also elicited personal confidences. In any group of five people she sat down with, Bronwyn found, at least one person would be harbouring a story about how tobacco-related illness had touched their lives; down the track, two chairmen would recuse themselves from votes about their funds' tobacco exposures, fearful of emotion clouding their corporate decision making.

Pregnant through some of this time with a second child, Bronwyn found that her most incisive pitch was illuminating the tobacco industry's exploitation of the young. The average age at which Australian smokers take the habit up, fifteen years and nine months, is actually high by world standards. Globally it's estimated that 80-100,000 children start smoking every day – so much for the notion of smoking being based on mature, fully-informed choice. What's more, according to the International Labour Organisation, up to sixty per cent of the 33 million engaged in tobacco farming worldwide are under sixteen. To those who challenged that tobacco stocks were historically good performers, Bronwyn had a brisk rejoinder: 'If a business can live with six million deaths and externalizing €2 trillion in health costs a year while employing mainly children, then it probably won't find it difficult making money. All it has to do is adjust its moral compass.'

Bronwyn was careful, all the same, not to scold. After all, much of this information was new to her too – and as a medical practitioner she might have been expected to know it. In fact, as she realized, medicine has historically divided between clinicians like herself, who treat people, and public health specialists, concerned with society. So she sought the latter out: the likes of Professor Simon Chapman at University of Sydney and Professor Mike Daube from Curtin University, whose experiences in tobacco control stretched back to the 1970s. They were impressed. 'I get a lot of approaches from people with crackpot ideas,' says Chapman. 'Bronwyn immediately struck me as different – someone highly intelligent, very organized, and street smart. Not to mention engaging and vivacious in an area that's stereotyped as deadly earnest and tinged with moralism.' Says the wryly humorous Daube: 'She's such a deeply unpleasant person, isn't she?'

While the tone of Bronwyn's campaign came naturally, she was shrewd enough to understand it as an attribute. She shrank from calling herself an 'activist'; she was simply an 'oncologist'. She denied hers was a 'cause'; she spoke instead of pursuing her 'interest'. She did not regard financial institutions as 'targets'; instead she was seeking 'partners'. She respected confidentiality, avoided confrontation, declined to court the media, and drew on her own experience as exemplifying the involition of much tobacco investment, which had its institutional counterparts. 'I presented to one fund that took sustainability very seriously,' Bronwyn recalls. 'They had a 'sustainable investment' option. I looked into it. They chose their international shares via the Dow Jones Sustainability Index – a best of sector index which BAT is part of...The board members of this super fund were...well, they felt tricked. Before I got home I had an email from their CEO saying: "We've issued a comprehensive tobacco free mandate across our portfolio." '

By mid-2014, Bronwyn's initial epiphany had become almost all-consuming. A dozen funds had divested more than $1 billion of tobacco stocks. With two small boys, she was not sleeping much anyway, but she was enjoying it. Tobacco Free Portfolios was winning support not only from business leaders but politicians, and of all stripes: Liberal health minister Sussan Ley, former Labor health minister Nicola Roxon, the Greens' Richard Di Natale and independent Andrew Wilkie all recorded video testimonials. Papers were being invited for the forthcoming biennial World Cancer Conference, which the Union for International Cancer Control happened to be staging in Melbourne. When Bronwyn impulsively submitted an abstract, she had her first glimpse of the world of global tobacco control, and an opportunity to spread The Story. It cast its now-familiar spell.

The only time Bronwyn falters in making the case for Tobacco Free Portfolios is in making the case for herself. And four and a half years after starting, she remained a one-woman band paying for things on her credit card. 'Fund raising is an art in which people specialise,' she says. 'I'm a doctor. Doctors aren't good with money. Most of us don't even really like talking about it.' Introduced to the CEO of the UICC, Cary Adams, she started talking about how much more she could do in Australia if she could afford it – just a little money to cover expenses. 'You know,' said Adams, 'you're not thinking big enough.'

Adams is a former banker: prior to this role, he had been chief operating officer of Lloyds TSB. Maybe it was time his new community started talking to his old industry. Unbeknownst to Bronwyn, the UICC every two years takes a local project to a 'global platform' – a 'president's pick' of the Geneva-based board. They were shortly to do again. 'Leave this with me,' Adams said. 'I've got big plans.'

*

There had been such plans before. Under the anti-tobacco sun, little is outright new. In the UK, activists eyeballed The City as far back as the 1970s, buying single shares in tobacco companies so as to lob questions at annual meetings. After one, Mike Daube recalls, he was taken aside by Rothmans chairman Lord Pritchard, who offered to fund the protest campaign of his choice...providing it had nothing to do with tobacco.

Divestment was trialled in the US in the 1980s, partly inspired by the boycott of companies invested in apartheid South Africa. Activists first cajoled the American Medical Association into urging medical schools to quit tobacco. In the 1990s several universities and state pension funds followed suit. But efforts petered out after 1998's Master Settlement Agreement, among whose perverse impacts was to align the interests of Big Tobacco and state legislatures who depended on them for future funds. And opinion on the efficacy of divestment remains divided. On the basis of the

American experience, veteran anti-tobacco campaigner Professor Alan Blum of the University of Alabama is sceptical: 'As long as another investor buys what a university, pension fund, or a health insurer sells, there's no net loss of investor confidence in the stock or capital in the company's coffers.'

Anything attached to what's conventionally abbreviated as CSR (corporate social responsibility) and ESG (environment, social, governance) also raises fiduciary questions. Does a manager of funds owe clients anything other than maximum returns? Is socially responsible investment even possible? In the 1990s, Philip Morris ran a stealth campaign against 'social investing', relying on an oft-cited 1980 paper by two distinguished American law professors. In 'Social Investing and the Law of Trusts', John Langbein and Richard Posner argued, actually in the context of disinvestment in South Africa, that 'the trustee who sacrifices the beneficiary's financial well-being for another object breaches both his duty of loyalty to the beneficiary and his duty of prudence in investment'; Langbein was subsequently employed by Philip Morris as a consultant.

Has the position changed? Professor Richard Daynard of Northeastern University, another veteran of the anti-tobacco movement, thinks so: 'The Chicago School position argued by Milton Friedman is that the corporation has only one objective, which is greed, or shareholder return. Which means that any organisation doing socially responsible investing can get away with it only if it is a complete fraud. That would be the logical deduction – that corporate social responsibility could only be legitimate if it is pure PR, and as long as it does not cost the company a penny. But nobody argues that any more. Lots of companies flourish their social responsibility credentials. They're good for business. And there are business judgement rules which enable a board of directors to do more or less what they want providing it's not unreasonable. That's actually a large amount of leeway.'

Leeway has been additionally widened by two multilateral instruments. Ten years ago, after consultation with a group of big institutional investors, the United Nations laid out six 'Principles of Responsible Investment': there are today 1500 signatories. The principles are aspirational and non-binding, but the first articulates a departure from circumscribed conceptions of fiduciary duty: 'We will incorporate ESG issues into our ownership policies and practices.' And while UN PRI does not single tobacco out, another UN treaty does: in force since 2005, the World Health Organisation's Framework Convention on Tobacco Control has been signed by 180 countries, representing 89 per cent of the world's population. The framework is exacting and comprehensive, committing governments to a wide variety of risk minimization measures, taxes, regulations and prohibitions – including on investment. Article 5.3 specifies that 'no branch of Government, including local government, should have any financial interest or investment in the tobacco industry.' So far, only three countries have complied: New Zealand since 2007, Norway since 2009, Australia since 2013. Some even seem unaware of it, and not just the usual delinquents: the UK is presently rolling local government pension funds including their tobacco investments into seven sovereign wealth funds.

So divestment, says Professor Chapman, has a different context, as well as a broader purpose. 'The standard critique that someone sells then someone else buys misses the symbolic importance of building the rank odor around the industry,' he says. 'That odor already exists in the health and medical professions and in the general population – when we poll them, we even get it from smokers. Building that consciousness among people making financial decisions furthers that delegitimisation.' Investment in tobacco, argues Bronwyn, is a devil's bargain. 'When you invest in a company, you want that company to thrive, don't you?' she says. 'But do you *really* want Big Tobacco to thrive?'

Like a lung cancer, tobacco is also metastasizing as a public health issue. When the UICC seeded Tobacco Free Portfolios to run its Global Task Force in March 2015, Adams appointed as chair the improbably glamorous figure of Princess Dina Mired, something of a darling of the anti-cancer movement. Since her son's diagnosis with leukaemia twenty years ago, Princess Dina has dedicated her life to improving cancer treatments in Jordan: she is director-general of the Amman foundation of the King Hussein Cancer Center, her country's largest.

Introduced to Bronwyn, Princess Dina loved The Story: 'It was one person seeing something shameful and deciding to do something about it, by herself, knocking on doors, showing commitment and never giving up.' More than that, she sensed the need for a form of tobacco control accented to supply rather than demand. It is poorer countries, where public health consciousness is weaker, that will chiefly bear tobacco's brunt: the World Health Organisation estimates that by 2030 they will account for four in five tobacco-related deaths.

The reasons are not far to seek. 'As countries like Australia, the US and Canada have been increasing regulation and hiking up prices, tobacco companies have made extra efforts in Middle East and Africa,' says Princess Dina. 'Since the Arab Spring, we are a stressed-out population, and we are game...They [tobacco companies] are zooming on our youth in a really big way.' Today more than a third of Jordanians smoke and the proportion is growing: the crop of tobacco-related cancers being sown prelude a bitter harvest. 'And if you invest in tobacco,' she adds, 'you are part of that killing machine.'

*

Heading a 'Global Task Force', Bronwyn still had unfinished business in Australia. But she now had a helpmate. Lawyer Clare Payne worked at Macquarie Bank for eleven years, and ran its integrity office for six, before founding an initiative called the Banking and Finance Oath: an attempt to popularize for finance industry professionals a code of practice akin to the Hippocratic Oath. So when she and Bronwyn watched each other speak consecutively at a Responsible Investment Conference in November 2014, they felt a natural kinship. 'Bron's achieved more than most people have in twenty years of responsible investment,' says Clare. 'She's got more than engagement. She's got action.' Clare joined Tobacco Free Portfolios as 'chief operating officer', a droll joke seeing that her 'office' was a cleared out built-in wardrobe in the Sydney cottage she shares with her young daughter.

Boards now faced two advocates, Clare with her corporate experience perhaps slightly steelier. Where Bronwyn was always sunnily optimistic, Clare groaned inwardly at counterarguments trotted out, like a board chair who couldn't see a problem with tobacco because an uncle had smoked till he was ninety-five, not to mention the familiar slippery slope fallacies. 'I remember one day this American saying to me: "Let me just play devil's advocate here...",' says Clare. 'And I thought: "Really? Aren't we beyond that now? Unless it's your view. Otherwise we're just proceeding from a silly starting point."' To Clare, the problem was straightforward: it was persuading the powerful to heed the people. 'Australian society accepts tobacco control,' she says. 'They don't want their children to smoke. If they smoke themselves, they want to stop. They want fewer people to die. Governments want better health outcomes. Funds should reflect that.'

Bronwyn, meanwhile, was pondering how to replicate across the world her Australian system. She tapped her 'partners' for contacts and introductions, never failing to follow up the feintest lead. She would start days at the Epworth with two sheets of paper: her patient schedule, and her Tobacco Free Portfolios to-do list. The patients came first, their needs acute, their questions poignantly familiar. ' 'How long?' ' says Bronwyn. 'That's what they all want to know. "My daughter's getting married. Will I make it?" "My daughter's having a baby in January. Will I live to see it?" "My son's graduating next year. Will I be able to go?" '

Of time, she was constantly reminded, there was never enough. So any minute before, between or after patientcare was an opportunity to make a phonecall, send an email, or dash into the CBD. Nights steadily became Skype marathons. One evening her husband walked in with a cup of tea suggesting she take a break. 'Quick, close the door!' she exclaimed. 'I'm about to talk to Kuwait!' Bronwyn laughs: 'He looked at me and it was, like, "Who *are* you?" He thought I'd lost the plot.'

Extending the filaments of her network also involved serious travel. In July 2015, Bronwyn made her first trips to Washington and New York. In September, she took in a Principles of Responsible Investment Conference in London and visited the World Health Organisation in Geneva. In November she travelled to Istanbul for the World Cancer Leaders Summit, and swung on to London for a first look at the City.

Where doors were now open in Australia, they were only tentatively ajar in the UK. Big Tobacco and City merchant banks align snugly. Rock star fund manager Neil Woodford has made a fortune from tobacco stocks for his eponymous investment boutique, explaining that clients expect him to 'exercise an investment judgement' not a 'moral judgement'. Notes Bronwyn: 'The influence of companies like BAT and Imperial Tobacco is enormous. They also set the low watermark for every metric of corporate behavior there is, and operate to make life difficult for anyone in public health trying to stop people dying.' Tobacco Free Portfolios hosted a roundtable for twenty investment professionals at the Whitechapel offices of Principles of Responsible Investment, a UN-supported NGO. It became an eye-opening realtime experiment in City attitudes.

> One guy, a very senior leader in UK finance, was quite difficult. He just kept saying: 'Our approach is to engage with the tobacco companies. We *engage* with the industry.' He was getting very fired up, and I just had to hold my ground. Finally I said: 'I understand engagement is a useful tool, and it's important to be a good steward of capital. But this is the exception. Engagement with the tobacco industry is futile. Positive influence is impossible. There's not one example in all the history of engagement leading to fewer deaths.'
>
> Of course, this was very uncomfortable for him. The City *does* engage with the tobacco companies. Suddenly, out of the blue, this other guy whom I'd not met says: 'We're getting bogged down in the nitty-gritty here. What about the big vision? Isn't this industry just killing six million people a year and we're part of it if we're investing in it?'

The interjector, Dawid Konotey-Ahulu, had arrived at the last minute, without particularly high expectations: 'I assumed it would be a run-of-the-mill discourse on the dangers of tobacco and the virtues of shunning it.' Now he was excited. A former Merrill Lynch banker, Konotey-Ahulu has for the last decade run an investment and risk management consultancy for pension funds, Redington. Bronwyn reminded him of a popular business concept: the Big Hairy Audacious Goal, or BHAG, coined by Jim Collins in his 1994 management bestseller *Built to Last*. Since the roundtable, he has become Tobacco Free Portfolios' City adviser, including on the recruitment of a new

London representative, Dr Rachel Melsom. 'We are living in an era where "Do the Right Thing!" is increasingly the guiding principle, and pension funds, by and large, want to do the right thing,' says Konotey-Ahulu. 'We are watching this area of sustainable investing very closely and it will not surprise me if in the near future, several large pension funds elect to disinvest from intrinsically harmful assets such as tobacco.' They now have an example.

*

On 28 February, after months of planning, Bronwyn landed in London on her first European mission: twelve days, six countries, forty-five meetings, with pension funds, insurers, sovereign wealth funds and health leaders, plus 'a lot of airports and a lot of taxis'. She had pursued every introduction, cadged every favour on offer. To her excitement, not one approach had been rebuffed. To her further excitement, she had arranged to spend the weekend in Paris with friends, the De Vienne family, for whom in 1997 she had worked as an au pair. Then, unable to help herself, she asked round her Australian business 'partners' with whom in France it might be worth meeting. The CEO of a major funds management business connected her with AXA.

So it was that six years after that meeting in her hospital's cafeteria, Bronwyn sat across a luncheon table at Café Chic on Rue du Faubourg from Sylvain Vanston, AXA's forty-four-year-old chief of ESG integration. A year earlier Vanston had been instrumental in AXA's ceasing to invest in coal; but since agreeing to meet, he had been musing that this was the first red flag ever raised about a vastly more significant killer. 'Tobacco has been a problem for health, but it has not been a problem for investors,' he observes. 'When I met Bronwyn, she immediately started putting together the pieces of the puzzle that we hadn't.'

In Bronwyn's telling, that puzzle of tobacco's unique iniquity has four pieces. Can the product be used safely? No: zero is the only safe number of cigarettes. Can an investor have a positive influence on the tobacco industry? No: the risks are indivisible from the product. Is the problem huge? Yes: the WHO forecasts a billion tobacco-related deaths in the twenty-first century. Is there a UN treaty? Yes: the FCTC has sought to limit tobacco usage for more than a decade. A concluding pith: would you set up an industry now knowing that in the next year it would kill six million people and cost the health care system €2 trillion? Vanston was taken aback: 'I thought I knew about tobacco, but in reality I'd missed important facts.' Did she have all this written down, he asked? Bronwyn fished a Tobacco Free Portfolios information kit from her bag. That night she rang Clare. 'I've got a good feeling about this,' she said.

Likewise Vanston. This was a far bigger deal than coal: four times the size, and entailing not insignificant financial sacrifices. But AXA's incoming CEO Buberl had been promoting a redesign of its health business, arguing that insurance must change from being a payer of bills to a helper of clients toward healthier life choices. And if AXA wanted clients to foreswear tobacco, it could hardly do otherwise. Besides, Buberl observes, the calculus has changed: 'Once, lung cancer meant a quick death. As treatment has improved and lives have been prolonged, it has gone from being a lethal to a chronic illness, and costs are exploding. It's a simple equation – the social, medical and taxation consequences of smoking have grown considerably worse.'

Vanston was commissioned to present to Buberl's management team; Bronwyn, now back in Melbourne after whirling through Geneva, Stockholm, Copenhagen and Oslo, contributed by email. Back at work at the Epworth, preparing prognoses, counseling patients about their survival chances, she messaged Vanston just before his presentation, three weeks after their single meeting: 'Good luck with your speech. Just imagine that you have every oncologist and every patient who has suffered from tobacco standing right beside you.' Vanston replied: 'That's a good point!' He didn't lack them, and his CEO actually needed little convincing. 'Decisions take longer when they're ambiguous,' says Buberl. 'There is nothing ambiguous about tobacco.'

*

Nor, it must be said, is there anything ambiguous about the money tobacco makes. It is a high cash-flow, low-volatility business – a classic defensive stock pick in times when they are scarce. Yet no industry could exercise so dark an allure – something accentuated by the profile of smokers, skewed increasingly towards the poor, the young, and, frankly, the darker-skinned and further away.

It is a problem of magnitude that occasionally dismays Bronwyn King, although never long. 'I'm an optimist,' she says. 'Some people I've met have been unconvinced by the arguments. Others have said "oh it's a bit early" or "can you come back with more information?" But I've watched literally dozens of people move from that position of initial resistance, to thinking ours is a reasonable position, to being completely convinced and ringing up a few months later asking: "Is there anything I can do?" I never hear "no" as "never"; I hear it as "not yet".' Since AXA, she has had contact with a score of European financial institutions: one sovereign wealth fund has already divested, although is yet to announce its decision. Bronwyn's travel schedule for the rest of the year looks unsparing, and she is resigned to foregoing sleep because of it. 'But if I knew what I knew and did nothing,' she says, 'I couldn't sleep at all.'

# GRAVEN IDOLS

## *The cult of the CEO* (2007)

First, a proposition: chief executives are among the laziest, most slovenly, most delinquent individuals in our society. When not simply staring out the window, they are inclined to spend hours sleeping under their desks, working on their tans, and playing endless games of Angry Birds. Given opportunity, their tastes tend toward erecting towering statues of themselves in poses reminiscent of Napoleon. Left unrestrained, they could easily just give away vast sums of company money to people met at random in the street.

Hmmm, you are thinking: none of this is true. The CEOs you know work incredibly hard. They have to ask their secretaries if they are still married. They last saw their children in 1994. The closest they come to reading a book for recreation is when they glance at the blurb on a Tom Clancy while passing through the airport. So how can I possibly say they are essentially slothful, workshy, feckless? Well, here's the news. It's not me saying it; it's a *reductio ad absurdum* of the modern conviction, in which we all collude, that the only way to obtain an executive's total absorption and loyalty is to pay him or her exponentially greater sums.

The best brains on the consulting block have been applied to the complex and apparently unending task of making sure that CEOs are adequately motivated and incentivated, otherwise they might...well, what exactly? Stare out the window in protest? Come on. Does anyone truly believe that CEOs would be less effective, less ambitious, less driven were they paid half as much, a quarter as much, a tenth? If not, then it is hard to argue that they would be twice as productive paid twice as much. Yet on we go.

The fact is that we pay senior executives as much as we do not because unassailable logic dictates it but because it has become a social norm. We are apt to speak of the 'entitlement culture' that is said to develop among welfare recipients. Yet nowhere in Australia does 'entitlement culture' flourish so unrestrainedly as its boardrooms, where directors take comfort from familiar platitudes.

They say: financial incentives, especially equity, drive company performance. Except that the evidence for this is elusive. Indeed, after reviewing no fewer than 220 studies on the correlation between equity incentives and financial outperformance for the *Academy of Management Journal*, Dan Dalton of the Kelley School of Business decided that there was 'no relationship whatsoever' between how much of a company was owned by its executives and how it did. Likewise a major study by the National Bureau of Economic Research concluded that most schemes to align managerial and shareholders interests failed, and principally became means for executives' personal enrichment. Analysing the intensive case histories that formed his best selling *Built to Last* (1994) and *Good to Great* (2001), James Collins stated flatly: 'The idea that the structure of executive compensation is a key driver in corporate performance is simply not supported by the data.'

They say: we must meet the market, because the market is always right. Except, of course, on the occasions when the market is wrong, when it overshoots, when it loses touch with fundamentals sometimes for years at a time, when the seeds of inflation are planted, when artificialities are introduced, as there are in the market for executives – full, as they are, of barriers to entry, inefficiencies, illiquidities, information asymmetries and old-fashioned superstitions. For as Rakesh Khurana points out in *Searching For a Corporate Saviour* (2002), the market for executive talent is actually an extremely restricted one, the defining attributes being chiefly three: previous position, performance of individual's previous firm, and status of that firm. The effect is an artificial scarcity, and a tendency to the choice of look-alikes. He states: 'Restricting the CEO labour market to a select set of candidates and then pretending that the outcomes can be justified as a consequence of the market process is a self-serving conceit.'

They say: we must be 'internationally competitive'. This is a phrase that has taken on conspicuously divergent meanings where top and bottom of the salary scale are concerned: workers are always being enjoined to price their labour to compete with the cheapest rival, even as executives seek convergence with the highest common denominator. Imagine a tender in which the successful bid was not the lowest price but the highest. Absurd!

But executive talent is a world of topsy-turvy values. No director ever says: 'Hey, look at this bargain-basement CEO we picked up.' They say: 'Hey, we're serious about getting the best, and we'll pay top dollar.' Or, even better: 'World-class talent deserves world-class pay.' One can only wonder how often availability of the latter confers the status of the former.

Bear in mind that it was never decided that corporate executives should be paid the extortionate sums they are paid today; it was theorised, early in the 1980s, that they should be paid differently, in such a way as to align their interests with those of shareholders. How to whip faceless, flaccid, unaccountable executives into shape? Why, make them owners: big ones, too, whether with MBOs, or through lucrative stock and option grants.

Now, imagine if there had been a theory fifteen years ago that one could make a better tenant simply by giving them half of the house they occupied. The tenants would have done pretty damn well, eh? All they would have needed to do was stand around and collect, and maybe paint a bedroom, or put in new curtains, to make it look like they were honouring their side of the bargain. But you'd have to have wondered about it from the vendors' perspective, wouldn't you? Well, that's not too dissimilar to what happened with senior executives. Although, of course, the vendors – the shareholders – actually had no say: all this was done on their behalf by a group of lodgers living in the attic who occasionally popped their heads down through the manhole to make sure the tenant hadn't set fire to the place. Also known as the board of directors.

Of course, our imagined tenant would scarcely have deserved the good fortune of their endowment during a housing boom. So how is it that executives are felt to deserve the fruits of long-running bull market cycles in equities and commodities and property? CEOs are not, of course, so passive as tenants, nor are corporations so easily and obviously improvable as houses, being at the mercy of a host of exogenous variables. But this makes it more complicated working out what an executive is due rather than less, and slides easily into assumptions that they are very much more capable of manufacturing superior performance than they are. In their recent book *Hard Facts, Dangerous Half-Truths and Total Nonsense* (2006), Jeffrey Pfeffer and Robert Sutton wrily recount a conversation with a senior executive from a Florida utility whose remuneration practices were determined chiefly by profitability:

> The utility's profitability, since in the short run most of its costs were fixed, depended mostly on the amount of electricity sold, and the amount of electricity sold depended on the temperature. The hotter the summer in Florida, the more power was sold, and the more profitable was the utility...This executive noted that this incentive system made no sense – unless you believed he could control the weather in Florida.

Acceptance of the limits of executive agency is not a counsel of despair; it is a cognisance of common sense. This is for the very good reason that it was meant to be this way. The whole objective of the modern industrial corporation is to combine the many in one. As Pfeffer puts it in *The Human Equation* (1998): 'In general, the greater the interdependence among various members of the organisation, the more difficult it is to measure their separate contributions. But, of course, intense interdependence is precisely what makes it advantageous to organise people instead of depending wholly on market transactions.'

This, of course, challenges all the pieties. If holding shares doesn't make feckless managers behave like responsible owners, what will? But the lack of correlation makes perfect sense. Shareholders are not collegial. Ownership is essentially a selfish business; the fortunes of other investors are not your concern. The historic evidence, indeed, is that big shareholders have concerned themselves little with smaller ones: think of the generations of entrepreneurs who have devoted lifetimes to screwing their minorities. Why is it assumed executives holding big clumps of stock will be any different, when they didn't even start the companies they are charged with running?

Money, moreover, is a blunt instrument for securing adherence to goals and authority. In his irreverent study of recognition and remuneration systems *Punished by Rewards* (1995), Alfie Kohn concluded: 'Rewards usually improve performance only at extremely simple – indeed, mindless – tasks.

And even then they improve only quantitative performance'. To return to where I began, knowing what we do of CEO's Stakhanovite work habits, why do we imagine that paying more will somehow extract from them greater effort, deeper insight, superior genius? Incentives over time, in fact, come to be seen as rights or entitlements, and to lose such effect as they have. To achieve continued levels of coercion, abundance can only be succeeded by greater abundance, with a steady diminution of returns.

Prime minister Kevin Rudd's recent appeal for executive wage restraint struck many as a shot across business's bows. And if we are about to see another bout of public recrimination on executive salaries – and these customarily coincide with stock prices moving south even as remuneration continues trending northwards – there is one area in which companies look particularly vulnerable: the mouth-watering tax advantages to the 'long-term incentive' component of executive remuneration.

With a bit of expert assistance, concessions offered by Section 139E of the Tax Act, originally devised to encourage employee share ownership plans, can reduce the tax payable on the equity portion of a pay package to less than a fifth. Exercise and sell after a year, and the capital gains tax impost is 22.5 per cent. If the research on the routine undervaluation of options packages is any indication, the $600,000 average equity handout to our top 300 executives is worth about $2.1 million each. That is a lot of money obtaining preferential tax treatment, and a sizeable burden for others to bear who aren't so lucky in the structure of their pay and conditions. Even if you assume that executives are worth every penny, it is hard to see how they deserve tax breaks as well.

For all the belief in money's motivating power among some, furthermore, there seems little recognition of its power to demotivate others. The exorbitant rewards of a boss they do not know, never see, and barely understand hardly stirs a worker to greater effort: more likely it leads to disaffection, resentment and the very 'free riding' that 'performance-related pay' is meant to banish. Some have criticised modern CEOs for being too obsessed with appearances; on the contrary, they care not nearly enough. Ken Iverson of Nucor, the last American steelmaker worth the name, pointed out in his *Plain Talk* (1997) what seems to have eluded so many others of his rank and generation:

> The people at the top of the corporate hierarchy grant themselves privilege after privilege, flaunt those privileges before the men and women who do the real work, then wonder why employees are unmoved by management's invocations to cut costs and boost profitability... When I think of the millions of dollars spent by people at the top of the management hierarchy on efforts to motivate people who are continually put down by that hierarchy, I can only shake my head in wonder.

Big salaries, then, are not merely hard to justify; they may be compromising the companies that pay them, turning the so-called 'war for talent' into a campaign full of pyrrhic victories.

# THE RICH, THE BAD AND UGLY

## *Rogues of the* Rich List (2009)

In the reams of quotations about wealth, a sizeable proportion relate to its powers to corrupt and debase human nature. Think Thomas Jefferson: 'The more money, the less virtue.' Think Andrew Carnegie: 'To die rich is to die disgraced.' By these lights, the *BRW Rich List* should be almost synonymous with *Australia's Most Wanted*.

For a long time in Australia, a school of thought held business similarly suspicious. *The Bulletin*, in its turn-of-the-century pomp, put it most succinctly, covering commercial matters beneath the droll headline 'Business, Robbery Etc', as though from one could be inferred the other, as if the bank manager and the bushranger were easily and obviously transposable. It was a cheap point, but a meaningful one. In a country of supposedly egalitarian principles, to be rich was to be a bit disreputable – it was, at least, to stand out, a form of offence in a culture of widespread conformity.

The *BRW Rich List* has both reflected and abetted a change in the culture, wealth becoming respectable, even admirable, as well as merely desirable. But it has also tweaked our latent misgivings by throwing up its share of spivs, chancers, and old-fashioned rogues. Sometimes, embarrassingly, they have attracted the list's attention just in that final last efflorescence before flaring out for good; a success story can be but a short distance from becoming a cautionary tale.

Recall, for example, George Herscu, a man who for whom the *Rich List* might almost have been devised. A headstrong, high-rolling collector of cars, planes and racehorses, he dressed with a dandified air and philosophised of his cheerful ostentation: 'Beautiful things like Rolls-Royces and Jaguars are made for people to enjoy. Money should be enjoyed. I love to enjoy myself. To spend money. To dance – do the cha-cha. I love people with life in them and love to live.' He had modelled his Whernside Avenue home on Tara in *Gone With The Wind* – a book he claimed to have read ten times, perhaps taking a little too much inspiration from Rhett Butler's motto: 'With courage, one can do without a reputation.'

For his reputation took a pounding when his corrupt relations with first the Builders Labourers' Federation then Queensland's local government minister Russ Hinze were revealed. In the *Rich List* of 1989, Herscu was valued at $300 million, and limned as 'a survivor', although he was admitted to have had a 'bumpy year'. His fall from grace was then sudden and utter. Not only did he file Australia's biggest personal bankruptcy, $496 million, but he was prosecuted for his indiscretions with Hinze. Perhaps no *Rich List* member has been pictured so abjectly as Herscu, crumpled in the back of the Black Mariah speeding him to prison for a five-year stretch.

For losing money alone does not a rogue make. No businessman worth their salt has not known some failure – sometimes costly, occasionally humiliating. Frank Lowy had his Westfield Capital Corporation, John Roberts his Wembley, Maurice Alter, Marc Besen and John Gandel their Max Green, Nicole Kidman her *Stepford Wives*. For some members of the *Rich List*, mistakes have been formative. Ask Lloyd Williams about what he learned during the property meltdown of 1974, or Lindsay Fox during his unhappy year running Linfox as a public company. 'I learned by making mistakes and not duplicating them,' Fox has explained.

No, the chief characteristic of the modern business rogue is a certain brazen incorrigibility – for which a nation of convicts might be felt to have a certain gift. After all, had there been a nineteenth century *Rich List*, it would have made up for in colour what it lacked in gross wealth. Wool tycoon John Macarthur, the 'rich Botany Bay purturbator', boasted that he had 'never yet failed in ruining a man who had become obnoxious to him'. Landowner Charles Ebden, first settler on the Murray, went down in history for his mock self-reproach: 'I fear I am becoming disgustingly rich'. Bank of Victoria owner Henry 'Money' Miller noisily advised embezzlers not to mess around: 'If you ever feel a desire to go wrong, don't prig cash or enter threepenny letters as sixpence. Collar £10,000 and be sure to burn the bally books.'

No *Rich List* exhibits this attribute in greater concentration than the gallery of 1987, which was probably read more avidly, and became obsolete more quickly, than any before or since. Much of the reporting has a certain piquancy. Brian Yuill is explained as having 'established a complex web of companies', as though the writer had simply been overcome by the headache of looking at them all. Kevin Parry is described as 'yet another aggressive WA entrepreneur' as if the stock of available adjectives had been exhausted by the state's sheer financial flair. The 'very widely respected Abe Goldberg' is praised for his 'commitment to the characteristically troubled textile and clothing industry' – just as he was losing interest in it. Little did anyone realise that the impending *annus horribilis* would off them all along with many others.

The scenery was also suggestive. In hindsight, one of the list's most eye-catching features is a two-page advertisement for Standard Chartered Bank, featuring a handsome fish on ice lying coldly next to a hook. The symbolism is as unsubtle as it seems. 'If we can see you've got a good idea and the drive and skills to make it work, we're hooked,' reads the explanatory text. 'From that point it's all straight lines with us...If you've got a good idea and you know what you need to make it work, come and say g'day, we'll probably take the bait.' Come take our money, in other words: we're so stupid, we'll hardly notice.

Nobody incarnated this spirit more completely than the Perth parvenu Laurie Connell. Borrowers knew him as 'Last Resort Laurie' for the open handedness of his merchant bank Rothwells, although the *Rich List* that year generously assessed his wealth at $80 million: 'His loud approach to almost everything has earned him some adverse publicity, but Connell dismisses this as "sour grapes".' At the time, he was planning Perth's largest home, having demolished seven residences on a one-hectare block in prestigious Dalkeith, and owned more than 400 racehorses. No wonder Rothwells' group treasurer would describe the effort of funding his boss as 'like having to put out a bushfire each night'.

Nine weeks after the *Rich List* hit the streets, that bushfire broke through its containment lines: there was a run on Rothwells in the wake of the sharemarket crash. Connell rang none other than Standard Chartered – perhaps he had seen the ad. In fact, the bank's local chief David Hurley recommended receivership – a course of action that might have changed history had it been taken. Instead, there commenced the first of three increasingly elaborate and hopeless rescue operations involving some of Australian business's biggest names: Kerry Packer, John Elliott, Larry Adler, Richard Pratt, and Robert Holmes a Court, all improbably aligned with Connell's close friend Alan Bond.

It gradually emerged that Connell was a commercial Typhoid Mary: he made a rogue of almost everyone he touched, including a Labor Premier, Brian Burke, of whom the same might now be said. A picture of Connell and Bond fishing with prime minister Bob Hawke and senator Graham Richardson embarrassed both politicians. Warwick Fairfax, Connell's biggest client, entered his circle a wealthy naïf and left it a poorer idiot. Rothwells, originally a gentlemen's outfitters, became a synonym for sleaze. A lurid Royal Commission revealed its finances to be a strange mixture of the sacred and profane. Among its biggest depositors was Perth's Catholic Archdiocese; roughly two-thirds of the debt was owed by Connell companies, about $600 million vanishing into his affairs over three years and never coming out.

Some felt feint at the scale of the depredations. Corporate lawyer Aleco Vrisakis, brought in to wrangle the first rescue, took one look at the loan book and quailed: 'I've got a very bad heart and I can't cope with this.' Others raged. At one famous conference with Connell's advisers, Burke's successor Peter Dowding prowled the room slamming doors and kicking furniture. 'We have just paid $400 million for a petrochemical plant worth nothing,' he roared. 'Now we're back to where we started. I am surrounded by liars and cheats. Now you want more money. Who are we saving from going to jail this time?' Jail certainly beckoned, although in the Al Capone tradition of crooks eventually brought to book for relatively trifling offences, Connell served his porridge for bribing a jockey, Burke for rorting travel expenses.

Jail finally awaited Bond, too, who in a gallery of rogues almost deserves an entire wing, having brought business to a pitch of unequalled shamelessness. The wide boy who never paid a bill on time because it was 'cheap money' and who painted Yanchep's sandhills green 'to make the brochures look better' turned into the big league buyer of breweries and blimps while scarcely changing his modus operandi. As Michael Grace told Bond's biographer Paul Barry:

> If he wanted something it was very hard not to say, 'Yes, I agree with you, Alan.' He just had that charm, that charisma, that complete belief in where he was going...No matter how many times we said 'That doesn't suit us Alan', he just brushed it aside and kept going ahead. And then when we said, 'Look, we can't do that legally', he said, 'Oh, we'll find a way around it.' It did not enter his negotiating position that it couldn't be done.

Bond wasn't the first West Australian entrepreneur to cosy up to a vicious dictator, Lang Hancock having expressed golden opinions of Romania's Nikolai Ceasescu. But nothing quite matches for crassness the photograph of a deferential Bond shaking hands with General Augusto Pinochet, preparatory to acquiring Chile's privatised telephone monopoly in August 1987. 'You feel safe on the streets and it's the best economy in Latin America,' said Bond; the generalissimo's serial human rights violations and massive money laundering were apparently just the price of progress. How piquant that the fates of both Bond and Pinochet should involve them staving off justice with claims of frailty and forgetfulness.

The rogues, of course, did not go quietly, some even taking out their ire on the system that had previously celebrated them. The *Rich List* of 1987, for instance, lauded the 'self-confessed workaholic and fitness fanatic' Allan Hawkins for having 'rocketed to the forefront of the Australian and New Zealand corporate scene'. He wasn't so enamoured of the magazine when editor Robert Gottliebsen wrote the obituary of his Equiticorp group a few months later. Before New Zealand's Serious Fraud Office sent him to jail, Hawkins complained in his *mea non culpa The Hawk*:

> This guy is a real tit – bald, horse-faced, and with a thin-lipped prissy mouth and an overall expression of extreme self-satisfaction. I don't know what he does at night because he spends most of his days dreaming. In fact he doesn't seem to inhabit the same real world as the rest of us...and

he's the sort of bloke who doesn't let the facts of a story interfere with a chance to increase the magazine's circulation.

Not every brush with the law leaves a reputation permanently stained. Developer Albert Scheinberg was caught in the same Fitzgerald Inquiry dragnet that snared George Herscu, but spared jail on grounds of his seventy-nine years. Bruno and Rino Grollo have lived down their day in the Supreme Court twenty-three years ago during the trial of Norm Gallagher. In meting out justice to the venal union boss, Justice Waldron described the developers' conduct in keeping him on side as 'devious, secretive and deliberately dishonest' and meriting 'custodial sentences'. Contemporaries were less censorious, knowing it a cost of doing business in an industry befouled with corruption.

Sometimes, though, corruption is a symptom of a deeper *folie de grandeur*: witness Tasmanian Edmund Rouse. Vindictive, overbearing, boorish and fond of political incorrectitudes, Rouse stood out all the more for the relative gentility of his state, which he described as 'a little pimple hanging on the arse end of nothing in international terms'. His ENT Ltd owned the *Launceston Examiner*, and both Tasmania's commercial television stations. Yet he despised the press: his idea of an annual bonus at the *Examiner* was walking through the newsroom each Christmas distributing all-day suckers. And he was contemptuous of the public, claiming to have bought his Rolls Royce for the effect it exerted on pedestrians: 'In Launceston it makes them spit; in Hobart they throw up.' Asked once if he would kick an opponent when he was down, he replied: 'Yes, if I thought he might get up.'

If an opponent remained standing, Rouse employed more emollient means. When the collapse of the Wesley Vale pulp mill scheme in March 1989 tipped Tasmanian politics into crisis, five Green independents agreed to an accord with Labor opposition that cost Liberal premier Robin Gray control of the House of Assembly. Rouse was also chairman of Gunns Kilndried Timber, whose free hand in reducing the state's forest to woodchip suddenly looked in jeopardy, and he counterstrategised: he would bribe a Labor member to cross the floor. It wasn't exactly United Fruit in Guatemala or ITT in Chile, and it is hard to know whether the plan was more crude than incompetent or vice versa. He didn't know his target; he merely theorized that a recent marriage breakdown would make Jim Cox susceptible to financial inducement; he was haphazard also in his choice of intermediary: 3UZ sales executive Tony Aloi had rung Rouse to obtain work experience for a friend, and hung up with a commission to bait a $110,000 lure.

Although the scheme unravelled almost before it had ravelled – Cox went straight to his leader – Rouse was stubbornly impenitent. Defending counsel at his trial, Jack Hedigan, pleaded that Rouse's public spirit had blurred his sense of right and wrong: 'It may be, your honour, that the benevolent exercise of power by this man, over a long period of time, may have blunted the perception of what he might, or might not do.' It was nonsense. Rouse knew his actions were illegal; he simply thought himself above the law. 'If I were drunk at the wheel and ran down a child in the street, I would suffer incredible remorse,' he stated in self-justification. 'But to try and rectify a situation which I believed would be disastrous for Tasmania – and was disastrous – of course I have no remorse.'

Rouse could not even claim credit for the interests he sought so urgently to defend. He had married into ENT's founding Rolph family – as he explained it, with characteristic felicity, he got his 'dick caught in the till'. And in inherited wealth, the *Rich List* has found some of its most dubious characters, as though a sense of entitlement instils a brisk amorality. Larry Adler, another fixture of early *Rich Lists*, loved his son Rodney – to a fault. Rodney's recollection, featured in Andrew Main's *Other People's Money* (2002), was suitably grateful: 'I bumbled through uni, I got through my chartered accounting, I got through my masters, and everyone thought that I was a pretty good mediocre person. Dad thought I would be great. Dad marketed me as if I was great.' The marketing was so good it persuaded the subject: 'Do you know what? I rose to meet his aspirations.' It wasn't an assessment widely shared. Adler was pungently summed up by his sometime American broker Jeffrey Pokross, a New York Jew with Mafia connections who didn't bandy words lightly: he was a 'fucking lunatic'.

Certainly the ASX has received few wackier communications than Adler's valediction as boss of FAI in January 1999: 'Dear Sir, Farewell. My tenure as chief executive is nearly over. My life at FAI is at the same stanza in time.' Its paean of praise to capitalism that read like a Productivity Commission edition of Adam Smith and William Shakespeare: without 'the invisible hand', the 'world as we have come to know it would disappear into a sea of mis-allocated resources'. Invisibility, in fact, was not Adler's *metier*. On the contrary, he loomed even larger in the affairs of the company to which FAI had been sold, until HIH capsized in March 2001 with debts of $5.3 billion. Many were dissatisfied by his two and a half year's jail time. Comedian Vince Sorrenti evolved a joke featuring a gunman with two bullets being confronted by Saddam Hussein, Osama bin Laden and Rodney Adler. The solution – shoot Adler twice – always met with an ovation.

The law fell more crushingly on the Nicholas family, whose wealth cascaded down the generations from the Aspro axis of Alfred and younger brother George. First the descendants of George became mired in a Jarndyce case against their trustees in the Victorian Supreme Court. Then Alfred's grandson David Nicholas, who had worked his fortune harder than most by introducing first Pizza Hut then Kentucky Fried Chicken to the country, fell spectacularly among thieves.

In the hothouse of the 1980s, David Nicholas was a hybrid, establishment roots topped with exotic branches, housed in Toorak and Portsea, but married to his beautiful Swedish stepsister, moving in the circles of both Alan Bond and Christopher Skase – and beginning to learn some of their habits. His first brush with the law was when the junior miner Mid-East Minerals whose board he chaired was rumbled warehousing shares in Metals Exploration: he was fined $40,000 and banned from holding a directorship for five years. His investment company Asiatic Pacific then squandered money on an investment in handcrafts, and Nicholas began topping up his finances by less orthodox means. When Asiatic Pacific collapsed in March 1988 with an $8 million deficiency, it emerged that he had bilked AGC of $2.2 million with fraudulent invoices for plant never built and equipment never bought. By June 1990 he was beginning a four-year term for fraud. 'Hopefully that will be the last chapter in (his) public humiliation,' said his counsel, with misplaced optimism.

Although the sentence was reduced on appeal, and he served fourteen months, David Nicholas did not savour freedom long. In September 1994, he and a Chinese business associate Lu Cjun Khe collected a bag from a contact at South Yarra's Hotel Como. The bag contained 8.4kg of heroin worth $12.5 million – enough, a few years earlier, to have won you a place on the *Rich List* on its own. But also tucked away was a listening device, while the contact himself was a Thai nark working with the AFP. Spectators at the trial struggled to reconcile the calm, courteous, well-spoken son of privilege who claimed mildly to have been in the wrong place at the wrong time with the desperations and deceptions of the hard drug trade, but the jury did not hesitate to convict nor the judge to impose a sentence of fifteen years.

If no family is without its dirty laundry, only one in the *Rich List's* history has chosen to hoist it on a flagpole. But then, Douglas Moran has had a habit of saluting himself regardless. He wrote to *BRW* welcoming its innovation in 1983: 'I firmly believe that Australia's prospects for greatness and recognition in the world rest entirely with those in the country who take risks and generate wealth.' Just how firmly he held that belief was illustrated in the instance of his son Brendan, who took ninety minutes to asphyxiate himself with carbon monoxide in a car in the drive of a North Epping house in February 1995.

Gentle, weak, troubled Brendan had been steadily and fastidiously disowned by the Morans, to the extent that he was sent a copy of a *BRW* profile of the family with the notation: 'Notice you didn't get a mention…Loser!' When Brendan's widow Kristina began a legal crusade to be compensated for the mental and physical cruelty inflicted on her late husband, the patriarch, who insisted on his children calling him 'Mr Moran' or 'Chairman' at work, dismissed it as 'simply blackmail'. Perhaps he should have paid anyway: in court he emerged as the poster father of psychological sadism.

Read one letter: 'You may like to consider the serious consequences that sheer stupidity can lead to…Your extravagance continues to lead to trouble. Unfortunately I believe it cannot be cured.' Read another: 'Your lack of discipline has been tolerated for some time with my expectancy that you should grow up…Your continued insistence that that you have been hard done by is difficult to understand.' And finally: 'Those who do not dedicate self-discipline and willingness to work and pull their weight end up being losers...No further financial support of any description will be made available to you both, nor do we accept any verbal or written response on your family affairs.' At the time of Brendan's death, it emerged, Douglas was sueing to recover for costs of a house his son had considered a gift.

That was not the family's only dysfunctional relationship. Brendan's brother Peter Moran, a violent man who came under a restraining order for bashing a teenage relative's head on a concrete pavement, had taken sibling rivalry to a new level when they worked together in the family real estate business. In one dispute around Christmas 1990, Peter had beaten Brendan brutally, and bitten his finger through to the bone; in another around August 1993 he had rendered Brendan unconscious by strangling him with his tie. According to Kristina Moran, Douglas's wife Greta had urged her to use make-up to cover the scratches and gashes on Brendan's face and neck. And the Moran parents, said Kristina, were used to giving orders and having them followed: 'You're told where you're going to live, what car to drive, where your children go to school. It was not unusual at all.'

Towards the end of the sensational court hearings, it transpired that all was not as it seemed with Douglas and Greta either, in spite of their cloying hand-in-hand arrivals each morning. She was revealed to have undertaken electro-convulsive therapy in 1984 to deal with her depression, and to have sought advice about a divorce six years later. A letter from her to Douglas presented in evidence described 'bashing' which had 'become a habit' and 'verbal abuse – absolute filth and obscenities...meant to humilate me and as vulgar as were the physical bashings', although worse still were the 'ultimate humiliations of your extramarital affairs' which were 'common knowledge'.

> Considering that you enjoy mentioning often having risen from humble beginnings and being justifiably proud of it, so many people would be delighted to hear of your present behaviour with a woman whose character leaves so much to be desired, showing that all your achievements have been only reasonably lucky and that the character

> that you have been showing publicly is a sham, that the real you is back to your original standards.

Case notes presented by a Northside Clinic doctor who counselled Greta in July 1993 gave a clear prognosis: 'To put it very mildly, the relationship with her husband is catastrophic. I think she has the option of going on as it is and probably dying from hypertension or doing something about it. She is very reluctant to face reality.' This last observation was verified when the matriarch was examined by Kristina Moran's barrister: Greta had simply forgotten it all. The family commenced to do something similar when the case was settled soon after. To Douglas, the proceedings meant only one thing: further evidence of Australian disrespect for the enterprise spirit.

> [The court case] disappoints me as an Australian. Friends in the US have said to me, 'Doug, if you were over here in the States, what you've done, where you have come from, you would be highly respected'. But we don't want that here...People say, 'Let's shoot him down'...We will kick on. It's a great family, dedicated to nursing care. So we will win.

All of which recalls another oft-quoted line concerning wealth, F. Scott Fitzgerald's about the rich not being 'like you and I'. For there are times when it seems fervently to be hoped.

# ENTREPRENEURS A-GO-GO

## *James Packer and Richard Pratt* (2009)

When *Business Review Weekly* inaugurated its classic 1980s institution, the Rich List, one of the first correspondences received was from the scion of a great family fortune. How dare the magazine invade his people's privacy? It was a disgrace, an outrage. And what was especially disgraceful and outrageous was that *BRW* had failed to send him a free copy. He'd have ten, thanks.

The Packer and Pratt families, Rich List stalwarts, have had similarly ambivalent relations with the watching world, with larger-than-life patriarchs who became instantly recognized public figures, but who also dealt peremptorily with unwanted attention paid their personal and commercial misadventures. Books by Paul Barry, and by James Kirby and Rod Myer, now purport to tell their tales; they have not been lightly given up.

Having brought the mogul to pungent, profane life in *The Rise and Rise of Kerry Packer* (1993), Barry's ostensible subject in *Who Wants To Be A Billionaire?* is Kerry's son James. But to use his beloved network's slogan, Kerry is still the one. He is the subject here of all the best stories, doer of all the biggest deals, maker of all the grimmest jests, such as checking himself into Cornell Medical Centre under the name 'James Fairfax', then leaving instructions to advise all visitors that he is dying. There are sections, meanwhile, where the perennially put-upon James diminishes almost to vanishing point; Kerry, it seems, dominates his luckless son even on the page.

But Kerry also dominates Barry. For all his years immersed in the culture and folklore of the Packer family, he has done little to develop his view beyond the idea that Kerry was a bully, his wife Ros was nice, their son used to be nice like his mum but became a bully under his father's influence, and errrrr, that's it...

This makes for psychology as repetitive as it is clumsy: 'Like many sons, he was desperate to win his father's love and approval. But he also loved his mother'; With a fair dose of his mother in him, he had always been a milder person than Kerry and had tried not to copy the old man'; 'He was half like his mother and half like his father and it was hard to discover the real James'. And you get the sense after a while that Barry isn't really trying very hard to do the necessary discovering.

As far as James' motivations are concerned, too, Barry sets great store by a 1994 interview that the young man gave to Peter Fitzsimons: 'If I sat back and decided to sell the product of my father and my grandfather's work, like a leech, you know I wouldn't be able to look myself in the mirror.' These, however, seem pretty commonplace sentiments; certainly they're hardly worth forgetfully dropping in again 300 pages later.

Between these psychologising sallies, because James Packer inevitably withheld cooperation from the book, there is rather too much unsourced and unsubstantiated material. For instance, it is anybody's guess how to assess the following: 'One of Kerry's closest friends tells a similar story in which James supposedly fell in love with a girl who seduced him, only to have his father reveal afterwards that he had hired the young woman himself. Kerry did this sort of thing "all the time", according to a family friend.' Well, what are 'family friends' for, but to impart vague tittle-tattle to eager ears?

Protection of sources by a cloak of anonymity is, of course, a legitimate journalistic practice; but here, because the reader is unable to distinguish between and judge the credibility of all the 'friends' and 'business associates' and 'former executives', the sibilance of whispers begins to seem vaguely unfair, even a little potty. 'Ched [James's schoolfriend Matthew Cseidei] was also famous for his parties, at which his wilder playboy friends snorted coke and had fun,' Barry pants at one point. 'One man who went to several remembers James appearing at one of them and complaining he was cold. Someone immediately rushed upstairs to fetch him a jumper.' The smoking jumper!

Barry has even developed the rather odd habit of quoting himself without attribution. Rupert Murdoch's News Corporation office on New York's Avenue of the Americas, for instance, is pictured as unremarkable, 'lacking the huge metal doors and acres of carpet that needed crossing in the fictional world of Evelyn's Waugh's famous press baron, Lord Copper'. If this has a familiar feel, it's because the same headquarters is described in Barry's narrative of the OneTel fiasco, *Rich Kids* (2002), as featuring 'no acres of carpet such as one has to cross in the fictional world of Evelyn Waugh's famous press baron Lord Copper'.

All of which is a shame, for two reasons. Firstly, it's that Barry in his time has been a seriously fine journalist, and still pens a nice line; you'd need a heart of stone not to enjoy the reference to John Alexander resembling a 'maitre'd in an expensive restaurant'. Secondly, it's that *Who Wants To Be A Billionaire?* presents enough of an agglomeration of material for an interesting picture of financial heredity to emerge, even if Barry does not make best use of it.

Commercially, it seems, Kerry and James are intrigueingly opposite and complementary. Kerry was a profligate and impulsive man, a famously compulsive gambler. But as a businessman, he was growingly conservative, sticking to industries he knew, shrinking from innovation and developing investment philosophies as bleak as his thoughts concerning mortality.

James does not seem to have inherited his father's personal risk-taking proclivities, becoming an owner of casinos rather than a habitué, yet has been prepared to take far greater business bets. All the same, the gaming industry, built as it is on the exploitation of weakness and delusion, somehow sits comfortably with Kerry's pessimism about human nature. In this sense, James appears genuinely his father's son.

Barry advances some other potential contrasts, some interesting, some less convincing. He wishes us, for example, to see a gulf between Kerry and James in the matter of their mastery of minutiae: 'That was the difference between father and son. Kerry had a gasp of all the detail needed to run a business. James was much more interested in making deals then moving on, like a venture capital investor.' That, however, seems more accurately a difference between father's and son's generations. Both father and son, furthermore, proved unsentimental about their respective birthrights, James exiting Channel 9 just as Kerry jettisoned the *Daily Telegraph*. James's decision to opt out of the media as soon as he politely could, indeed, seems an altogether saner strategy than John Fairfax's of holding assets they neither appreciate nor understand.

Ultimately, *Who Wants To Be A Billionaire?* is summed up in what passes for a climax, when Barry finally comes face to face with his subject at the opening ceremonies for his grandiose City of Dreams casino complex in Macau. Barry has by this stage been dogging the billionaire's steps for two years to no avail; suddenly they are close enough to make eye contact, and to exchange a few faltering words.

> 'Off the record, off the record,' he insisted as he bent down to shake my hand
>
> 'I just wanted to ask you...'
>
> 'Off the record, Off the record,' he repeated.
>
> 'I just wanted to ask you...'
>
> Then he saw the TV cameras bearing down on him and broke away angrily, obviously thinking he had been set up.

The cameras actually have nothing to do with Barry – piquantly, they are those of Channel 9, the network, and the past, on which Packer turned his back. Documentary makers like Michael Moore and Nick Broomfield have milked whole films from the long-deferred, anti-climactic interview; Barry wrung some current affairs gold from a brief, brusque confrontation with Alan Bond twenty years ago. Here, however, it's all a bit of a non-event; we don't even find out what Barry intended asking. And by this stage, we don't really care.

The circle of Richard Pratt have hazarded a different solution to journalistic curiosity, apparently choosing to cooperate with the authors of *One Out of the Box*, which appears only eight months after the death of the Visy billionaire. Publishers at John Wiley, in fact, had something of a head start: *One Out of the Box* originated in *Richard Pratt: Business Secrets of the Billionaire Behind Australia's Richest Company* (2004), for which James Kirby, then at *BRW*, received a generous degree of access. This 'How-To' guide has been bulked to the size of a slim life story by Rod Myer, formerly of the *Sunday Age*, who made a fair fist of another Jewish commercial family saga *Living The Dream: The Victor Smorgon Story* (2000).

To the publishers, this must have seemed a bit of a wheeze. Pratt made a fortune out of recycling. Why not us? Well, *One Out of the Box* is the reason: a thin, trite, palpable quicky that is neither one thing nor the other, and feels suspiciously like Visy pulp in the making. The original Kirby book was actually a pretty passable study of management principles in practice, but it required a great deal more than Myer's once-over-lightly additions to transform it into a full scale work, let alone the 'compelling biography' promised by the blurb.

*One Out of the Box* opens with 'the Cardboard King' at Raheen in 'the leafy Melbourne suburb of Kew', a 'fighter and a visionary who was accustomed to shaping life according to his whim' brought low by cancer. Uh-oh. 'The Cardboard King' may be intended as an echo of 'The Cattle King', Sir Sidney Kidman, but it sounds oddly derogatory, like The 'Paper Tiger' or 'The Plaster Saint'; and why are these suburbs always 'leafy'? Anyway, people visit. Then he dies. 'Rosebud'? Not a bit of it. We're off on a terribly pedestrian recapitulation of Pratt's road to riches via refuse, on which, whether out of gratitude for the apparent blessing or sheer lack of imagination, no blot is permitted to fall.

Wiley was correct in one respect: Pratt would make a fascinating biographical subject. His business sense was a homespun mix, of old-fashioned *fingerspitzengefuhl* with an almost post-modern aversity to the idea of a centre. There are legion stories of Kerry Packer, feet on his desk in Sydney, berating some hapless underling - or, indeed, son. If Pratt was known for one thing, it was his wholehearted distaste for offices: his natural habitat was the shop floor. Like Henry Ford II, who immortally stated that 'Ford World Headquarters is where I am on any given day', Pratt traveled ceaselessly and communicated compulsively; hell was being alone.

There is, however, communication and *communication*. And it doesn't really cut it to begin a chapter by saying that Pratt was a 'natural communicator' whose 'communication was extended to his competitors, as he thought it was important to maintain a culture of openness that would enable him to remain alert to the nuance and culture of the industries in which he worked'. Because, you know what's coming next, don't you? Yes, that 'lunch' with Amcor's Russell Jones, and the prosecutions arising, of which it also doesn't quite suffice to conclude: 'It would have been a difficult burden to bear towards the end of what was in many ways a very successful life and career.' Nor is this the happiest of sentences: 'By this time in the proceedings another ingredient had made its way into the Shakespearian-like drama – Richard Pratt's prostate cancer had returned.' Proceedings? Ingredient? Shakespearian-like?

It's hard to blame Kirby and Myer entirely here: turning a $5 billion man into a $5 book was simply a lousy idea to begin with. In some respects, Barry's volume is the more disappointing, and the bigger pity, for it is the work of a journalist of talent, has been publicized extensively by reputable outlets, slagged off by all the right people, and amounts to two-thirds of nothing much. If Allen & Unwin receive a phone call from James Packer, it won't be demanding ten copies.

# HERO OF THE MARKETS

## *A review of Alan Greenspan's* The Age of Turbulence (2007)

A story is told of Arthur Burns, Eisenhower's chief economic adviser, appearing before a congressional committee on unemployment. Peering through thick glasses from under his thatch of centre-parted hair, Burns dilated on the issue for some time in a sombre monotone, then seemed to stop. 'If I infer correctly,' said a Connecticut congressman at last, 'what you are saying is that the unemployment problem is really one of women and young persons.' Burns paused ominously, fixed the congressman with an icy gaze, took a long drag of his pipe, and finally replied in his New Jersey drawl, 'I said a *great deal* more than that.' The room waited. Further elaboration came there none.

Burns, Friedman, Galbraith, Heller, Samuelson, Keyserling: the hand-picked economic mandarin has been a familiar figure stock character in the Beltway since the New Deal. And no representative of this clerisy has had the presence of Alan Greenspan. Burns, as it happens, was his mentor, when Greenspan was a young analyst at the National Industrial Conference Board in the 1950s; like Burns, Greenspan followed spells as a domestic policy co-ordinator (for Richard Nixon) and chief economic adviser (to Gerald Ford) by casting the interest-rate runes as chairman of the US Federal Reserve (for Reagan, Clinton and Bush *père et fils*, over 18 years). His status was attested in 2000 by the ultimate certification: a biography by Bob Woodward, *Maestro*, which made up for its thinness with pure schoolgirl gush. 'With Greenspan, we find comfort,' Woodward wrote. 'He helps breathe life into the vision of America as strong, the best, invincible...Each of us is a character in the nation's great economic soap opera; Greenspan is both director and producer.' Well, maybe if it was *Revenge of the Nerds*.

To be fair, the 'economic soap opera' was always vested with a certain jokey self-awareness. At the zenith of Greenspan's influence, the financial-news network CNBC got into the habit of filming his arrival for Federal

Open Market Committee meetings, submitting to analysis the size of his briefcase. The operating principle of the Briefcase Indicator was that the slimmer the case, the lighter the owner's heart and the more buoyant his market prognosis. In fact, according to Greenspan's new autobiography, *The Age of Turbulence: Adventures in a New World*, the choice of case was dictated by whether he had packed his lunch – but to say so at the time, of course, would have spoiled the game of the market watching him watching the market watching him.

The book, for which the publisher paid an advance of US$8 million, finds Greenspan still playing up to his role as the wonk's wonk, all owlish specs and oracular pronouncements, a man who once jested of himself, 'I guess I should warn you, if I turn out to be particularly clear, you've probably misunderstood what I said.' On a first date with his future wife, he talked about monopolies and asked her back to his flat to read an essay he'd written on anti-trust. So dense is his expression, even in repose, that it later took five attempts before she realised he had proposed; on their honeymoon in Venice, he exasperated her with remarks like, 'What is the value-added produced in this city?' He imbues with great gravity such personal philosophies as, 'I have always argued that an up-to-date set of the most detailed estimates for the latest available quarter is far more useful for forecasting accuracy than a more sophisticated model structure.' He fell into a virtual swoon when that monetarist minx Margaret Thatcher introduced herself with a flirtation: 'Tell me, Chairman Greenspan, why is it that we in Britain cannot calculate M3?'

Greenspan makes so much of this as to cast doubt on whose is the voice in *The Age of Turbulence*: is it Himself or that of his amanuensis, *Fortune*'s Peter Petre? There are a few of the subject's trademark terminological train wrecks – for example, 'inherent anchor in a fiat-money regime' and 'decontrol-engendered affluence' – but otherwise the reasoning is pretty clear. The vernacularising process might even have gone a little far. The book is burdened by tired colloquial personifications of the market: from 'roller-coaster' to 'eight-hundred-pound gorilla', and inevitably as a '*Titanic*' on course for an 'iceberg'. One searches in vain for an insight as arresting as the delightful aperçu of the Fed's longest serving chairman, William

McChesney Martin Jr, who said his role was to 'order the punch bowl to be removed just when the party is really warming up'. Greenspan doesn't do much better than, 'Panic in a market is like liquid nitrogen – it can quickly cause a devastating freeze.' And the dullest passages read like a recitation of rote-learned clichés, such as:

> Had we turned the screw one time too many? We were groping through a fog. The FOMC has always recognized that in a tightening cycle, if we stop too soon, inflationary pressures will resurge and make it very difficult to contain them again. We therefore always take out the insurance of an additional Fed funds increase. Ending the course of monetary antibiotics too soon risks the re-emergence of the infection of inflation.

Or: 'My concern about a bubble had changed my mind. I told the committee we might need an interest-rate increase to reign in the bull. I was choosing my words carefully because we...were playing with political dynamite.'

Certainly the book contains no economic idea quite so compelling as one to which Greenspan has regular recourse: Joseph Schumpeter's 'perennial gale of creative destruction'. This is the book of a nimble, adaptable but small-scale thinker. Perhaps this made him a good bureaucrat; it doesn't make him the ideal memoirist. *The Age of Turbulence* has to be read closely for other than merely incidental pleasures.

In the main, Greenspan's personal judgements are unsurprising. Nixon was the smartest and angriest of leaders, while Reagan lent a 'sunniness and benevolence to the presidency that never wavered'. Greenspan's relationship with Bush senior was tense, with Bush junior tenuous. Of all the presidents, he testifies most glowingly of the humble and hard-working Ford, but was most enamoured of Clinton, captivated by his charm and intellect, oblivious to his immorality and opportunism.

And for all Greenspan's intellectual insouciance, that capacity to be charmed is perhaps the real story. Greenspan found he could not cheerfully serve Nixon and retreated to consulting on Wall Street; taxed once by a question about his former boss's alleged anti-Semitism, he replied pithily, 'I don't know anybody he was pro. He hated everyone.' By the '90s, however, Greenspan was the quintessential insider – and, as he says, 'I have to admit, I was having fun.' His account of the Clintons' Millennium Dinner is almost starry-eyed, even to the extent that he notes his wife's 'cut-velvet burgundy and black Badgley Mischka'.

Greenspan was also far from uninvolved in the manufacture of his own myth. The phrase for which he will be recalled, he relates, came to him in the bathtub shortly after the Dow broke 6000 in October 1996. He kicked it round for a couple of months with colleagues, debating its adequacy, pondering its consequences. 'Are you sure you want to say this?' asked a senior colleague before the American Enterprise Institute dinner at which it made its inaugural public appearance. Greenspan enjoyed studying the reactions as it reverberated round the room: 'On the podium that night, I delivered the key passage, watching carefully to see how people would react...No one guessed. But I'd seen people in the audience sit up and take notice, and as the evening ended, the buzz began.'

'Irrational exuberance' suited the circumstances exquisitely; in its donnish dubiety, it soon became not merely something Greenspan *had* said, but also what he *would have said*. In reality, it was scarcely the cry of 'Fire!' in a crowded theatre, being expressed in the form of a question: 'But how do we know when irrational exuberance has unduly escalated asset values...?' In congressional testimony the next week, indeed, Greenspan denied he was talking share prices down. But this, for the speaker, was perhaps the episode's most intoxicating part: recognition, even reverence, for not saying very much at all; merely for sounding measured, informed, yet non-committal.

The Fed's autonomy is guaranteed by the *Banking Act* of 1935; it funds itself, and the chairman is answerable only to his board of governors. Greenspan's immediate predecessor, Paul Volcker, once received a note from Reagan asking if the president could come see him; Volcker replied tersely that this was 'inappropriate'. Yet after 'irrational exuberance' gave him global profile, Greenspan's White House contacts grew increasingly regular. He allowed himself to be courted by the Clintons and then by Bush junior, members of whose cabinet he knew exceedingly well, especially Dick Cheney, Donald Rumsfeld and Paul O'Neill: all veterans of the Ford administration. At regular White House lunches, Greenspan recalls, 'I talked so much that I don't recall ever having time to eat.'

This is a telling admission. It smacks of Greenspan reverting to his previous role as chairman of the president's Council of Economic Advisers, rather than preserving the distance and impartiality incarnate in his own office. And it is hard not to speculate that it bore on his testimony to the Congressional Budget Committee in August 2001 when, during the American economy's five minutes of surplus sunshine, he appeared to bless the Bush tax cuts that led the US deeply into deficit. Again, this was a premeditated step from which colleagues strove to dissuade him. 'The issue isn't so much what you're saying,' said the former treasury secretary Robert Rubin. 'It's how it's going to be perceived.' Greenspan gave a wilful reply: 'I can't be in charge of people's perceptions. I don't function that way. I can't function that way.' But he was, he did and he always had; and while Bush would probably have forged ahead with his tax cuts regardless, Greenspan's fiat gave them an irresistible momentum. In *The Age of Turbulence* he excuses the lapse as statistical: the effect on the tax base of the dotcom bust was greater than expected. The suspicion lingers that it was more personal, an undue relish for the role of maker and breaker of policy.

Greenspan spends a good deal of the rest of his recollections dissing the Bush White House for its comfort with deficits, its cynicism in distributing spoils and its connivance in the unstoppable growth in 'earmarks': budget line-items directing funds to specific projects without public hearing or review. Yet in his five years as Bush's chairman of the Fed, he was largely docile and accepted at face value his re-appointment for a fifth term a full year ahead of schedule. Greenspan is right to upbraid Bush for failing to wield his veto, and strangely reticent in talking about his own, theoretical but powerful.

The best of *The Age of Turbulence* is actually not the very limited self-assessment but the parts of the book devoted to economic themes.

Particularly good is Greenspan's account of visiting Moscow two months before the fall of the Berlin Wall and meeting his counterparts in Soviet economics at the planning bureaucracy Gosplan, where he obtained insights into the genius of capitalism from the decrepitude of communism. 'The Fed's job was challenging,' he writes. 'Gosplan's was surreal.'

He shows an enthusiasm for the illuminating datum and a flair for the counter-intuitive fact, especially where consumerism and oil consumption are concerned. Unfortunately, this is not what readers have come for. And, having stepped down from his bully pulpit in favour of Ben Bernanke in February last year, Greenspan is really just another economist – which perhaps he knew all along. His views are now simply views; on his pauses, nothing hangs.

# UTOPIA LIMITED

## *For and against universal basic income* (2016)

In the echoey theatre of modern political gesture, welfare has recently had one of its periodic stagings. A minister has honed his ideological credentials; columnists have extracted culture war content; tabloid journalists have parroted shamelessly grossed-up figures and patrolled Bondi beach for dole bludgers.

Yet for once it was worth cocking an ear. For if the world of employment is facing upheaval, then so is its counterpart of unemployment. And if the future of work is, as many argue, increasingly flexible, casual, various and scarce, it's arguable that those short of it will steadily face exacerbated economic risk. What might a welfare system of the future look like? What is the potential of ideas such as a universal basic income or a negative income tax, long discussed by economists, mostly beyond the ken of politicians?

Despite its regular depiction as a peeler of lotuses for layabouts, Australians have reasons to be proud of their social safety net. Australia's taxes are steeply progressive, moderating inequalities of income, and its welfare system comparatively cheap, certifiably efficient in delivering to those in greatest need. Most of the bill is absorbed not by the dole but by the aged pension, even if no tabloid has ever sent reporters to scour those opulent retirement homes and bingo halls in search of the spongeing workshy elderly.

But being fit for purpose is no help if purpose should change. 'What we have now is a welfare system designed around a whole bunch of policy settings that aren't there any more – a parsimonious dole predicated on a protected economy in what's now a dynamic, unprotected, trade-exposed economy,' argues Tim Lyons of the thinktank Per Capita. 'The dole makes sense if you're a cook and you lose your job as a cook and you want another job as a cook in the same town you live in. But it's not going to get you through a long period of unemployment without a decline into poverty, it won't help you retrain and it's not sufficient to help you move.'

Possibilities of gales of creative destruction are mitigated somewhat by slow growth in the supply of new workers. 'One thing that's happened over the last five years is that the growth rate in supply of workers has shrunk quite rapidly,' notes economist Saul Eslake. 'Since 2011, we've seen slowest growth in working age population since the great depression...and unemployment has fallen by more in the last three years than in any other three-year period.' Average job duration, too, has changed relatively little in the past 30 years and the much-discussed gig economy is as yet small, its impacts anecdotal rather than substantive – even if that may partly be a factor of official measurability.

In some respects, Australia is better prepared than other economies for the challenges of job churn. 'We're well ahead of a lot of other countries that tie a lot of things into the employment package,' observes the shadow assistant treasurer, Andrew Leigh. 'For example, when you tie healthcare into employment, it makes it much harder to move between jobs. When you have defined benefit pension plans tied to a particular job, that makes transition towards an economy in which people start working multiple jobs far more problematic. In that sense, we're starting in the new economic world with less lead in our saddle bags than much of North America and Europe.'

Developing a sense of future employment prospects, moreover, is something about which humility is advisable. Says Eslake: 'While it is easy to point to jobs that are threatened by technological change, what economists, futurists and others have been very bad at is pointing to the jobs that will emerge, whether people will be appropriately equipped to do those jobs and whether they will produce adequate incomes.'

Yet some facts can now be constituted as trends. Wage growth is anaemic, with all manner of entailments, including a property boom that is the empowered consumer's response to income insecurity. Casual work, meanwhile, is as profuse as full-time employment is flat. In 1988, just over a fifth of workers were employed part-time and adult full-time wages were 21% higher than wages paid to all. Today almost a third of workers are employed part-time and the wages gap yawns at 36%. Employers are ever more reliant on the ranks of casuals, part-timers, workers on short-term contracts, migrants on short-term visas and even full-time school students, who now constitute

2.3% of the workforce. The underemployed – those who would like to find more work but cannot – have reached unprecedented proportions, their circumspection acting as a drag on demand.

The Turnbull government's peculiar mix of effervescence and inanition suggests a superficial engagement with future possibility – imprecations to 'nimbleness' have replaced the valourising of 'working families'. But its rhetoric about welfare – variations on lifters and leaners, workers and shirkers – sounds more like a pandering to constituencies.

The benefits of the laissez-faire approach have been whittled away, leaving concentrations of prosperity, a more general residue of exhaustion and discontent. 'We're about to fall into that low-inflation trap that we've previously avoided, even though we're still growing – wage growth is the lowest it's been since they started collecting that data,' reports George Megalogenis, author of *Australia's Second Chance* (2016). 'You can't say people are slack and don't deserve a pay rise. They're working harder than ever and productivity has boomed. But the profit share has swung too far to capital without it being reinvested. So we need a reset, for same reason as you always need a reset – to maintain stability and smooth out the cycle.' Says veteran economist Ross Garnaut: 'There will be a certain number of jobs in future that give very good incomes, with a degree of luck involved in who gets those – even people of talent could work their guts out and not get one. We want a system of transfers that help the rest, the people who are unlucky, enjoy a reasonably secure life.'

But how? There are big ideas abroad. At the cutting edge is one with paradoxically ancient antecedents. Universal basic income, a form of social security involving the state paying its citizens a regular unconditional lump sum regardless of whether they work, claims a 500-year intellectual pedigree, the notion of providing 'everyone with some livelihood' having been countenanced by Thomas More in *Utopia* (1516) as an antidote to crime. It has since been approved by a remarkable range of reformers and redistributionists. In *Agrarian Justice* (1797), Thomas Paine envisioned a national fund, provisioned by the levying of a 'ground-rent' on landowners, which would make two kinds of payments to every person: a fifteen-pound lump sum at the age of 21 'to enable him or her to begin the world' and a ten pound annual stipend to everyone over 50 'to enable them to live in old age without wretchedness, and go decently out of the world'. In *The Road to Serfdom* (1944), FA Hayek argued that the universal assurance of 'some minimum of food, shelter, and clothing, sufficient to preserve health and the capacity to work' was 'no privilege but a legitimate object of desire' and could be provided 'outside of and supplementary to the market system'.

For a long time, then, universal basic income has looked like an elegant solution in search of a problem, including in Australia, where it was first mooted in the context of postwar reconstruction in a 1942 monograph by the radio journalist RG Lloyd Thomas and was a proposition entertained in Prof Ronald Henderson's landmark *Report of the Commission of Inquiry into Poverty* (1975). Lately it has found another articulate Australian advocate, the academic Tim Dunlop, whose *The Future is Workless* (2016) deems it 'suddenly very sexy' – not a description often applied to social security schemes.

'To me the real efficacy of basic income is that even if we're not headed into a workless future, we're destined for a future where work will be based on short-term contracts,' Dunlop says. 'That might be very lucrative for some people. And you might be able to string together a lifetime of that stuff. But, for a lot of people, even if there is plenty of that sort of work, there are going to be periods where you've got nothing. And if you have a society based on that insecurity, that's a bad society.'

The argument is being heard in a number of countries. Swiss voters pondered such a scheme this year, before rejecting it; Finland is running a non-universal pilot program next year; Y-Combinator, a Silicon Valley incubator firm, will sponsor a similar test in Oakland, California. And one of the most interesting features of a universal basic income is its variety of advocates, from wings of the egalitarian left, who see it as decommodifying labour and transforming labour relations, rallying behind such works as Guy Standing's *The Precariat* (2011) and Nick Srnicek and Alex Williams' *Inventing the Future* (2016), and the libertarian right, eager to winnow the welfare bureaucracy away, inspired chiefly by Charles Murray's *In Our Hands* (2006).

Dunlop finds common cause with both. 'The way the welfare system works now is insane,' he says. 'It's all outsourced to private providers, yet neither the government nor the provider can get you a job, only an interview. So the government is paying all this money to providers for getting people into interviews without access to the most obvious performance metric: did they get a job? All they can ask is are people "job ready"? So they come up with all these measures. Have you done a CV? Have you done training? Have you done this or that? All this government money is being spent basically on compliance costs, on policing people. I'm all for the libertarian argument in that sense. If we can get rid of that, I think everyone's better off.'

The trouble with having some supporters on left and right is that annoys others. Many on the left hear the echo of 'to each according to his needs'; a sizeable proportion of right still yearn to distinguish between 'the deserving poor' and 'the undeserving poor'. Welfare in Australia long ago sheered away from a social insurance model; it has traditionally been targeted, generally been niggardly. The idea of money for nothing would go against a deeply grained idea of a reciprocal bond between state and citizen – embedded in our national anthem, of course, is the notion of 'wealth for toil'. Given work's perceived ennobling characteristics, a basic income would strike some as morally corrosive. But most now uncontroversial forms of income support were first condemned. And a universal basic income might prove less of a disincentive to work than generally imagined. In the most famous basic income experiment, Mincome (1974–79), residents of a poor town in the Canadian province of Manitoba were sent monthly cheques. Working habits among males in Dauphin changed hardly at all, households remained thrifty, and other life measures were enhanced: teenagers remained in school longer; mental health outcomes were better.

Mincome was doomed by a conservative shift in Canadian politics and its findings were buried – perhaps in part because they cast doubt on an abiding assumption that the poor immiserate themselves by carelessness with money. On the contrary, it seemed, for having had little, they were all the more careful.

Occurring as it did only on a local scale, however, Mincome only takes the argument so far. A truly universal basic income would reach many who neither need nor want it. 'If the proposition is for a basic income, then, as someone who earns more than $200,000, I say: "Don't cut me a cheque",' says Labor's Andrew Leigh. 'It will do nothing to change my behaviour and it will be produced either by raising taxes unnecessarily or, worse still, by taking money away from people who need it more than me. And we would be doing it in a country where the total burden of tax is one of the lowest in the advanced world.'

A basic income would, indeed, be exceedingly expensive: even calibrated at the minimum wage, it would require the disgorging of almost the entire tax take. 'Our system isn't perfect,' says economist Eslake. 'It can be improved on the expenditure and the revenue sides but that can be done. Whereas if you were to say to the Australian people we need to raise the level of tax by 10% of GDP, I can't see that flying. It is less of an issue for Scandinavian countries who recycle a lot more through the tax and transfer system.'

Dunlop is not so starry-eyed that he sees the universal basic income as an idea whose time has come. 'I guess I end up at the view, as I do with lots of things about the future of work, is that we actually have to get to the crisis,' he says. 'That you don't argue your way into this, because the social and cultural norms are so entrenched that you need to come to a point where alternatives demand it. We only got a welfare state because of two world wars. You've also got to convince the one per cent that their income is being legitimately redistributed. They're very powerful and it's not like society is falling down around their ears – not yet anyway. In the meantime they can insulate themselves from it. Things will have to get very bad to get their attention.' As Tim Lyons notes: 'At the moment we're a country that can't come to grips with increasing the dole by $35 a day, which everyone, even the Business Council of Australia, accepts is a ridiculously low level.'

Sometimes drawn into discussion of universal basic income is a less ambitious but more robust welfare variation – that of the targeted cash transfer. Its advocates first stirred in the mid-1990s and again have numbered some interesting individuals. In his maiden speech to parliament in 1994, for example, young backbencher Tony Abbott outlined an inchoate plan for a broad-based, non-means-tested 'family wage' of $100 a week payable to the principal carer of dependent children. Again the allure was simplicity, reduced bureaucracy.

While voters have shown an innate mistrust of radical change to the tax system, everyone understands and hardly anyone objects to a cash payment. A family wage is quite different from welfare. It is a recognition of responsibilities, not need. It is a payment for services, not a handout. It means that personal choice could replace economic necessity as a rationale for family decisions. One beauty of a family wage system is that it would take one public servant, just one, and a computer to administer. Payments would start the moment a birth is recorded on the registrar of births, deaths and marriages database and finish 16 years later.

The showpiece, however, has come from the left of politics, specifically Lulism in Brazil. Now 13 years old, Bolsa Familia is a mean-tested basic income allocated to poor families through the female head of household, delivered via a citizens card that operates on a debit basis, conditional on contrapartidas (counterpart responsibilities) such as children attending school, receiving vaccinations and medical check-ups. It is overwhelmingly popular, a quarter of Brazilian households being eligible recipients. It is also disarmingly cheap, absorbing less than half a per cent of GDP.

Bolsa Familia has its critics, from the right, including the Catholic church, and from the left, who see it as too paternalistic and consumerist – the contrapartidas are arguably as much about legitimising the scheme in the eyes of the middle class as improving public health outcomes. There have been the inevitable issues of abuse, enforcement and burden on overtaxed social services. Yet many initial objections have been disarmed: the evidence is against it breeding improvidence or dependency, with the bulk of the money spent on basics such as food and clothing, while three-quarters of adult recipients still undertake paid work.

If the disbursement of cash might seem a crude device, a third device has already been run up a mainstream political flagpole. The negative income tax, in which those earning below a set amount receive supplemental pay from the government, has described a zig-zagging intellectual course, one of its most committed advocates being Milton Friedman in *Capitalism and Freedom* (1962), who saw it as eliminating the need for a minimum wage, addressing disincentives to work posed by high marginal tax rates, and consolidating overlapping welfare circles.

A negative income tax was first mooted here by the classical liberals Wolfgang Kasper, Dick Blandy, John Freebairn, Douglas Hocking and Robert O'Neill, who in *Australia at the Crossroads* (1980) envisioned it being financed by 'a reduction in the provision of 'free' government services and subsidies to private producers' (they also promoted life-endowment grants: sums of 'the order of $20,000' payable to young people 15–21 as a start in life or 'stake' in society). It was subsequently promoted as an anti-unemployment measure by Freebairn, Peter Dawkins, Ross Garnaut, Michael Keating and Chris Richardson in their Five Economists' Letter of October 1998.

Garnaut, a former senior adviser to prime minister Bob Hawke and an ambassador to China, now a professorial fellow of economics at University of Melbourne, remains an advocate: 'A simple way of making it work would be to give all Australian citizens or residents [an] automatic payment into their bank account every fortnight, subject to a means tests, principally an assets test, [and] you'd be taxed at a basic rate from the very first dollar of income... It's just a much simpler system for employers and you don't get high marginal tax rates discouraging people on social security as they do now.'

Its attractions were noted by the McClure review of welfare in 2000, which recommended a single 'common base payment' to people of working age replacing all other pensions and allowances, with a few add-ons for those with special ability and housing needs. Tony Abbott, by then the employment minister, thought that it 'should be possible to build a consensus for a single working-age payment with supplements based on special needs and participation in the community'.

But the push lost momentum: its outgrowing instead was the low income tax offset and to a degree the raising of the tax-free threshold. The only political party in Australia still advocating a negative income tax is the Pirate Party, whose platform in the last election included a tax designed to ensure of minimum income of $14,000 for everyone over the age of 18.

Whatever transpires, a shift in the paradigm of work poses a challenge to the recently evolved bargain between citizen and state. For much of last 20 years, Australian governments have explored variations on the theme of shifting costs back to the electorate, coaxing voters along the route of private provision for education, health, infrastructure, services and retirement. This slow but steady heaping of expenses on the household table has exacerbated domestic financial precariousness.

'You go underwater very quickly without a wage,' says Megalogenis. 'Which suggests that, technically, if your open market model can't provide your working-age population with a steadily rising income any more, you've reached the limits of that cost shifting, especially in education and health. That's a big problem for the economy overall. It was a shortcoming of laissez-faire capitalism in the 19th century: it could never get its mind around the idea that when it got rid of a worker, it was robbing itself of a consumer. We face something like that problem now.'

To Megalogenis, the global financial crisis should be recognised as the day the future began: 'The last few years in politics have diverted us from the great lesson of 2008–9. We now have a federal government looking at a structural budget deficit, a Reserve Bank that has lost its discretion on the price of money because global interest rates are now so low and a wages system not rewarding the worker for what the open market has demanded they do for the last 20 years, which is adapt – a model that's broken but exhausted. Yet knowing how successfully the state leaned against the GFC, basically all the levers working exactly as you would wish, you could be pretty confident of it getting things right.'

The future requires, he believes, a state more active and more robust in alleviating the cost of day-to-day living. 'Before the robots take over, I'd be thinking about where the state can get back in, with the commonwealth as the borrower and the states as the spender,' he says. 'Most people want to feel that government is on their side. Not because they want a handout, which is the way it's frequently been misinterpreted. They want government involved. So the state should be thinking hard about keeping on its books the costs it can bear on behalf of the community. Without an active state you can't prepare the population for the next big hit, which is coming anyway, whether we're ready or not.'

The welfare nostrums of the Turnbull government? Largely pointless, argues Tim Lyons. 'What this mob has returned to is a view that it's necessary to punish people who are unemployed, to get them in a headlock,' he says. 'It's a recurrent rightwing fantasy of the last 25 years that there's this vast imaginary army of malingerers and a ton of money to be saved in welfare – the idea that we're going to save the federal budget by finding a whole bunch of Paxton kids.'

In fact, believes Garnaut, the stakes could hardly be higher. 'We're testing how democracy works when wages are stagnant or falling,' he says. 'Well, I think we already know how it works, which is badly. In fact, unless we get used to the idea of doing something systematic and non-stigmatising to support the incomes of ordinary people, it may not be viable as a political system.' The answers will not be found on Bondi beach.

## REQUIEM FOR A BRAND

### *The death of Holden* (2020)

Sometimes that an event is greeted as news is as noteworthy as the event itself. Thus the coverage this week of the retirement in Australia of the Holden brand name by its American owner, General Motors.

The name traces its lineage to a saddlery and carriage maker founded in the days of Cobb and Co. The business belongs to the pioneering era of automotive globalism, when GM also scooped up the likes of Opel and Vauxhall on the way to becoming the world's most valuable commercial enterprise.

But Holden's significance had already been vastly attenuated by its owner's decision just over six years ago to wind down local manufacturing, which ceased in October 2017. The brand had gone on being slapped on imported makes for continuity's sake, but such goodwill as remained had long since leeched away.

The obsequies, then, were over an empty casket – last opportunities to show the stock footage of the original Holdens receiving Ben Chifley's benediction, featuring in cheesy advertisements, circling Mount Panorama, rallying in rough terrain. It was as though people were just catching up with the news, that Australia had lost a car industry in the way the British were said to have acquired an empire – in a fit of absent-mindedness.

Or maybe it was a stage in grieving, a belated acknowledgement of the loss, not so much of the cars, now seldom bought, as the way of life they connoted, the four-door, rear-wheel drive sedan having for so long been the natural carapace of the nuclear family.

There were those jobs too, for Holden made lives as surely as cars. Henry Ford is conventionally, if a little tendentiously, credited with the idea of creating his own customers by paying workers a generous wage. Automotive manufacturing had a similar impact on Australia. When General Motors-Holden in February 1935 foreshadowed plans to manufacture engines at Fishermans Bend, it alleviated a burden of depression, economic and psychological. The speech of welcome by Victoria's lands minister Albert Lind elucidates as well as any how industry conduced to the building of a healthier, wealthier society.

> A large number of men will be engaged immediately on the construction work, and later in the factory on its completion. Further employment will be provided in connexion with reclamation, sewerage, water supply and road construction.
>
> At a time when unemployment is so widespread, and such large amounts are being expended on sustenance and unemployment relief, the government is pleased to have proposed to it this fine offer involving legitimate employment, and affording permanent relief for out-of-work sufferers...
>
> The weekly distribution of such a large amount of regularly-paid wages must favourably react on every section of the community ranging from the smallest retail trader in the metropolitan area up to the revenue of the government itself. This must result in a material improvement in the general prosperity of the state.

From manufacturing, in other words, benefits cascaded, in ways they did not from the exploitation of agricultural and mineral commodities – a foundational principle of a mixed economy. For decades onwards, the arrival of an automotive plant in your neighbourhood, dragging auxiliary businesses along with it, was something devoutly to be wished.

When GMH outgrew Fishermans Bend in the 1950s, for example, its expansion transformed the area around Melbourne's Clayton and Doveton: International Harvester moved in next door, Volkswagen, the spare parts business Kirkall-Repco, the component manufacturer Robert Bosch and the paint maker BALM nearby. Such areas became havens for postwar migrants, the factories enacting workplace diversity *avant le lettre*. In the history of Australian workplaces, perhaps only the goldfields have been so ethnically and culturally multifarious.

Automotive work, furthermore, was purposeful work – complex, precise, demanding, fulfilling, dignified, steady. The sort that allowed long-term domestic decisions to be made, encouraged interdependence, thrift, social progress; the sort that instilled a certain pride.

Cars remain the biggest, dearest and most complex machines that Australians use. Manufacturing them ourselves was an assertion of self-sufficiency significant to a heavily derived and imported culture. Previously Australians had been lumbered with a range of anaemic English vehicles. At the time of the original FX Holden, Australia's biggest selling car was the meek Austin A40 Devon; John Brack's *The Car* (1955) envelopes its passengers in a boxy Triumph Mayflower. The Haighs owned a Hillman Imp with lap belts and two cylinders, only one of which worked.

The FX and FJ, followed by the Kingswood, Monaro, Torana, Commodore et al, suggested a way of life rather than merely a means of transportation, captured in the photographs of Athol Shmith in the 1950s and Henry Talbot in the 1960s, associated with the feats of Peter Brock and Jim Richards in the 1970s and 1980s.

So did the Holden come to pervade vernacular culture. The Kingswood was conspicuous and virile in *Homicide* (1964–77), invisible but immanent in *Kingswood Country* (1980–1984). An eroticised Monaro dominated Henry Williams' novel *My Love Had A Black Speed Stripe* (1973); a rakish FJ accelerated Michael Thornhill's movie *The FJ Holden* (1977); Kingswood panel vans oozed sexual possibility in adaptations of *Puberty Blues* to the big screen (1979) and small (2012–14). Peter Brian, a young chartered accountant from Price Waterhouse seeking a distinctively Australian stage name as he embarked on a musical career, found inspiration in his father's old ute – and Frankie J Holden, as he observed, sounded better than Victor Lawnmower.

Murray Bail christened his protagonist Holden Shadbolt advisedly in the novel *Holden's Performance* (1987): Holden is steady, strong-bodied, a 'car maniac...indoctrinated by the mathematics of the streets', for whom the odour of hot oil is 'French perfume to his nostrils' and car keys represent 'an outer world of noise, speed and limitless space'. The Holden, as the historian Graeme Davison puts it in *Car Wars* (2002), 'coded unambiguously male'. And after a while, of course, Australian society no longer did. As protection abated, Australians were offered wider automotive choices and took them, compromising the volumes available to local manufacturers.

Manufacturers did a better job of adapting than they are given credit for in what is by world standards a small market. They also rather failed to update impressions of their industry, which ended up stuck with the image of a quaint form of metal bashing, when to mass produce precision engineering of the kind involved in making a car requires very advanced techniques – the kind, in fact, that nations have historically aspired to.

There is no need here to reprise the decline and fall of Australian automotive manufacture – a car expert, as the late John Button put it, can be found on every street corner. The industry has long been a favoured subject for wonks, columnists and economists, opinionated usually in inverse proportion to their direct experience. Everyone has a favourite culprit: the dollar, the unions, industry protection or lack of, the cost of energy, the overhang of foreign ownership. In the end, however, the dissolution of the car industry was, like its inception, not an economic decision so much as a political one.

For a long time, the automotive industry in Australia had been able to depend on a broad consensus between the forces of capital and labour. Members of its well-paid managerial class and of its solidly unionised workforce might lean differently in the polling booth, but their interests were otherwise aligned. The industry's prosperity was deemed generally efficacious.

But as political tectonics shifted, that changed. The car has lost some of its aspirational significance; the activity of making, rather than buying, selling and marketing, is felt unfashionable, or best left to others. So the industry's friends dwindled. There were none among the desiccated calculating machines of the right, severe about perceived subsidies, leery of organised labour; none among the carbonphobic left, alienated from working class culture; none among the Davos pilgrims and Ted talkers who fantasise of saving the world one app at a time. And an industry that had always needed incentives to stay could no longer find them.

At around the time car manufacturing's future was being debated, I spent several enjoyable months reporting it for a short book, visiting automakers, component manufacturers, unions, consultants, politicians and pundits. In the industry, I had half-expected low morale, corporate inertia. In fact, the mood was disarmingly buoyant. Not because the challenges were unrecognised: these people lived in an environment of constant challenge, in which the movement of a few cents in the dollar or the slightest slack in taut supply chains could wipe profits away.

But the actual work was, still, great – intricate, fascinating, at the forefront of technology, constantly moving, profoundly satisfying, with deep local and intergenerational roots. This was a business, I was repeatedly told, to which one could dedicate a life and never be bored, with dimensions no economic model could capture.

Perhaps I saw the best of it. Yet it was difficult to reconcile this experience with the common depiction of the industry as moribund, workshy, cadging, twentieth century – an image which, in the end, counted for more. For in due course, automotive manufacturing in Australia fell victim to the ambivalence of its owners and to the frivolous gesture politics of the day. Some commentators have since described treasurer Joe Hockey's stance as 'principled'. Maybe in the Groucho Marx sense: if you didn't like these principles, he had others...

Australia is, after all, plunging headlong into naval shipbuilding at astronomical cost to the taxpayer to the benefit of far fewer workers. The car, meanwhile, will be busy being revolutionised; yet in that development, Australia, with a century of automotive skills, knowledge and heritage, will play no part. We will have instead a museum of memories, cliches and stock footage.

# DEATH OF A BOSS

## *Lee Iacocca (1924–2019)* (2019)

'Someone has to speak up. I hardly recognise this country anymore... I'll go a step further. You can't call yourself a patriot if you're not outraged. This is a fight I'm ready and willing to have.'

Today the words have a familiar 'drain-the-swamp' feel, the times calling for very stable geniuses. Yet they were uttered by Lee Iacocca, who died last week aged 94 long after his 1980s zenith as a business personality and wannabee populist – a kind of proto-Trump, with the twist that he was a proper businessman and not the mime act of one. Long before Trump emblazoned the slogan on trucker caps, 'Making America Great Again' was title of the last chapter of Iacocca's eponymous autobiography, otherwise chronicling his storied career at Ford and Chrysler.

The parallels run deeper. Both came from immigrant stock – Iacocca's Italian, Trump's German – with entrepreneurial patriarchs. Both married thrice (so far, in Trump's case). They had common associates, such as the creepy lawyer Norman Cohn, and the celebrity enabler William Fugazy. In 1986, brought together by the man Trump called 'Willie The Fug', the two businessman even bought a condominium project together. Despite their seeming combination of star power, Trump Plaza of the Palm Beaches was a flop. Trump had to buy Iacocca out, and later surrendered the development to bankers during one of his numerous financial embarassments.

The sheen of both was burnished by that signal American honour, the cover of *Time*, which Iacocca first achieved aged 39 off the back of the success of the Ford Mustang, and which Trump first landed aged 44 for being a tacky show off ('Flaunting it is the game and TRUMP is the name'). Both went back regularly; Trump is now difficult to keep off it.

Both presented their credentials, as it were, in hugely successful books: *Iacocca* was America's best-selling non-fiction book in 1984 and 1985, *The Art of the Deal* (1987) spent 51 weeks in the *New York Times* bestseller lists.

In politics, both arrogated to themselves the status of 'outsiders', insofar as hugely wealthy white males can ever be outsiders, or at least individuals who owed no allegiances: Iacocca was a registered Republican who skewed Democrat out of distaste for the Bushes, Trump a registered Democrat whose rematerialisation as a Republican involved a showy loathing of the Clintons.

Iacocca's obituarists last week concentrated on his Detroit legend, where he was the only man to run two of the big three. They rather neglected his significance as the first real incarnation of the modern phenomenon of the celebrity CEO, whose fame rivalled that of the organisations he led.

The US had a great tradition of commercial barons, dating back to Carnegie and Rockefeller. But the salaried executive had to that stage been a relatively inconspicuous figure. Iacocca's revival of Chrysler was very much a team effort – he recruited no fewer than forty-eight executives from Ford. But if there is proverbially no 'I' in team, there certainly was an 'I' in Iacocca, who emerged from behind his desk to deliver a series of reverberating advertising pitches ('You can buy a Chrysler, or you can go with someone else – and take your chance'; 'If you find a better car – buy it!').

Some of his catchcries had a nativist ring. Iacocca routinely lambasted Japan for its one-way protectionism – a drum that Trump has beaten successfully in the case of China. 'Let's make America mean something again!' he thundered in one advertisement – which led to speculation as to how far he was prepared to take this.

In June 1982, *The Wall Street Journal* ran a front page story bruiting Iacocca's presidential ambitions – it seemed hardly less likely than the election of the star of *Bedtime for Bonzo*. 'If a Hollywood star can,' asked Amanda Bennett, 'why not a Detroit car salesman?' Iacocca ostentatiously disclaimed interest in political office: 'I'm too outspoken to be a good politician. If a guy's giving me a bunch of baloney, I tell him to buzz off because he's wrong. Somehow I don't think the presidency works that way.' Pregnant pause. 'But I *do* think,' Iacocca continued, 'that our national leadership consists of too many lawyers and not enough people from business. I'd like to see a system where we brought in twenty managers to run the business side of the country.'

There grew currency in the idea that the US was like a commercial turnaround opportunity, a la Chrysler. In April 1985, *Time* again plonked Iacocca on their cover in shades of red, white and blue, with the famous headline: 'I Gotta Tell Ya: America Loves Listening to Lee.'

Iacocca claimed to be flattered by the attention: 'I get a lot of mail about running for president. It's made me aware there's a real vacuum out there. People are hungry for someone to tell them the truth – that America isn't bad, it's great – or at least that it can be made great again if we just get on track.... People are hungry to be led.' Privately he envisioned a campaign, to the extent of hiring an experienced speech writer, producing a more overtly political follow-up book called *Straight Talk*, and arriving at a slogan – although he rejected the nostalgic belligerence of making America great again in favour of doubling down on the vertical pronoun: 'I Like I.'

In fact, as Reagan's folksy charm won the American people over, the opportunity narrowed, and he was in the end probably sincere in his avowals that he was not a natural fit for politics. Iacocca's friend Tip O'Neill, Republican speaker of the house, counselled: 'You're used to running a big corporation. When you make a decision in the morning, you either earn a profit that day or you don't. You can't run government that way. It would drive you crazy.' If you have a patchy profit record anyway and are already three-quarters crazy, the obstacles are more surmountable.

If not for the US, it is probably a shame for Iacocca that he did not run. He stayed so long at Chrysler that Iacocca was said to stand for 'I Am Chairman of Chrysler Corporation Always', and he admitted later to 'flunking retirement', finding nothing to which to harness his daemonic energies. His last testament, *Where Have All The Leaders Gone?* (2007), is tinged with sadness, that Iacocca remained possessed of strong views, while also seeming to grasp that America no longer loved listening to him quite as much, and that without his job and its trappings he was just another voice.

Yet holding no brief for anyone freed him to roll out a heterodox set of political beliefs. He remained a robust capitalist, a red-tape hacker, a trade thunderer, an advocate of nuclear power, a champion of the self-made. He quoted approvingly Milton Friedman, Oral Roberts, Bob Hope, General

Patton. He also deplored George W. Bush's truckling to tyrants ('If our goal is to spread democracy through the middle east, why don't we do our friends a favour and call for regime change in Saudi Arabia?') and claims that 'the jury is out on climate change' ('Which jury is that? The OJ jury?'). He decried as Unamerican the punitive treatment of illegal immigrants ('Walls don't work...America doesn't build walls, it tears them down') and of Guantanamo Bay prisoners ('Hey aren't we supposed to be the good guys? I'd like someone to explain to me how torturing prisoners has become the American way').

Iacocca probably sensed he was out of step with the increasingly partisan times, for he was also no longer quite so enamoured of the American people's intrinsic virtues, and admitted to wondering whether 'a bunch of overeating, pill-popping, TV-watching, iPod-wired, shopaholic, attention-deficit-disordered people' was 'going to make it'. Then he lived long enough to see one such person actually elected president.

# DEATH OF AN INVENTOR

## *A review of Walter Isaacson's* Steve Jobs *(2011)*

'It's your book,' Steve Jobs told his hand-picked biographer Walter Isaacson two years ago. 'I won't even read it.' He was as good as his word: the Apple mogul died in October without having done so, leaving *Steve Jobs* as an apparently unvarnished account of his life and times.

Now, there is something a little odd about this. Jobs was gravely ill with cancer. His ostensible purpose in commissioning the book was so that his children, to whom he had for many years been an absentee father, might come to 'know' him. But most people in a similar predicament would simply have talked to their children, spent time with them, shared memories, made amends. Jobs instead gave forty rambling and none-too-revealing interviews to a journalist that mainly corroborate Carlyle's dictum about genius being 'always a secret to itself'.

Did Jobs not trust his interpersonal skills? Was he hoping someone else might be able to understand him better? Isaacson is not the biographer to speculate. In fact, he's not the biographer to do much more than take dictation. The result is a book that describes often in quite fine detail what Jobs did, but imparts precious little sense of who he was.

Isaacson's recurrent motif in exploring Jobs' character is that he possessed what peers call a 'reality distortion field'. 'In his presence, reality is malleable,' says a contemporary. 'He can convince himself of practically anything.' This seems like a fancy name for a relatively commonplace idea – that Jobs invested most heavily in facts that suited him, ignored those that didn't, and intimidated those whom he could not cajole into sharing his vision. Perhaps the most interesting thing about it is that the expression was borrowed by a former colleague from the classic *Star Trek* two-parter, 'The Menagerie', in which the phenomenon is a gift of a doomed alien people, the Talosians: in Silicon Valley, sf was a lingua franca.

Jobs undoubtedly had the capacity in rare measure, but it doesn't really get a biographer very far, and repeated references to it, as though it is an explanation sufficient in itself, lend the book a kind of relentless superficiality. Again and again, we're told that Jobs was 'charismatic and inspiring' while also 'an asshole at times'. Isaacson had access to all the major figures in Jobs' personal and commercial life, and he has interpreted their banalities as profundities. There are numberless variations on: 'Steve is a one-of-a-kind guy. You know that about him when you do business with him.' The business transactions tend to be narrated in a bland magazine prose, such as when Jobs is negotiating with Disney's Bob Iger about the acquisition of Pixar.

> 'I want you to know that I am really thinking out of the box on this,' he [Iger] said. Jobs seemed to encourage the advances. 'It wasn't too long before it was clear to both of us that this discussion might lead to an acquisition discussion,' Jobs recalled.

Opportunities to delve more closely into Jobs himself, meanwhile, go begging all too regularly. In May 1978, for example, Jobs' sometime girlfriend bore him a daughter, Lisa. Jobs wanted nothing to do with her. 'I didn't want to be a father, so I wasn't,' he told Isaacson succinctly.

What Jobs did instead was name an ambitious Apple computer project the Lisa, while claiming ludicrously that this stood for 'Local Integrated Software Architecture'. This, says Isaacson, would have caused 'the most jaded psychiatrist to do a doubletake'. As a biographer, alas, he does no more than nod.

Isaacson also allows Jobs to repeat, for the umpteenth time, an urban myth that *Time* intended to make him Man of the Year in 1982, then decided, after he skirmished with journalist Mike Moritz, to honour the personal computer. 'We're the same age, and I had been very successful, and I could tell he was jealous and there was an edge to him,' says Jobs. 'He wrote this terrible hatchet job, so the editors in New York get this story and say "we can't make this guy Man of the Year". That really hurt.'

Bizarrely, Isaacson reports that he knows this story to be untrue. He was privy as a *Time* junior editor to cover discussions, and the personal computer was always designated for the mantle, never Jobs. Does he confront his subject with the unreality of his man-eating grievance, a case of the 'reality distortion field' serving as an instrument of self-torture? Does he heck.

Isaacson is not altogether imperceptive. He is best when he has someone to contrast Jobs with, whether it be Bill Gates, or John Sculley, the PepsiCo executive whom Jobs lured to Apple who then engineered his 1985 ouster. When he has Jobs on his own, however, he lapses into the lamest cod psychology. Isaacson is excited to learn, for instance, that the youthful Jobs read *King Lear* and *Moby Dick* with pleasure, then rather let down: 'I asked him why he related to King Lear and Captain Ahab, two of the most wilful and driven characters in literature, but he didn't respond to the connection I was making, so I let it drop.'

The daftest passages are where Isaacson plagues Jobs for what is 'on' his iPod, citing Steve Levy's assertion in *The Perfect Thing* (2006) that this is one of the 21st century's crucial character tests: 'It's not just what you like – it's who you are.' So to what does Jobs listen? Nothing special. Early Dylan and Beatles; no Eminem. Ho-hum. But Isaacson goes on and on, extracting from Jobs such deathless judgements as: 'Donovan did some good stuff, really.' What he actually provides is counterevidence to the whole gushy consumerist crock that we are simply composites of our tastes in popular culture. But he's in too deep to see it.

In the end, the definitive testament to Jobs is not what was on his iPod, but the iPod itself, and the whole suite of related products, iMacs, iPhones, iPads and all, in the sense that you're never quite sure whether you're in the presence of simple beauty, sterile fetishism or both. A personal disclaimer seems in order. This review was written, amid an iPod's shufflings, on a MacBook Air, whose box is still sitting in the corner of the room because it was somehow too neat to throw out straight away. *Si monumentum requiris, circumspice.*

# FEEDING THE HAND THAT BITES

## *On Reviewing* (2010)

Everybody wants to go to heaven, as they say, but nobody wants to die. So it is in the world of book reviewing. Everyone is in favour of frank and fearless criticism, up to the point where a work of theirs might come off the worse for it.

It was, arguably, ever thus. But the books pages of Australian newspapers and magazines have become such a wasteland that traditional timidities no longer suffice as a satisfactory explanation. Sections that should contain some of a publication's sharpest, shrewdest, most incisive and irreverent writing have become hodgepodges of conventional wisdom and middlebrow advertorial.

Newspapers bear some blame for this. Although you'd imagine that anything contributing to an informed and discriminating print culture would be advantageous to them, newspapers publish books pages with a grudging air, regarding them as a financial burden because they attract little advertising support.

Reviewers, by extension, are the lowliest of contributors. Some newspapers and magazines in Australia have ceased paying for reviews at all, believing that the thrill of a free book alone will summon the definitive notice. Others are winnowing costs away by on-selling reviews to sister publications, buying reviews from overseas (usually of books three people in the country might read) or using staff journalists (generally, whether out of incompetence or envy, the dopiest reviewers of all). Then there is the popular institution of the capsule review, one hundred words or less, executed for beer money, and there to convey the illusion of comprehensiveness by breaking up the page, one superficial but reverberating assertion at a time.

In his classic essay 'Confessions of a Book Reviewer', a touchstone for every 'down-trodden, nerve-wracked creature' who has toiled in the craft, George Orwell opined that one thousand words was the 'bare minimum' for a review of consequence, and that the 'standard middle-length review of about 600 words' was 'bound to be worthless'. Yet in newspapers today, six hundred words constitutes a veritable meander.

No wonder, then, that there's little incentive for sticking one's neck out, for actually taking a position, for arguing that a book is bad, or sloppy, or stupid, or two or three iterations short of finished – an affliction staggeringly common among Australian books. Who needs the aggravation? Far easier to summarise the contents, recapitulate the blurb, describe the author's reputation, or examine the author's politics in a thinly veiled op-ed – is he or she 'one of us'? After all, the author might be reviewing us one day, or perhaps already has. In which case, it may, of course, be payback time.

Yet there's much less of this last phenomenon – both the time-tested revenge fanging and the newfangled pre-emptive fanging of the sort recently perpetrated in *The Monthly* – than is commonly imagined. The besetting sin of Australian book reviewing, curious in an age in which newspapers are chock-full of try-hard humourists and blow-hard opinionistas, is its sheer dullness and inexpertise.

A successful review has two qualities. First, it is a lively and engaging piece of writing. It informs and invigorates. It detains and delights. Yet how often in Australia do you read a book review that is a sparky, spunky, memorable bit of prose? And how many reviewers can you name whose work you would cheerfully read regardless of the book being discussed?

Second, a competent book review should be a form of inquiry into what makes books *good* – an inquiry with, as unfashionable as it sounds, the courage of its elitism. Without a benchmark of what constitutes excellent writing, scrupulous research and intelligent discussion, a reviewer is locked into a world in which 'liking' and 'not liking' are the only options – the *Beavis and Butthead* world, as the American literary critic Curtis White has put it, in which 'this sucks, that rocks, this is awesome, and everything is just finally a lot stupid'.

As well as setting standards, a competent review gives context, deepens understanding and clarifies debate. This requires some discernment, some rigour, even some dedication. If you're reviewing a work of fiction, it might be expedient to have read, or if not, to read, the author's earlier publications; if you're critiquing a work of non-fiction, it will require an acquaintance with the subject in question, even if it is a general one. Whatever the case, reviewing is a discipline, a form of argument demanding logic and evidence as well as 'taste' and 'opinion'. And it is a discipline in barely acknowledged decline.

What is perhaps just as troubling as the lacklustre infomerciality of so much Australian reviewing – gushing over the latest vogue, avoiding anything that cannot readily be pigeonholed – is that the situation suits so many vested interests in Australia's small, snobbish, fashion-conscious, self-celebrating literary scene. It veils the publishing industry's lazy, parsimonious, hidebound practices. It reinforces the everyone-has-won-and-all-must-have-prizes racket of festivals, fellowships and grants. It makes our culture a cosy, matey, happy, heavenly place, while reminding us of Mark Twain's dictum: 'You go to heaven for the climate, hell for the company.'

# DEATH OF A PUBLICATION

## *The demise of* The Bulletin (2008)

Few Australians have loitered so long at the brink of death as Kerry Packer, and perhaps none so ambivalently. Tens of millions of dollars were lavished on the campaign to prolong his life. He was saved first by timely defibrillation, then by a transplanted kidney, and finally by a constant cycle of surgery and steroids, trailed everywhere by the best minds in clinical care. But, heedless of the medical consequences, Packer was resolved to make no changes to his life whatsoever. His addiction to junk food remained unaltered by diabetes; his smoking continued unabated, despite six coronary angioplasties. 'Light my cigarette, son,' he famously told a prominent cardiologist. Upbraided for his lifestyle by a specialist at the Cornell Medical Center, he made his priorities perfectly clear: 'All right, son, you've given me the fucking lecture...Now are you going fucking fix me up or aren't you?'

No title in his print empire was closer to Packer's heart than the weekly *Bulletin*. And in its last two decades, no title seemed quite so shaded by its proprietor's personality. Tens of millions of dollars were allocated to the *Bulletin*'s survival. There were constant transfusions of journalistic talent and executive expertise. There were regular relaunches and recalibrations. But the venerable masthead, dedicated to the week's news, geared to rapid response, found it hard to break the habits of a lifetime, and outlived its legendary master by barely two years.

On the morning the *Bulletin* finally closed, Thursday, 24 January 2008, editor-in-chief John Lehmann went for a haircut. There were bound to be television cameras; he might as well look his best. Lehmann was right. The news crews duly came, but they camped out the front of ACP Magazines, at 54 Park Street, Sydney, unaware that for four and a half years the *Bulletin* had been round the corner in Stockland House, at 175 Castlereagh Street. It was a happy accident allowing *Bulletin* employees to stroll mainly unmolested to their impromptu wake at Darling Harbour's Pier 26; it also attested the magazine's marginal position in the Australian media.

Newspapers the next day rushed to tell the story of the suits at CVC Capital Partners, who now control ACP Magazines through the 75% stake in PBL Media they secured last year, and who had now trampled the traditions of 128 years. 'Welcome to the brave, but soulless, new world,' said John Lyons (former *Bulletin* national-affairs editor) in the *Australian*. 'It was the last bastion of the long view,' said Tony Wright (former *Bulletin* national-affairs editor) in the *Age*. At word that the *Bulletin* was losing about $4 million a year, eyes moistened in memory of the dear departed. 'Kerry would win or lose that [$4 million] in a weekend in Las Vegas or London,' observes David Haselhurst, for 35 years the stock-tipper extraordinaire behind the magazine's 'Speculator' column. 'The money the carpetbaggers [CVC] were losing in the *Bulletin* was an eighth of what they had just paid themselves in executive bonuses,' notes Patrick Cook, for 20 years the voice of its satirical 'Not the News' page.

Squirming at the scrutiny, the venture capitalists proceeded with a hugger-mugger interment. The magazine's website was switched off within a day. Its name was swiftly removed from the downstairs listings of its building, while mail was soon being returned to senders with blunt stickers advising, 'NO LONGER AT THIS ADDRESS ... BULLETIN CLOSED.' On the day I visited, the door of the magazine's eerily silent office was still blazoned with its last cover, 'Why We Love Australia'.

Yet there's no doubt that this passion of the *Bulletin*'s was, towards its end, unrequited. Audited circulation had halved since the 1980s, its ageing subscribers were not being replaced and its newsstand visibility had dwindled. When one former senior staffer sought a souvenir of its last edition at Central railway station on 24 January, he searched a big newsagency high and low, to no avail; finally asking for help, he was directed to two copies hidden almost out of sight.

*Schadenfreude* is always possible when one magazine reports the closure of another with which it is widely supposed to be in competition. That's not the case here: this writer enjoyed a happy decade as a contributor to the

*Bulletin* and counts a number of former employees as friends. In studying the decline and fall, nonetheless, one can't help hearing the echo of its erstwhile proprietor's famous deathbed comment: 'Am I still there? How fucking long is this going to take?'

*

The last 18 months of the *Bulletin*'s deathbed vigil had been gruelling; there was a sense in some of its more panting covers of a publication running hard to stand still. There had been a constant cycle of farewells, 20 staff reading the signs and moving on. Most of the senior staff members were replaced by less seasoned reporters, where they were replaced at all.

Much of Lehmann's time had been devoted to doing more with less, sometimes with nothing at all, as when he invited politicians to contribute to the *Bulletin* during the election campaign. 'Who can I get?' was the question by which he became known. Sometimes this had an unconscious comedy. 'Who can I get to do a cartoon?' he said, emerging from his office one day, apparently oblivious to his having just let go his last two cartoonists.

In these austerities he was watched over by his publisher, Paul Myers, a short, bossy figure installed by PBL Media CEO Ian Law, who had previously run the RM Williams magazine, *Outback*. Myers might have fitted in a century earlier, when the *Bulletin* had rejoiced in its reputation as the 'Bushman's Bible'; staff now referred to their cheese-paring publisher as 'Small Pliers'. Some economies were noticeable, such as the replacement of Jana Wendt as 'Lunch with' columnist by the lighter and less costly Juanita Phillips; some seemed niggardly, like canning *The Chaser*'s droll headline news summary. Others became the stuff of legend. Book reviewers? Who needed them? 'Why do we have to pay these people?' griped Lehmann one day. 'Don't they like reading?' Myers stormed: 'We've got 26 people on staff! Get one of them to do something!'

The *Bulletin*, nonetheless, had soldiered on, and continued to punch above its diminishing weight. Its ace Darwin correspondent, Paul Toohey, broke the story of Therese Rein's business interests; its dogged investigator Jennifer Sexton revealed the shady past of Paul Keating's business associate

Bruce McDonald, and the bizarre mores of Rene Rivkin's inner circle. The magazine had unearthed one excellent young reporter, Katherine Fleming from *Medical Observer,* and manufactured another, Joey Catanzaro, promoted from manning the front desk to touring Iraq. By the end of last year there was the kind of euphoria that comes from having apparently cheated the hangman. Cook remembers that where the Christmas lunch of 2006 had been 'thinly attended and resentful', that of 2007 had involved 'a vast amount of enthusiasm, goodwill and yippee'. Despite all the grim tidings, it came as a shock when group publisher Phil Scott introduced ACP Magazines CEO Scott Lorson in the *Bulletin* office that Thursday morning.

Lorson arrived like a man bearing bad news – dark suit, navy blue shirt, scuffed loafers – and wasted no time sharing it. He herded staff into a tight group in front of him, as though they were soldiers on parade or children at a school assembly, and told them they had published their last issue, efforts to sell the magazine having failed. Phones in the office were ringing before he had finished his address: a press release announcing the closure was already in circulation. How long did it fucking take? In the end, about 20 minutes. In hindsight, probably closer to 20 years.

*

During his three vigorous years as editor-in-chief of the *Bulletin,* Lehmann's predecessor, Garry Linnell, toyed occasionally with the strapline 'Setting Australia's Agenda Since 1880'. His news editor, Tim Blair, would laugh: 'Are you sure you want to remind people of some of the agendas we've set?' After all, earlier straplines had included 'Socialism In Our Time'; then 'Australia for the Australians'; and, most infamously, 'Australia for the White Man and China for the Chow'.

For much of its history, the *Bulletin* was chauvinistic to the point of isolationism, denouncing foreign wars and foreign capital with equal ardour; it was also unblinkingly anti-British, especially when the empire was in its view insufficiently racist. 'There is nothing to lead us to believe,' it editorialised a hundred years ago, 'that [John] Bull, bloated with pride over the possession of over 300,000,000 nigger subjects, has a vestige of sympathy with, or comprehension of, the White Australia ideal.' It was variously anti-Semitic and anti-communist; it was happy to yield Spain to Franco, and Italy to Mussolini; it advised appeasement of Hitler ('Far from being a megalomaniac,' said the *Bulletin*, three weeks before the invasion of Poland, 'Adolf Hitler is probably the most modest man in Germany') and counselled scorn for Churchill ('Mr Churchill is the Dangerous Dan McGrew of Imperial politics,' said the magazine in January 1940, 'and he is far more dangerous to us than to the enemy').

At its best and boldest, however, the *Bulletin* was more than a periodical. 'It was *Australia*,' said the writer–adventurer Randolph Bedford. DH Lawrence's alter ego, Richard Somers, exempted the *Bulletin* from his drear view of Australian culture in *Kangaroo* (1923): 'He liked its straightforwardness and the kick in some of its tantrums. It beat no solemn drums. It had no deadly earnestness. It was just stoical and spitefully humorous.' There were the writers: not just Henry Lawson and Banjo Paterson, but Steele Rudd, CJ Dennis, Joseph Furphy, John Shaw Neilson, Dorothea Mackellar, Katharine Susannah Prichard, Frank Dalby Davidson, Christopher Brennan, Ethel Turner, Barbara Baynton, Vance and Nettie Palmer. There were the artists and cartoonists: Hop (Livingston Hopkins), Phil May, Norman Lindsay, Fred Leist, Will Dyson and David Low. 'Perhaps never in the history of world journalism has a paper stood nearer to the heart of a country than the *Bulletin*,' thought Sidney Baker, who studied the publication intently for his classic *The Australian Language* (1946). 'Perhaps never again will so much of the true nature of a country be caught up in the pages of a single journal.'

Every journal has a lifespan, of course, and founder JF Archibald had no illusions about the *Bulletin*'s, foretelling that his 'clever youth' would inevitably 'become a dull old man'. His prophecy seemed to have been fulfilled 50 years ago, when the *Bulletin*'s circulation was barely 27,000, having more than halved since World War II, burdening the Prior family, its owners since 1927, with heavy losses. It's survival was a fluke. Frank Packer, publisher of the *Daily Telegraph* and impresario of Channel Nine, wanted to neutralise the Priors' *Woman's Mirror*, a rival to his own *Australian Women's Weekly*. Packer was not quite sure what to do with the unprofitable, inert *Bulletin*, which came as part of the purchase, in October 1960. He rang Donald Horne, editor of his new fortnightly, the *Observer*. 'I've bought the *Bulletin*,' he said. 'Which will we kill off? It or the *Observer*?' The *Bulletin* endured on Horne's whim: it was, if you like, the Lucky Publication.

The *Bulletin* scarcely deserved its good fortune. Horne found it 'a clumsy souvenir of long ago', printed on inferior stock, sustained by infestive readers: 'Of the dozen and a half jokes in each issue…there was always an "Abo" joke, and often a reffo joke, although the reffos no longer had Yid noses, but the largest single category was jokes about the daftness of old women and the bodily curves of young women.' Horne rewrote its manifesto, committing it to give 'an informed picture of the life we lead in this country and its extraordinary diversity', and forbore the frenzied hostility of the response to his changes: at least one reader sent several used pieces of toilet paper.

Horne's two spells as editor, separated by the tenures of Peter Hastings and Peter Coleman, more than doubled the circulation. The editorships of Trevor Sykes and Trevor Kennedy doubled it again, seeing off challengers like Gordon Barton's *Nation Review* and John Fairfax's *National Times*. The by-lines were as bejewelled as Barry Humphries, Xavier Herbert, Hal Porter, Thomas Kenneally, David Williamson, Frank Moorhouse, Tim Winton and Gwen Harwood (who took her leave with piqued acrostics whose first letters spelt S-O-L-O-N-G-B-U-L-L-E-T-I-N and F-U-C-K-A-L-L-E-D-I-T-O-R-S). Few Australian journalists of note, meanwhile, did not serve at least a brief tour of duty at the magazine, including some with big plans. Wannabe Labor player Bob Carr never stopped networking: he used his position as state political roundsman to introduce the likes of Paul Keating, Graham Richardson and Barrie Unsworth to his proprietor. Aspiring conservative politician Tony Abbott was known for his iron discipline: after running at lunchtime, he would plant his head on a cleared desk, sleep for exactly ten minutes, and immediately resume work. Speaking at Malcolm Turnbull's thirtieth birthday, Kennedy jested that the prime ministership was a mere bauble: Turnbull would be satisfied only by world domination.

The *Bulletin* duly became part of the Packer inheritance that Kerry valued. If he no longer had the *Telegraph* at his disposal, like his old man, the *Bulletin* lent him perceived influence – almost as good, when it came to it, as the real thing. It was fun, too, a sort of knockabout intelligence unit. The scion got to muck about with a few of his father's old retainers, such as Alan Reid and David McNicholl, and to cultivate a few of his own, like Laurie Oakes, a peerless political seer, and David Haselhurst, whose tips for the 'Speculator' column outstripped the All-Ordinaries index in 30 of 34 years, including nine years of triple-digit growth.

In the 1970s, in fact, Packer actually trusted Haselhurst to run two investment companies on his behalf, with discretion to place buy-orders up to $40,000. Some might have found the experience of punting their boss's money daunting. The insouciant Haselhurst spent it with abandon, on one occasion leading a plunge into Launceston Gas that inadvertently netted him scrip worth $60,000, the surplus third of which he laid off among *Bulletin* colleagues. It happened that Packer chose that day to whisk staff to Chinatown in four stretch limos, where he was confused by the lunchtime chatter. 'Why is everyone talking about Launceston Gas?' the mogul demanded. 'I've been meaning to tell you, Kerry,' said Haselhurst hastily. 'You're now the biggest shareholder there, and we're in it with you.' Packer grinned at his minions: 'Ah well, when Haselhurst takes me down the gurgler, at least you'll all be coming too.' Haselhurst became such a favoured son that when his marriage broke down, Packer lent him $50,000 free of interest to buy a house in Darlinghurst.

Expensive to adequately resource, the *Bulletin* was never massively profitable. And when in the 1980s newspapers invaded the glossy-advertising market by expanding their weekend editions with colour supplements and news reviews, it again became financially marginal. It was even cramping the style of its sister publications. Fairfax, for example, was building a profitable franchise with its *Business Review Weekly*, but Packer dithered over gearing up the fortnightly *Australian Business* as a challenger, out of consideration for the *Bulletin*. For all his personal caprices, Packer was a proprietor who hastened slowly.

To shake the ACP tree, Packer hired Richard Walsh, the former wunderkind of *Oz*, *POL* and *Nation Review* who for the preceding 14 years had run Angus & Robertson. In Walsh's opinion, the magazine market had been changed irrevocably by the arrival of the American news magazines *Time* and *Newsweek*, reliant upon cover prices of almost give-away cheapness to build the circulation that would in turn impress advertisers. But where such businesses could amortise their costs worldwide, the *Bulletin* had only a slow-growing domestic base. The newspaper glossies *Good Weekend* and the *Australian Magazine*, moreover, also had an edge on the *Bulletin*, being spared the newsstand gauntlet by coming out free each Saturday, with a guaranteed circulation. Walsh spent a lot of time considering the *Bulletin*'s predicament and came up with...well, not much. 'I couldn't work out how on Earth we were going to get out of it,' says Walsh. 'When you looked at it logically, there simply didn't seem any strong reason for the magazine to exist.'

Above all was the inhibition of his proprietor's conservatism. Walsh's first idea was to eliminate some of the *Bulletin*'s discretionary costs. He planned to merge the commercial, marketing and distribution structures of the *Bulletin* and *BRW* in a 50–50 joint venture with Fairfax, and sell the magazines as a subscription package. Initially interested, Packer cooled on the idea. 'Kerry seemed to understand,' says Walsh. 'Then he decided he would rather lose money.' Walsh next reconceived the *Bulletin* as a journal of 'vigorous opinion', a weekly in the style of the *Spectator* or the *New Statesman*. He headhunted David Dale – the pithy 'Stay in Touch' columnist of the *Sydney Morning Herald* who had written for *Oz* as a teenager at Randwick High School – and mandated him to perk the magazine up. With Fairfax in disarray after Warwick Fairfax's botched buyout, others were willing to follow, among them Patrick Cook, business columnist Glenda Korporaal and photographer Lorrie Graham.

Dale ran a very readable, very attractive magazine. Cheeky covers and an accent on the 'back of the book' – its arts, books and entertainment coverage – substantiated a Carey McSpeddin advertising campaign boasting of the *Bulletin*'s new 'brio'. But Dale's style and ACP's ways remained oil and water. To Trevor Kennedy, now ACP's managing director, the *Bulletin*'s makeover was too clever, too cute, rather effete. 'There's only one thing you need to save this magazine,' he lectured. 'Fucking good stories.' It was the voice of the veteran newsman, at home with scoops, scorchers, bombshells and balltearers. Nor did Dale warm to ACP's testosterone- and profanity-laden culture, where success seemed to be based on 'your capacity to fit the word "cunt" into the sentence more often than the next person'. Enemies outside and inside the *Bulletin* were ready to exploit any misstep when Dale gave them opportunity.

In July 1988, Dale and his colleagues selected 'The 100 Most Appalling People in Australia', an undergraduate but ecumenical exercise that lumped Paul Keating in with Joh Bjelke-Petersen, Manning Clark with Geoffrey Blainey, Patrick White with John Farnham, with a few *Bulletin* alumni – among them Phillip Adams and Malcolm Turnbull – for good measure. It also included several of Packer's 'pick and stick' circle – Alan Jones, John Singleton, Graham Richardson – and news of their displeasure was firmly communicated to Dale. 'Kerry didn't read the *Bulletin*,' says Walsh. 'But he knew people who did.' For Packer, the cover resonated with his own impression of news-media negativism, and he inveighed against journalists to one of his loyal foot soldiers, Bruce Stannard, in the *Bulletin* in November 1989: 'Unfortunately, many Australians want to pull down anyone who achieves. And journalists are no exceptions. They have become a law unto themselves.'

Dale's attempt to reprise the cover as 'The Great Australian Balance Sheet', with assets as well as liabilities, was never likely to endear him to his boss. Today the *Bulletin* of 20 March 1990 reads like a fairly mild survey of *bien-pensant* opinion, with a few disarming twists: John Howard was an asset ('demonstrates a loyalty to party and principle that makes it possible to believe that politics isn't all bad'), Joan Coxsedge a liability ('bores for Australia where possible'). At the time, it loomed rather larger. Most of the barbs were safe enough, like Susan Renouf ('Enouf! Enouf!'); but Singleton was given another touch up ('Good at playing to the lowest common denominator and making a virtue of the vulgar Australia'), while Jones received a rather low blow ('Created an eternal mystery by surviving a spot of bother with the police in London. His friends at home stood behind him').

Uneasy calm prevailed for a few days, and Dale's next issue was one of his most profitable, Toyota paying a premium to buy every single advertisement in the magazine: the sort of deal for which advertising departments break out champagne. It counted not, and the story of Dale's sacking haunts him rather as Sir Peregrine Worsthorne will forever be associated with the story of his sacking as *Sunday Telegraph* editor over perfectly poached eggs on buttered toast at Claridges. When Walsh resigned, rather than comply with Packer's request to sack Dale, Packer did the job himself. 'I'm going to fire you,' he told Dale. 'Can I speak?' Dale asked. 'You can speak,' Packer replied. 'But it'll do you no good.'

Walsh has no doubt that Packer loved the *Bulletin*: 'Kerry was pretty much a philistine, but he had his own pretensions. He would scoff, of course, at anything that smacked of high art. But he had a certain respect for Australian traditions, and he understood that his own dynasty was rooted in one of the golden periods for Australian culture, the period of *Smiths Weekly* and *Australian Women's Weekly*, Ross Campbell, Lennie Lower, Ken Slessor. In that sense he understood the idea of continuity.' But Dale's dismissal was a warning to all his *Bulletin* successors – indeed, all editors at ACP – that in the impresario of *60 Minutes*, *Cleo* and World Series Cricket now beat the heart of a true reactionary.

*

The 1990s were mainly fallow years for the *Bulletin*. Walsh, who was induced to return by Trevor Kennedy, promoted Lyndall Crisp as editor: the first woman to hold the job. But the young James Packer, who had come into the family business as a general manager reporting to Walsh, then advocated the installation of former *60 Minutes* producer Gerald Stone as editor-in-chief. Stone filled the magazine with the flaccid clichés of television current affairs. Apathy prevailed. 'Sure, progress brings about great social upheavals but it doesn't change human nature,' Stone droned in the *Bulletin*'s 6000th edition, in December 1995. 'A good read is a good read.' That the world was thoroughly over-endowed with such 'good reads' did not seem to penetrate Park Street. The *Bulletin* had Laurie Oakes at one end, Patrick Cook at the other, and David Haselhurst making money in between. Otherwise the magazine stood for an awful lot of nothing in particular; yet the formula was not to be tampered with for almost a decade.

Again, the catalyst was an outsider, John Alexander, former editor-in-chief of the *Sydney Morning Herald* and *Financial Review*, a news executive with elbows as sharp as his instincts. Joining ACP as group publisher, he made the *Bulletin* a special project – partly, some felt, because he understood it as a short cut to an affinity with his proprietor. Running into Packer at Park Street was a possibility few relished. Not everyone was so poised as Jack Marx, then a senior writer at *Picture* and *Ralph*, who once found himself in a lift stuck between floors with the mogul and had the presence of mind to say, 'I sure hope this lift starts moving soon. I don't know about you, but I've got work to do.' But suddenly Packer was to be glimpsed in the *Bulletin*'s office – a sight not seen for 20 years, and an auspicious one now.

Alexander gained Packer's permission to assemble a hand-picked team of former Fairfax cronies: Max Walsh as editor-in-chief; Paul Bailey as editor; national-affairs editor John Lyons; business correspondents Alan Deans, Deborah Light and Peter Freeman; Melbourne-based feature writers Garry Linnell and Virginia Trioli. These heavy broadsheet hitters he complemented with a gifted magazine specialist. After spells running the *Independent Monthly, Rolling Stone* and *HQ*, Kathy Bail had the perfect CV and sensibility to take on the deputy editorship. On the day of her farewell lunch from *HQ*, at Tetsuya's, her mobile rang constantly with calls from Alexander, brimming with bonhomie.

Suddenly the *Bulletin* was the place to work, with big opportunities and salaries to match. One of Walsh's first recruits was Maxine McKew, who had been his co-host on the ABC's *The Bottom Line*, and who now received $3000 a pop for her weekly 'Lunch with' column. A former staff member recalls being taken to lunch by Catharine Lumby, who insisted on picking up the bill because she earned more from her fortnightly column than as an associate professor. Contributors accustomed themselves to a $1 a word, and the coincidence of the relaunch with the irrational exuberance of the dotcom boom meant that there was plenty to go around. In truth, the magazine still occupied an insecure market niche, and was still spending money faster than it was making it. Former subeditor Jim Hope recalls, 'When we did the first of our big issues, [chief subeditor] Col Klimo told me that Packer had given an assurance we would not go below 132 pages for at least six months. Within two months we had started shrinking again.' But Alexander's close collaboration with Packer did the trick: in March 1999 he succeeded Colin Morrison as chief executive of ACP.

Alexander is cast these days in media circles as the dark prince of Packerdom. Certainly, it is hard to find much affection for him among refugees of the *Bulletin*. 'If he decides you're worth knowing, he's all over you,' says one. 'If he takes a set against you, he's vindictive and spiteful.' Says another: 'You look at most key media figures in Australia and they've all created *something*. All Alexander has created is a career for himself.' This is harsh. At the *Bulletin*, Alexander secured significant resources from a hard-to-please proprietor, and paid talent sometimes-exorbitant tribute. It is arguable, nonetheless, that he was as interested in what the *Bulletin* could do for him as vice versa. For when the *Bulletin*'s unresolved problems re-emerged later, he was a force neither so present nor so positive.

*

Under editors-in-chief Walsh and then Bailey, the *Bulletin* put on an impressively brave face. But the magazine remained a captive of the news cycle: when in doubt, it was always easiest to home in on the week's biggest issue. Such a configuration has advantages: a weekly news magazine can be choosy about what it throws resources at. Yet Australian news is seldom naturally national. As Rupert Murdoch has learned from his stewardship of the *Australian*, a lot of what Australians want to read is local and regional. This funnels the resources of anything with countrywide ambitions towards Canberra, business and sport: fields already amply covered by the metropolitan dailies.

Selling advertising was tough. How did you placate picky corporates who wanted to know what might be the cover of the edition they supported? News, alas, is unpredictable: the *Bulletin* slumped into the habit of relying on promotions of Channel Nine programmes to fill the gaps. And exactly who were you reaching when you placed an ad in the *Bulletin*? The readership was now so fragmented that nobody was quite sure. 'The magazine was always sold on the basis that it was read by the powerful, by the influential,' says one senior executive. 'When you drilled down, there were a lot more Cs [the second-tier demographic, after the much-sought-after ABs] there.' The magazine was also eternally beset by its size. As other magazines worked towards creating 'beautiful' and 'inspirational' artefacts with edgier layout and higher-quality stock, the *Bulletin* looked increasingly inky and dowdy. The *Bulletin* probably put together the best subs desk in Australia – all full-time staff and all genuine wordsmiths – and had eye-catching artists and cartoonists. But its pages remained obsessively busy, jazzed up with entry points that sometimes had the effect of confusing readers about where to start. The executive with the most magazine experience, Bail, was attractively making over the 'back of the book' when space came under pressure with the shrinkage of advertising, following the collapse of the tech boom in April 2001, and the last-minute confiscation and cancellation of pages became routine.

Structurally, the magazine seemed stuck in the past. Certainly, it was stuck on Wednesday. That was thanks to the strange archaism of the *Bulletin*'s selection of stories from the American *Newsweek*, an arrangement which dated to July 1984. When it was decided to renegotiate the deal, the original contract was found to be so ancient that it had been prepared on a typewriter. 'Everything about the *Bulletin* seemed very old,' says *Newsweek*'s assistant editor, Ron Javers. But there was no shifting the *Bulletin*'s publication day without also shifting *Newsweek*'s, which was never going to happen. As for the theoretically limitless vistas of cyberspace, the *Bulletin* took one step forward and two back. In August 2001, it launched an online edition on ninemsn, the Packers' joint venture with Microsoft. But it was just that: the *Bulletin* online, which probably cost the magazine more newsstand buyers than it gained. For reasons nobody at the magazine understood, moreover, the online edition was not searchable by Google News, and it was possible neither to blog nor to post pictures much bigger than a postage stamp. The *Bulletin* had access to one of Australia's mightiest pictorial archives – that of the old *Daily Telegraph* – but almost no means of using it.

Only one factor made the *Bulletin* model viable: Packer. His commitment never weakened, and even won him a certain admiration. It made him *un homme sérieux* in the Australian media, as his combustible father had never been. Yet his indulgence was a mixed blessing, for he seemed happier to brazen out losses than to take the chance of succeeding by another means. And in a sense, this rather suited his journalists. Journalists are vain. We will always want to believe that our writing can change the world; that if we break good stories and find the right words, then the market will flock to us as a matter of course. Week in, week out, the *Bulletin* was actually demonstrating that news, in commercial terms, was scarcely worth the trouble of breaking it. When Laurie Oakes divulged Gareth Evans' long-term affair with Cheryl Kernot in July 2002, for example, the *Bulletin* had no way of monopolising the story: such profit as accrued to anyone did so across all news outlets. Yet here was a proprietor who, albeit for reasons less to do with his munificence than with his own distaste for change, apparently subscribed to journalists' belief in the redemptive qualities of their craft. When Packer anointed Garry Linnell as editor-in-chief in December 2002, he issued him resoundingly simple instructions: 'Son, just make 'em talk about it.' What journalist would not feel their sap rise, given such a charter? The trouble was that the arrangement would never outlive Packer long. The leading indicator of the *Bulletin*'s fortunes in its last years, then, was not its circulation, but Packer's vital signs.

Linnell and his editor, Bail, loved the *Bulletin*. When a portrait of JF Archibald was located on the executive floor at Park Street, Linnell commandeered it for his office; when readers reported that Archibald's grave at Waverley Cemetery had fallen into disrepair, Bail dedicated herself to its refurbishment. Pound-for-pound, they marshalled probably the most accomplished journalistic unit in Australia. News editor Tim Blair led a triple life as an acerbic columnist and Australia's savviest blogger. Business editor Alan Deans was a 30-year veteran of the trade from the *Sydney Morning Herald* and *Australian Business*. Features editor Susan Skelly, who had followed Bail from *HQ*, was a former chief sub at the *Australian Women's Weekly* under the legendary Dawn Swain. Together they brought out the most consistently fresh *Bulletins* since Dale, with a capacity for breaking news that made them compulsory reading in daily newsrooms. Jennifer Byrne prodded Anita Keating into discussing the dissolution of her marriage over lunch in

April 2004; Tony Abbott acknowledged a lovechild to Julie-Anne Davies in March 2005; Eric Ellis and Preston Smith caught up with fugitive financier Abe Goldberg in November 2005; Paul Toohey owned the Schapelle Corby and Bali Nine stories; the survival of the Beaconsfield Miners, Brant Webb and Todd Russell, was recounted in exhaustive detail by Tony Wright. Bail, meanwhile, instigated the *Bulletin*'s 'Summer Reading' issues, which brought together long pieces by well-known writers in an attractive perfect-bound package that lingered on newsstands for a month – a formula that was an instant hit. The office enjoyed an enviable esprit de corps. When staff members weren't busy making the *Bulletin*, they were busy talking about it. In the absence of a marketing budget, public-relations man Brian Johnson of Fingerprint Communications arranged scores of radio interviews every week, in which Linnell's reporters trumpeted their work.

In the *Bulletin*'s 125th year, Linnell had the nerve to offer a $1.25-million reward to anyone who found a Tasmanian tiger. But when Packer died at the end of that year, it was the *Bulletin* itself that went from being merely an endangered species to one under threat of extinction. The staff's initial response to the passing of their patron was unforgettable. Without complaint, they returned in droves from summer holidays to assemble a comprehensive and colourful tribute issue, wrangled in three days mainly by chief subeditor Andrew Forbes. They received a suitably grateful email from the ACP group publisher.

> From: Scott, Phil
> Sent: Thursday, 29 December 2005 7:11 PM
> To: ACP Bulletin Mag
> Subject: Thanks
> Right now everyone is knackered. Give it a day or two and you will realise you have been part of publishing history this week. Sure, we'd all prefer to have been down at the beach but if we'd stayed there we'd have pondered on what *The Bulletin* should have done to commemorate KP's passing. You should all take great professional and personal pride in the job you've turned around in the last 72 hours. I know the family

> has been touched by what you have done. The fact everyone wanted to be here to turn this around, without a grumble, has been deeply appreciated. It's a bloody good read and a fitting tribute.

The edition sold out faster than it could be reprinted, scaling six-figure circulation heights not touched in 15 years. It was one of the *Bulletin*'s finest hours, and its last certifiably great one. A little more than two years later, Scott would be introducing Lorson as the bearer of bad tidings.

*

Linnell had run a vibrant, headline-hunting *Bulletin* through three years bulging with big news – the Boxing Day tsunami, the War on Terror, a host of juicy government scandals – without making it essential reading; in fact, tightening circulation audits were eating away the means by which the magazine had previously plumped its numbers. It produced often-excellent journalism, but it was journalism of a sort not uncommon in newspapers. For it is a paradox of the profession that where 2000 words can sometimes be too many, 6000 on the same subject may not feel like quite enough. A thorough professional feature quoting all the relevant individuals on a current news story at the lesser length can never be much more than introductory; by contrast, the nutritious long-form journalism of the *New Yorker* or *Atlantic Monthly* is often inordinately satisfying. *The Bulletin* never confronted the implications of this paradox. 'There was a real lack of imagination at the top of the company,' says one former executive. 'Nobody had the commitment necessary to honestly analyse the *Bulletin*'s problems. Most of the people were out of newspapers who got stressed about news and had no interest in how it was presented. There was this endless bullshit about getting the exclusive, getting the Walkley, then you're a legend.' The magazine's dilemmas, notes Tim Blair, were somehow as intractable as they were obvious: 'The *Australian Magazine* and *Good Weekend* were coming out on Saturdays. We were coming out five days later, smaller, on poorer stock, with fewer resources. You were always having these conversations about the future direction of the *Bulletin*...but you could never find a way out.'

Only once in its last years did the *Bulletin* kick the jams way out – and then, in decidedly peculiar circumstances. In January 2006, with channels Seven and Nine at each other tooth and claw in the C7 action before the Federal Court, *Today Tonight* ran crude recapitulations of the One.Tel fiasco on consecutive nights, singling out James Packer. In his famous affidavit that added 'bone' to the media vernacular, Nine's former news and current-affairs chief Mark Llewellyn told of a foam-flecked tirade from John Alexander demanding that collateral damage be inflicted on Seven's Kerry Stokes. According to Llewellyn, Alexander told him: 'Nine has failed to go on the front foot previously with Seven and I am sick of that!...Stokes is a terrible man, and a terrible businessman. Everyone who has come into contact with him knows he is an appalling human being.' With his reluctance to comply, Llewellyn apparently marked his card at Nine.

Linnell was interested in a piece on Stokes on his own account, and business reporter Nick Tabakoff did not need to be press-ganged. 'Nick heard that they were scouting around for someone to do a big story on Stokes,' says a former staff member. 'So he went to see Garry and put his hand up, but on condition it did not become a vendetta.' It soon became a source of tension. Challenged by his business editor, Deans, Linnell argued with some force that Stokes was a figure of national significance about whom relatively little was known. In the event, the industrious Tabakoff worked for three months on a story that swelled to 15,000 words: from all accounts, a sprawling but fair-minded profile full of hitherto-unpublished information. The piece was then canned, ostensibly for legal reasons to do with the C7 action, although also after rumours that Alexander had complained it was 'too soft'. Bizarrely, a chunk was printed, mangled and manhandled out of context, in an article under the by-line of Tabakoff's successor, Rebecca Urban, formerly of the *Age*, in August 2007 – a stage by which events at the *Bulletin* were being dwarfed by events around it.

For with the death of the patriarch, the Packer empire came into play. The fourth Packer, after RC, Frank and Kerry, is the first without regard for print. His chosen route to the sunny uplands of gaming was the staged sale of majority control in PBL Media, incorporating ACP Magazines, Channel

Nine and ninemsn, to the Asian arm of CVC Capital Partners, a 25-year-old Luxembourg-headquartered venture-capital firm. Chaos was breaking out. As part of the grab for talent being dispersed, Linnell was wooed as Nine's new news and current-affairs chief, only to arrive on the same day that 95 redundancies were announced. Without a boss, meanwhile, the *Bulletin* looked agonisingly without a future. From time to time over the next six months, a senior publishing executive would breeze into Stockland House and announce that there was no danger of the *Bulletin* closing, which had the same perversely opposite effect as a football club's president stressing his confidence in a coach.

Bail, not only hugely capable but hugely popular, was Linnell's obvious successor. But her relations with Alexander, now chairman of PBL Media, had chilled, for reasons on which nobody was clear: he would not even return her calls. She decided to pitch herself to PBL Media's CEO, Ian Law, formerly CEO of West Australian Newspapers. At a detailed presentation, she explained that the *Bulletin* needed an injection of style: it should free itself from the news cycle and aim to be an up-market monthly, using the 'Summer Reading' issue as a model. With a smaller core staff and more contributors, it would be cheaper to run. With the kind of eye-catching design and premium-quality stock that would entice the luxury-goods advertisers that other magazines were tapping so successfully, it should have a better advertising profile. It was as coherent a plan for the *Bulletin*'s resuscitation as had been put – and it fell on deaf ears. When the appointment committee of Alexander, Law, Scott and PBL Media director Chris Anderson made their choice, in July 2006, it turned out to be neither Bail, nor Matt Price, nor Bruce Guthrie, nor any of the other rumoured candidates.

When Scott came into Stockland House to announce that the new editor-in-chief was John Lehmann, there was dead silence. 'Nobody could look at Kathy,' says one former executive. 'Of course, she never lost her sangfroid. But people were shattered.' Others detected a latent misogyny at work. 'It was horrible, just horrible,' says another former staff member. 'And so disappointing, because she so deserved to do it. And for women it was a particular blow, because it suggested that a boy was needed to do the job.'

When Scott left, Blair jumped up and started googling Lehmann's name. Who was this guy? He was little the wiser after the exercise. Blair was later irked when they met for a drink by Lehmann's airy assertions regarding global warming, not so much because of his views as because someone who purported to read the *Bulletin* closely should have known that Blair was an unapologetic sceptic about anthropogenic climate change.

As an act of courtesy to Lehmann, so that he had time to settle in, Blair, Deans and Skelly mapped out an issue on the Battle of Long Tan. They also shared their disappointment with Scott, and asked if he could do something to make it worth Bail's while to stay – a request at which Scott bridled. 'It's my decision,' he insisted of Lehmann. 'And I'll stand or fall on it.' But that wasn't the story that began spreading. Lehmann, it transpired, had come to Alexander's attention while a media writer for the *Australian*. There he had become involved in PBL's interminable politicking, being leaked an exclusive story about Nine CEO Sam Chisholm's attempt to oust John Lyons as executive producer of *Sunday*, an attempt thwarted by Alexander. Shortly before Lehmann departed the *Australian*, he had come into possession of the fabled Llewellyn affidavit. But where *Crikey* published the document – deeply embarrassing to Alexander – Lehmann refrained. He left the paper with the curse of his editor-in-chief, Chris Mitchell, ringing in his ears: 'I wouldn't want to be the last editor of the *Bulletin*...'

Fairly or unfairly, Lehmann was burdened with a reputation as a cat's paw of Alexander and Anderson. Blair became one of the first departures in a steady exodus that soon after included Bail. Into her role as editor slotted the chief sub, Forbes, although into her office moved the publisher, Myers. This was to be the new budget-*Bulletin*, living within slender means. In fact, the new regime made a positive start, responding with alacrity and special issues to the deaths of Steve Irwin and Peter Brock. Lehmann proved to be an irrepressible enthusiast with a well-developed news sense, honed by covering politics in Queensland and crime in New York. He still rallied a good staff. 'There were no slow ants or time-servers at the *Bulletin*,' notes David Haselhurst. 'They ran a very lean ship.' He also showed some chutzpah. When the *Australian* ran a powder-puff profile of the Rudds by

Mitchell's wife, Christine Jackman, Lehmann had the temerity to reveal that Rudd was godfather to their first son – quite an act of cheek, given Mitchell's legendary capacity for enmity. The *Bulletin* belatedly got its online house in order under Rod Dalton, a former night editor from the *Sydney Morning Herald*: its 'Bullring', a site dedicated to the election campaign, was informed and irreverent.

When the news did not provide an obvious direction, however, Lehmann struggled, displaying little aptitude for the *Bulletin*'s non-news component. 'We need more celebrities,' he would complain. 'That was part of my pitch.' So it was that the magazine of Lawson and Paterson published an interminable extract from Geoffrey Cousins' business bodice-ripper *The Butcherbird*; then it ran an interview with the author; *then* it ran a (deftly non-committal) review. So it was that the magazine of May and Low was reduced to Patrick Cook's weekly cartoon for Oakes's column, but still published a flatulent column by Alexander's friend Leo Schofield. Anything more heterodox was a challenge. On one occasion, Skelly planned to take an extract and photographs from Kaavous Clayton's *Abandoned Chairs*, a delightfully dotty collection of images of discarded chairs in incongruous settings. Lehmann hated it. 'We're just not on the same page here!' he barked. 'I don't care about chairs!'

Perhaps it was hard to care about chairs when there was a publisher so apt to stress how many feet there were under desks. Myers acted like a census-taker, obsessed with staff numbers. A hundred years earlier, the *Bulletin* had 112 employees; with a workforce a quarter the size, Myers now considered it way too large. He offered himself as a travel writer, but his prose was execrable. Glee was universal when he left early in the new year. It was short-lived.

*

Phil Scott took four scenarios to the PBL Media board: sale or closure; business as usual; a radical slimming; a monthly. There was no taste for further cuts, nor was there a zeal for experimentation that might cost money. The bids solicited were circumspect. News Ltd had previously flirted with inserting the *Bulletin* in the midweek *Australian*, and did so again, but pulled back; Lachlan Murdoch probably came closest to putting his hand in his pocket, and might have proceeded had Illyria Holdings not joined the syndicate to take over Consolidated Media Holdings. Yet he would have been caught in the same cleft stick as the Packers. 'The problem was that the *Bulletin* no longer had any editorial raison d'être,' says one bidder. 'If you reformatted the best content in the *Weekend Australian, Age* and *Sydney Morning Herald* in any given week, you'd end up with something that looked like the *Bulletin*. As for this revisionist bullshit about Kerry keeping it alive...'

'They stuffed the place up,' complained Kerry Packer of the work of his minions at Channel Nine, towards the end of his life. Mistaking money for faith, investment for imagination, he didn't do a bad job of the *Bulletin*, the billionaire with such an uncanny flair for sensing public taste in television steadily and obdurately losing his touch with print. Journalists with a sentimental attachment to a proprietor prepared to lose money have let him off lightly, partly because of their collusion in his faltering vision. The *Bulletin* served in concentrated form a news journalism that is now mass-produced – slick but very similar – with which the public is surfeited. What its failure tells journalists is that our old tricks are no longer so impressive. In the end it took a fucking long time – but it was always going to fucking happen.

# A CENTURY OF STUDS

## *A profile of Studs Terkel (1912–2008)* (2012)

Studs Terkel was in a buoyant mood in the spring of 1963 when he welcomed Marlon Brando onto his popular Chicago radio program. He had just won the Prix Italia for his celebrated documentary of nuclear dread, *Born to Live*; he was shortly to record passengers on board the Freedom Train to Washington for a haunting voice montage, *This Train*. And notoriously taciturn Brando, promoting his new film *The Ugly American*, proved at first no more than averagely contrary ('I don't understand'; 'I don't think that's true'; 'I don't think it's related to that at all'). But as Terkel continued gently to harry him, the interview took an unexpected turn.

'Now I want to ask you a question,' Brando said abruptly. 'You sit and ask many questions...You have an obligation to describe some of your feelings and point of view. What is it about a particular kind of work that interests you? Why are you preoccupied with these questions? What is the nature of your furrowing out this information from all manner of people? What kind of contribution does interviewing make to you?'

There was a pause. 'This is a reversal,' Terkel responded uneasily. 'I don't know.' He hemmed. He hawed. He was anxious, he said equivocally, not to be voyeuristic; he guessed he was simply curious about an artist's concept of art. Brando was unconvinced: 'When I asked you simply to describe what you feel about your work, you became tense and concerned, perhaps a little confused, unsettled. When you ask me something, I could give you a glib answer, spieling. But if I want to answer the question honestly, I have to search my mind. When asked a simple question, it's not easy to give a simple answer.'

The moment passed – Brando was too egotistical to pursue the inquiry, Terkel sufficiently adept to deflect it. But it was a rare moment in the storied career of perhaps the most admired chronicler of the last American century, when the spotlight was turned on *him*, when the biter was bit. On his death in October 2008, Terkel's fellow Chicagoan Barack Obama exalted him as a 'national treasure'; the *Independent* deemed him 'the world's greatest interviewer'; the *Guardian* claimed that 'to register him as "writer and broadcaster" would be like calling Louis Armstrong a "trumpeter" or the Empire State Building an "office block."' Yet despite his compilation of *Working, Hard Times, The Good War, Race* and other epics of national memory, Terkel successfully threw a thick cloak over his 'private domain' – ironic given how dedicatedly Terkel pursued untold stories and unheard voices. This week, Chicago marks the centenary of the birth of one of its most popular sons with a schedule of celebratory events, from showcasing some of the fruits of Terkel's 9000 recorded interviews to rededicating a bridge named for him twenty years ago. So how might he have answered had Brando pressed him?

*

Louis Terkel was born on 16 May 1912, the third son of Russian Jewish immigrants, tailor Samuel and seamstress Annie, inhabitants of a Bronx tenement. Theirs was an impecunious and eerily infirm household. Louis, regularly incapacitated by asthma and mastoiditis, shared a bed with his father, afflicted by chronic angina. He ascribed a lifelong love of music to its soothing properties when he was 'bound to the hearth'; he would hear it wafting from other apartments, and from the gramophone his gentle, soft-spoken father purchased so he could listen to Caruso. 'As I listened to that voice, my breathing came more easily,' Terkel recalled of first hearing Verdi's *Celeste Aida*. 'Caruso had succeeded where the doctors had failed.'

Yet the predominant sounds of his boyhood were those of domestic discord. Terkel's mother, Annie, was a domineering figure with a waspish tongue, who, when Sam grew too infirm for regular work in August 1921, uprooted the family and dragged it to Chicago, where she leased two boarding hotels: first the Elite, perfectly ill-named, then the Wells Grand, christened simply for the cross streets on which it sat. Terkel likened his mother to Eliza Gant, the implacable boarding hotel mistress in Thomas Wolfe's *Look Homeward, Angel* (1929), whose first response to any claim of weakness or indisposition is a haughty 'Pshaw!' but who is also prone to self-pitying lamentations: 'Nobody knows what I've been through!' Terkel grew to regard Annie as the essence of deluded American striving – indefatigable, inconsolable, dedicated to her little fortune, unable to comprehend its cost.

Chicago instantly captivated Terkel. He loved reciting Carl Sandburg's famous 1916 poem: 'Hog Butcher for the world / Tool-maker, Stacker of Wheat / Player with Railroads and the Nation's Freight Handler / Stormy, husky, brawling / City of the Big Shoulders...' He also grew fascinated by the city's reputation as a crucible of social struggle: the site of the Haymarket bombing, the setting of Upton Sinclair's *The Jungle* and Theodore Dreiser's *Sister Carrie*, the location of the archetypal settlement house Hull House and the headquarters of Eugene Debs's International Workers of the World (aka the Wobblies). And in some respects, Terkel's politics never outgrew his formative encounters with that heritage. Wobblies were conspicuous among the Wells Grand's guests, their debates with the disciples of the demagogic right-wing radio propagandist Father Charles Coughlin reverberating through its thin walls: 'Theirs was the American yawp. Every man a king. Every man a Demosthenes.' Terkel also revelled in the soapbox oratory of nearby Washington Square Park, known to locals as Bughouse Square: 'The stars of the square were representatives of the Socialist Party, the Communists, the vegetarians, and, of course, the moody Bible Institute orators. To tell you the truth, they outspoke in fervour, and certainly outsang, their Godless opponents.' Terkel's earliest inspiration, and his abiding benchmark for political heroism, was Senator 'Fighting Bob' LaFollette, an anti-corporate progressive and anti-war isolationist.

Yet for all these romantic influences, young Terkel was not a young turk. He drifted into studying law without urgency or aptitude, narrowly passing the bar exam at second attempt; after applying unsuccessfully for a job as an FBI fingerprint analyst, he took low-level New Deal roles in the Federal Emergency Rehabilitation Administration and the Works Project Administration as 'a tiny cog somewhere along the line in that vast machine'. He affected the garb not of the provocateur or the proletarian but, in the city of Capone, that of the gangster: trench coat with upturned collar, grey fedora, gravelly voice, lounging menace. It was this that earned him his nickname, from James T. Farrell's fictional hoodlum Studs Lonigan: an elaborate affectation indeed, sickly Jewish law graduate identifying with a brawling, ghetto-Irish anti-Semite. His happiest times, in fact, came to involve pretending to be somebody else. He obtained work in radio serials specialising in roles as the tough-talking mobster; he gravitated to the genre of labour drama popularised by New York's Group Theatre.

Terkel's political thespianism began quite accidentally, when he attended a rehearsal of the first Chicago production of Cliff Odets's famous *Waiting for Lefty*, inspired by the 1934 taxi cab strike that had recently immobilised New York: a script was thrust into his hand when the actor cast as Joe did not turn up. And like Joe, who in the play is a reluctant radical, and like Odets, who admitted he 'had never been near a strike in my life,' Terkel was a sympathetic voyeur on the labour movement rather than an instant disciple. Cast in a production of Sinclair Lewis's famous anti-fascist polemic *It Can't Happen Here* as the brutal gauleiter Shad Ledue, his reaction was not to run off to read Marx or to join POUM, but to wonder about those who gravitated towards the likes of the America First Committee and the Silver Legion: 'Who are the guys who join these kinds of groups? Who are the guys who become like him? Who are the ones who fix the lock on the door, who put the bulb in?...There are millions who, deep, deep down, feel disdained.' As it happened, he had some personal insight into such sensations.

In the early 1990s, Terkel was interviewed at length by his English peer Tony Parker, best known for his searching interviews with soldiers, single mothers and long-term prison inmates. In his autobiographical writings, Terkel usually gave in to his raconteur's instincts. But Parker drew him painstakingly out, especially about the death of his father and the life of his mother.

It was nineteen-year-old Terkel who came upon Sam's body after a fatal heart attack, glasses askew, seemingly asleep. His father's health had always been precarious, but the loss was devastating. 'I was riding the streetcar a few days later, sitting on my own,' Terkel recalled. 'Not thinking about him – then suddenly I did, and I burst into tears. Can you imagine that? I was helpless, uncontrollable, I had to get off the streetcar. I've never had a moment like that in my life, before or since.' It may have been the realisation that he was abruptly alone with his increasingly embittered mother, who on the brink of the Wall Street crash had had the prescience to withdraw her hard-won savings from a doomed bank, only to reinvest them in the empire of a doomed utilities magnate; she hung on grimly to the Wells Grand before finally losing it in 1937, becoming what Terkel called a 'cantankerous old woman, who almost, though never quite, caught the brass ring'. They were never truly reconciled – an idea, Terkel confessed to Parker, that haunted him even as an octogenarian.

> Odd the way thoughts of her come floating to my mind for no reason. It's not because I see something or hear something that reminds me of her...I'm not conscious of thinking about *anything*, and then I find I *am* thinking, just in a generalised kind of way, you know what I mean, and it's about *her*...I'd like somehow to have come to know her better when I was older, know what I mean? To have been able to sit down and talk with her sometime and try to understand her...You have to understand this about people, don't you? For most of them, life's been a disappointment.

It is not that Terkel was unconsciously addressing his mother when he later 'sat down and talked' with subjects; but there is a sense in which his belief in the therapeutic properties of talk to reconcile, rehabilitate and redeem 'disappointment' was rooted in personal opportunities forgone. In his later work, he explained, he never sought out 'types': 'The individual is the key to everything.' In his case, it had been.

*

If one half of Terkel's story was about personal reticence, the other was about tactful embroidery, not all of it his own. On his death, many eulogists grouped Terkel with other victims of McCarthyism like Dalton Trumbo and Lillian Hellman. In truth, his politics were rather more veiled than those of the average proselytising liberal or fellow traveller. Although an avowed pacifist, Terkel did not identify as a conscientious objector during

World War II. Although he hosted events for the Progressive Party's 1948 election campaign, Henry Wallace never quite replaced Robert LaFollette in his affections: at an alumni dinner of the University of Chicago's law school that Terkel attended before the 1960 election, a vote was taken on the next president: there were forty-four notes for Kennedy, forty-one for Nixon, and one for 'Fighting Bob'. Terkel's radio program *The Wax Museum* on WENR became notable for its promotion of black musicians such as Mahalia Jackson and Big Bill Broonzy, and when he and his social worker wife, Ida, became parents they named their son Paul for the singer and activist Paul Robeson. But when Robeson became a shill for Stalin, Terkel recoiled.

Between 1949 and 1952, Terkel hosted a warmly remembered NBC variety show, *Studs' Place,* an outstanding example of what has been called the 'Chicago School of television,' which eschewed scripts and elaborate scenarios in favour of a relaxed, intimate, naturalistic air. The conceit was that Terkel was the owner of a diner; musical guests breezed in and out; the atmosphere was warm, folksy and frankly apolitical; and he was ignored by the infamous *Red Channels,* the widely-read right-wing pamphlet on 'Communist Influence in Radio and Television' that named 150 actors, writers, musicians, broadcast journalists and others as politically suspect. Although Terkel ascribed the cancellation of *Studs' Place* to NBC's misgivings about his ideological leanings, its homespun style was also at odds with the slick, homogenised variety shows rolling in from each coast by this time.

Soon after, a witness before the House Un-American Activities Committee, a Chicago radio producer, came forward to claim that Terkel had many years earlier invited him to join the Communist Party. But Terkel was never subpoenaed and, according to James Thomas Baker, author of a 1992 monograph about Terkel's works, the broadcaster's main persecutor was not the malevolent Senator Joe but a single buffoonish American Legionaire, Ed Clamage, a florist who spread rumours of Terkel's liberal sympathies – unpleasant, but hardly the weight of a vicious police state.

'I'm confident they had a fairly rich dossier on me,' Terkel said of the FBI, but the file when released proved to be mundane. In one memoir, Terkel self-dramatisingly quotes the slur of an FBI informant, whom he says was a university professor: 'Slovenly, didn't care much, a low-class Jew. He is not one of our type of boys.' In fact, the informant was a tutor and not so astringent: 'While it is true that Terkel worked diligently, I did not consider him any more than average. His appearance was somewhat sloppy, and I considered him to be not the best type of boy.'

Above all, when Terkel found a home at radio station WFMT in 1952, he was embraced, and his radicalism proved to be of a subtler sort, as an abettor and amplifier of the voices of others, first of all in the long, sympathetic, well-informed and adeptly edited interviews on *The Studs Terkel Show*, destined to run for forty-five years. Initially, Terkel spoke mainly with his favourite musicians, such as Louis Armstrong, Pete Seeger and Woody Guthrie; his evening sign-off was borrowed from Guthrie: 'Take it easy, but take it.' Gradually he widened his range to include writers, thinkers, directors and performing artists. Interestingly, he never interviewed politicians ('I don't have any of those'). But whether he was interviewing Leonard Bernstein, Simone de Beauvoir, Arthur Miller, John Kenneth Galbraith, Tennessee Williams, Andrés Segovia, Margaret Mead, Jacob Bronowski, Bertrand Russell, Birgit Nilsson or Bob Dylan, there was always an underlying democratic sensibility. The questions were simple but often acute; they sought answers for an intelligent but not an intellectual audience; they were based on exhaustive preparatory research: Terkel never referred to a book he had not read or a performance he had not seen. Unlike his famously relentless British counterpart John Freeman, Terkel sheered away from his guests' private lives, effectively issuing them a solicitous invitation to reflect on their work. With a jazzman's knack for improvisation, a bluesman's feel for trouble and a folk singer's ear for the vernacular, he flitted so lightly from subject to subject that the interviewee barely knew they were being drawn, although Margot Fonteyn can be heard at the end of a lively 1958 interview acknowledging Terkel's artfulness.

> Terkel: Thank you very much indeed, Margot Fonteyn. Is there any last thing you'd like to say?

> Fonteyn: Only thank you – and I'm glad I'm a dancer. And I think you're a dancer too.
>
> Terkel: Well, maybe. At heart perhaps.
>
> Fonteyn: Yes, yes. At heart you are.

Terkel's interviews obtained such a local following that virtually no creative identity visited Chicago without providing him an audience, and that WFMT began publishing transcripts in their program guide. But Terkel might have remained largely a regional identity had it not been for a brief vogue for the work of a Swedish lunar leftist Jan Myrdal, who just before the Cultural Revolution was permitted to spend a month in China, and obligingly provided a starry-eyed apologia for Maoism. Acclaim for the English translation of *Report from a Chinese Village* (1963) sent its publisher, Pantheon's Andre Schifflin, in search of a writer who could compile an equivalent text for everyday urban America.

Terkel found the village motif unsustainable, his town having no concentrated area where ethnic, racial and income groups met. On the contrary: Martin Luther King had just deemed Chicago 'the north's most segregated city,' where a black population of 800,000 laboured under 'educational and cultural shackles that are as binding as those of a Georgia chain gang'. 'I think the people from Mississippi should come to Chicago and learn how to hate,' said King. The only place that Terkel's seventy black, white and brindle interviewees mingled was between the covers of *Division Street* (1967) – the name of an actual Chicago street, now connected to Halsted Street by the Studs Terkel Bridge, but a title chosen for its symbolic resonance. For divided they proved to be: the small businessmen and the janitors, the advertising men and the nuns, the steel workers and the social workers, the spokesman for Young Americans for Freedom and the former American Nazi Party member. There is the anomie of a black ghetto teenager shortly to be shipped to Vietnam, and of a white house painter who thinks Hitler 'wasn't all wrong'. There is the loneliness of a friendless sixty-year-old man living on oatmeal in a rooming house across the road from Chicago's

Urban Progress Center, and of a mother of eight in a high-rise project without electricity. There is the shame and suffering of a closeted 35-year-old gay man living with his mother and of a relief clerk in a men's hostel still stricken by the memory of selling dirty postcards to working men while he was a boy. The assemblage, Terkel claimed, came together as randomly as the composition of pedestrian traffic.

> A tip from an acquaintance. A friend of a friend telling me of a friend or non-friend. A face, vaguely familiar, on the morning bus. An indignant phone call from a listener or a friendly one…I realised quite early in this adventure that interviews, conventionally conducted were meaningless. Conditioned clichés were certain to come. The question-and-answer technique may be of some value in determining favoured detergents, toothpastes and deodorants, but not in the discovery of men and women.

*Division Street,* then, was to Terkel more than a book: it was the first stirrings of a cause, the celebration of the 'non-celebrated' to which he would dedicate himself the rest of his life, from *Hard Times* (1970), a compilation of interviews with survivors of the Great Depression, to *Will the Circle Be Unbroken?* (2001), a collection of reflections on death and dying, all brought together with a workaholic zeal. Never able to cope with his mother's disappointments, Terkel developed an untiring patience for those who felt similarly 'disdained'. 'Listen,' was his repeated admonition to aspiring interviewers. 'If you do, people will talk. They'll always talk. Why? Because no one has ever listened to them before in all their lives. Perhaps they've not even listened to themselves.' Terkel listened his way to greatest prestige for the Pulitzer Prize-winning *The Good War* (1985), which humanised World War II as seldom before, from a gay marine describing Iwo Jima, to a Jewish social worker spying the Nazi high command in captivity at Nuremburg: 'It was a group of well-dressed men, with brief cases, newspapers and magazines in their hand. You would think these were members of the board of directors of IBM prior to a meeting.' The listening could be confronting indeed. Recently reprinted on its twentieth anniversary, *Race* (1992) contains an interview with C.P. Ellis, formerly the Exalted Cyclops of the Ku Klux Klan, strewn with chilling vignettes: 'When the news came over the radio that Martin Luther King was assassinated, I got on the telephone and begin to call other Klansmen...We just had a real party...Really rejoicin' 'cause the son of a bitch was dead.'

Terkel listened no more raptly than for *Working* (1974), in which 124 interviewees reflected, unsparingly, on 'what they do all day'. Terkel detected little nobility in modern labour, dwelling on its monotony and degradation, while also marvelling at the energy, resilience, fortitude and humour of his subjects, from a burned-out former child prodigy seeking solitude by toiling as a nurseryman to an old steel worker whose priest son was leading campaigns against the pollution caused by his father's mill. A plastics manufacturer told Terkel that he was so in thrall to his work that he identified with his material: 'I take the position that I'm the plastic and how would I travel through the machine and what would I see.' And *Working* is itself a little masterpiece of plasticity, Terkel moulding and being moulded by the testimony of his subjects, collecting, condensing and juxtaposing them so that they almost seem to be involved in their own conversations, each interview subtly informing the next. A hard-pressed stewardess mourns: 'Even if we're sad we're supposed to have a smile on our face.' A bored model finds her work ridiculous: 'They say: "We want you to be sexy, coy, pert, but not too effervescent."' A prostitute likes being her own boss: 'As a bright, assertive woman, I had no power. As a cold, manipulative hustler, I had a lot.' So does a woman advertising executive: 'If you're in the business, you're in the business, the fucking business! You're a hustler.' But an actor feels like a slave: 'We're nothing but goddamn shills.'

The scale of Terkel's oeuvre bespeaks more than intellectual engagement; for him, interviewing was profoundly personal. He identified with the nervousness of his subjects because he himself found the process traumatic. Just as he never learned to drive or to ride a bicycle, for example, Terkel suffered waves of panic about his tape recorders, even after he swapped a Sony cassette machine for his original reel-to-reel Uher: 'I don't know how to open it, I don't know how to put in a cassette, which way up it goes, how to close the lid when it's in, which is the button to press to get it to start recording, which is the button to press to make it stop.' He adapted by making these anxieties part of his shtick: 'Would you be frightened of a little old guy who wants to tape record a conversation with you – and he can't even work his tape recorder?' Compulsion then got him through. 'It's not just the tape recorder I can't switch off, it's me I can't switch off either,' he confessed. 'There's always some part of me that's outside, detached, observing.' He told a story against himself of spending a whole day yarning with a New York fireman, who when they had finished taping invited him to share a meal; Terkel declined on grounds he had scheduled another interview. 'Hey,' said the fireman. 'I've just shared my life story with you and you can't share spaghetti and a beer with me?' Although a chastened Terkel cancelled his second interview and stayed, such moments did not come naturally. While reflexively repelled by Nixon, he came to feel a peculiar kinship with the president on account of their shared 'neo-Cartesian' obsession with tape recording: 'I tape therefore I am.'

On his centenary, Terkel is rather a *sui generis* figure: not quite a journalist, not quite an academic, not merely a broadcaster, not simply a historian, in sympathy with the Left, but more from sentiment than intellect. Especially in later books, Terkel's formulae grew cruder, more cloying and more repetitive: conservative pundit Joshua Epstein's description of him as a 'virtuecrat,' placing 'all virtue in a fictional common man,' has some force. Yet that elusiveness says as much about the modern news media's forces of conformity, its institutionalised incuriosity, its drearily mechanical nature, its excitement about so much and care about so little. Terkel never lost his excitement at the thought that there was a world out there just waiting to be heard, and ready to be opened by the simplest of questions – and these, he well knew, were often the most challenging to answer.

# CHURNALISTIC STANDARDS

## *A review of Nick Davies'* Flat Earth News (2008)

Not so long ago, I found myself in the newsroom of the newspaper at which I spent my reporting youth almost a quarter of a century ago, but in which I had not set foot since the early 1990s. Much had changed. I am just old enough to remember the frenzied clickety-clack of typewriters; the soundtrack was now the distant pocketa-pocketa of the commotion of keyboards. The sprawling open plan was gone; staff had been dilbertised by partitions. Perhaps partly as a result, they even looked a little different to hacks of yore; at least, they were notably better dressed. Only one reporter I knew wore a suit those many years ago: he wore it every day and it was purple.

I saw lots of people I knew, many more I didn't, and realised only on leaving how unsettling this was. These people – they were *there*. It was 3pm in the newsroom and they were...*in the newsroom*. At 3pm in the corresponding newsroom twenty-five years earlier, you could have fired a gun in safety – you might have hit a feature writer, but their absence would scarcely have been noticed. Everyone would have been out on a story, pursuing their round or duchessing a contact. I cast one last look over my shoulder at the modern mise-en-scene. Yes, there they all were, huddled in their cubicles, either scrolling up and down their screens, or on the phone wearing those headsets that are standard issue in call centres – galley slaves chained to their electronic oars as the newsdesk drubbed the news cycle drum. It explained a lot about the paper, *The Age*, and its slick, shiny malaise; all its sexed-up stories, soundalike columnists and weightless supplements, the general air of excitement about everything and care about nothing. And according to Nick Davies' *Flat Earth News*, this reinvention of newsrooms as dark satanic content mills is central to the collapse of journalistic standards everywhere.

Davies, a dogged investigative journalist for *The Guardian*, pulls no punches: office-bound, dependent on the phone, the web and the daily papierkrieg of press releases, the modern reporter produces not journalism but 'churnalism'. Davies even has statistical support. When he asked Cardiff University to survey a fortnight of content from Britain's five quality dailies, it emerged that eighty per cent of stories consisted either wholly or partly of information from wire services or public relations firms. The accent of the news business now falls so heavily on speed and productivity that checking is discretionary where it is not actively discouraged; it pervades even non-commercial media. Davies cites a BBC style guide that counsels: 'Your story MUST be accurate, impartial, balanced and uphold the values of BBC news...NEVER publish anything that you do not understand, that is speculation or inadequately sourced.' Then, in the next breath, as though the sentiment reconciles easily with the foregoing: 'Get the story up as fast as you can...We encourage a sense of urgency – we want to be first.' Davies also describes how staff numbers at the Press Association, Britain's premier wire service, have been winnowed away. Where once PA was famous for its coverage of the justice system, the eighteen courts of the Old Bailey are now covered by two people, the ninety-six courts of the Royal Courts of Justice by five; there are no dedicated reporters of local government *at all*.

The result is the title phenomenon: Davies defines 'flat earth news' as 'an unreliable statement created by outsiders, usually for their own commercial or political benefit, injected via a wire agency into the arteries of the media through which it then circulates around the whole body of global communication'. Some examples are hilarious. Just before the last World Cup, PA produced a story about an England fan, Paul Hucker, who had insured himself against traumatizing results: the story was widely circulated, on radio, television, in print and online, including at the *Sydney Morning Herald*. In fact, it was a scam to promote the insurance company involved; a near identical story had been trotted out four years earlier. 'There are loads of little Huckers out there,' says Davies – and the bigger ones are purported to pack WMDs.

So far, so bad. And when he is being a foot-slogging reporter, Davies provides case after case of media failure, from the bigging up of tenth-rate Iraqi nutbar Abu Musab al-Zarqawi into the Moriarty of international terror, to the amazing whitewash of the 'Natwest Three', the sleazy British bankers mixed up in Enron's meltdown who fought extradition with a scandalously effective PR campaign. It's when Davies tries contouring material to fit his thesis that *Flat Earth News* begins careering out of control, because he can't concentrate on any area long enough than to administer a few swift kicks.

Davies starts his saga with the millennium bug, in whose virulence the media invested so heavily, perhaps because 'Y2K', like 'BSE' and 'DVT', fitted so economically into a headline; whatever the case, Davies sees the squishing of the bug of millennium eve as a 'terrifying night for journalists', being a 'stunning example of a failure in truth-telling by the global media', because 'for journalists the defining value is honesty – the attempt to tell the truth'.

Are these, though, exactly the same thing? Journalists were certainly wrong. But is there evidence that they were dishonest – that is to say, actively purveyed information they knew to be false? A page or two on, Davies slightly modifies his critique: 'They [the journalists] did it because, just like their sources, the journalists themselves did not know the truth – even though truth is their primary objective. And that is commonplace. Ignorance is the root of media failure.' But this is as helpful as saying that heart failure is the root of death. Journalists will always be trespassing on areas, debates, and causes of which they know next to nothing – it's the nature of the craft. Davies might here have advocated the media seeking more specialist knowledge: instead of mechanically hiring graduates with useless degrees in journalism and media studies, why not, say, recruit a scientist to write about science, a doctor to cover medicine or a lawyer to report law? Is it because we're too arrogant to think that there's nothing our steel trap journalist minds cannot grasp, or because we just don't care about getting it right? Instead his rather self-serving analysis leaves a point half-made.

While Davies chooses good examples of media failure, he also chooses some bad ones. Enron might well have seduced media observers, but it seduced plenty of market analysts too, and the former, especially Bethany McLean of *Fortune* and Kurt Eichenwald of the *New York Times*, got it right before the latter. The allegations leading to Bill Clinton's impeachment weren't merely 'promoted by a group of right-wingers who were determined to destroy Clinton'; if anything, as Michael Isikoff showed in his *Uncovering*

*Clinton*, the president had many more media protectors, happy to reinforce the vanguard of lies around him.

Nor is the fact that British broadsheets carried 800 lines of parliamentary debate a day in 1988 but only 100 by 1992 merely because proprietors 'shifted their focus to stories which were more likely to sell their paper' and 'the now familiar destruction of reporting staff'; it is an outcome both of the broadcasting of parliament since 1989, and the Westminster system's increasingly presidential style. A commitment to the serious business of politics is certainly virtuous, but too much of anything is bad for you. On 16 August 1977, America's CBS began its news bulletin with six minutes on the Panama Canal treaty. 'Serious', to be sure – but it so happened that Elvis Presley had died that day.

When it comes to an overarching theory, too, Davies struggles to do other than repeat his original assertion. The ten 'rules of production' he enumerates in Chapter Four are wearyingly axiomatic. 'The great blockbuster myth of modern journalism is objectivity,' Davies says, 'the idea that a good newspaper or broadcaster simply collects and reproduces the objective truth.' Can this really *still* be a myth? Even conceding the unattainability of absolute 'objectivity', to simply discard it as a goal is a pretext for the kind of slapdash journalism Davies affects to deplore. OK, so 'balance' can be cosmetic, and betray an intellectual timidity – or, as Davies puts it: 'Balance means never having to say you're sorry – because you haven't said anything.' But to undertake journalism with no sense of obligation to unearth the inconvenient and contradictory as well as the revelatory and alarming is simply to become the mouthpiece of one's preferred vested interest. Indeed, Davies later quotes with approval Hugo Young 's criticism of the support his old employers at the *Sunday Times* lavished on Margaret Thatcher during the miner's strike of 1984: 'Whereas the old *Sunday Times*, if functioning properly, would have stood back and asked difficult questions of both sides, the new *Sunday Times* became the accomplice of one side only.' But, then, 'great blockbuster myths' can be useful when they allow a chip to be taken off Rupert Murdoch.

Davies is in a muddle about Murdoch. In Chapter One, Davies plays the Dirty Digger down. He's evil, but he doesn't actually have a 'coherent political platform'. News Corporation is evil, too, but not because Murdoch is an interventionist proprietor: 'We could replace him with Rupert Bear: the Murdoch newspapers and television stations would continue to pump out falsehood, distortion and propaganda.' (For some reason, this really tickled me: I now keep thinking of a stuffed toy in plaid trousers saying 'We Report; You Decide').

By Chapter Two, however, Davies has decided that the triumph of media mammon is all Murdoch's fault: 'It is rare in history to be able to identify the precise date of a turning point. In the case of the fall of Fleet Street, however, we can.' That date, 25 January 1986, is when News moved to Wapping, freezing out the street's volatile print unions: 'Those unions were notorious for their greed and bad practice, but they were also the only force strong enough to resist the new corporate owners.'

This is 'mine enemy's enemy' logic at its crudest. In the latest volume in *The History of The Times*, Graham Stewart provides a rather different estimate of the move. In the decade before Wapping, *The Times* lost 96.5 million papers to industrial action and a standard edition featured five misprints a page; afterwards it lost none, and misprints dwindled to one every three pages. For courageous journalists in the field like Robert Fisk in the Middle East, says Stewart, working for *The Times* before Wapping was soul-destroying: 'Periodically a message would be returned thanking him for his report and apologising for the fact the unions had called another strike and so it would not be appearing after all.' The climactic expose of the *Sunday Times'* famous campaign against Distillers over the harmful effects of thalidomide was, thanks to a stoppage, read by next to no-one. If Fleet Street's print unions were certainly strong, they helped nobody but themselves. Then when he is examining press analysis of the case made for invading Iraq and really has a chance to hold Murdoch's feet to the fire, Davies picks on...the *Observer*. Oh dear.

Davies ends up showing that he has more in common with his peers than he would perhaps freely concede. Harold Evans argues that the press is better at handling single events than social processes with no obvious beginning or end; likewise *Flat Earth News*. Beginning with what on its own would be a very good chapter about ethical corner-cutting in British newspapers, Davies loses interest in ideas, and flits instead from story to story, veering back and forth between past and present so that it's not clear whether things are a lot worse or just a little, vivid and impressionistic but also shapeless, tendentious and bitchy, so that the result is much less than the sum of its parts – rather like, in fact, a modern newspaper. He presents as in acute need of a competent editor. Rather like *The Age*.

# THE JOURNALIST AS HERO

## *A review of Seymour Hersh's* Reporter (2018)

The cover image on Seymour Hersh's memoir, *Reporter,* could hardly be improved. Taken in 1974 in the newsroom of the *New York Times,* it shows Hersh with his left elbow propped on a typewriter with blank paper in the roller, sleeves rolled up and patterned tie loose around an unironed collar. He is leaning confidentially in to the receiver of what must be a rotary dial phone, listening intently, gazing into the middle distance. It could be a still from *All the President's Men* or *The Parallax View,* although Hersh is in black and white, as befits a giant of print, bane of governments and scourge of spies from Watergate to Abu Ghraib.

As he describes it, Hersh was born into a school of American journalism already saturated with romance. His first job was on Chicago's City News Bureau, made famous by alumnus Charles MacArthur in *The Front Page* (1928), whose 'shabby desks, dirty floors, old typewriters, and marginal lighting' occupied by 'wise guys full of badinage' were dazzling to this 'punk Jew'. Here he absorbed cardinal nostrums of tenacity and precision, such as 'being first is not nearly as important as being right' and 'if your mother says she loves you, check it out'. He also, it occurred to him later, acquired a chameleonic knack of 'getting to know and exchanging views with a wide variety of people', stemming originally from 'being raised and working in a racially diverse part of Chicago'. This is a rare bout of introspection in *Reporter,* which lives up to its title in reading a little like a news feature on Hersh himself.

Not that this precludes excitement because, like anything involving Hersh, *Reporter* contains its share of scoops. The most fascinating concern the only interruption to his sixty years as a newsman – his time as press secretary to the quixotic 1968 presidential campaign of Gene McCarthy, about which he has never before written, and which is a minor classic of the campaigning life. McCarthy emerges as a noble dilettante, skiving off a fund raiser in Milwaukee to see *Ulysses* at the cinema because 'I understand they use the word "fuck" in the movie'. Asked by Hersh what he should tell the audience, McCarthy says airily: 'Tell them I'll part the waters.'

The story behind the story of Hersh's epoch-making My Lai reports also starts here, because he divulges that his original tip-off about the atrocity came from a fellow worker on the McCarthy campaign, and the key detail of the name from an angry colonel he had befriended at the Pentagon. Asked casually about the rumour of a 1968 massacre of men, women and children in a village in Vietnam, the colonel stormed: 'This Calley is a madman, Sy.' With a name, Hersh could go places – and did.

The two chapters concerned with My Lai, where it's now estimated around 500 civilians were killed in cold, khaki blood, are some of the finest I have ever read about the high ideals, low cunning and DIY ethics of the pavement pounding reporter. Yeah the war, and all that, but what matters above all is *the scoop*. 'I liked being the best, the leader of the pack,' Hersh confesses.

Hersh pursues Lt William Calley less like an avenging angel than a bounty hunter, charming, cheating, winking and wheedling. He pretends to take notes of a conversation with Calley's lawyer while actually reading and transcribing the charge sheet upside down on the man's desk. He prowls Georgia's Fort Benning, where Calley is being held, more or less pretending to be an officer. He feigns sympathy with Calley, who is, perhaps inevitably, a disappointing villain: 'I had wanted to hate him, to see him as a child-killing monster, but instead I found a rattled, frightened young man, short, slight and so pale that the bluish veins on his neck and shoulders were visible.' Proprietorial about the story, he rejects entreaties to tell it in the *New York Review of Books* and *New York Times* which would have slightly lightened his watermark. The public have a right to know, but what Hersh seems keenest they know is his byline.

It's unclear how well he recognises this about himself, but Hersh comes across as arrogant, boorish, a braggart and a prima donna, throwing typewriters through windows, raining insults left and right. And unlike his great contemporary Bob Woodward, who becomes a kind of White House court historian, Hersh stubbornly refuses domestication. His abiding frenemy is the *Times'* Abe Rosenthal, similarly volatile and profane, who heads off one

Hersh kvetching with: 'Shut the fuck up and get the story ready.'

Which is fun – a nice antidote to journalism's tendency to pious attitudinising. But after a while, it conduces to rather a one-note book, on which the paranoia lies heavy and in which the characters are mainly ciphers, even the admirable ones like the *New Yorker* editors William Shawn (who cooed to Hersh: 'Stories are never too long or too short. They're too interesting or too boring') and David Remnick (who rang Hersh before the second tower was hit with the instruction: 'You are now permanently assigned to the biggest story of your career').

Story follows story, but the larger one Hersh is meant to be telling, of himself, goes by the board. The lack of an interior life is one thing; the absence of a sense of what his work might stand for is another. Hersh is apt to cite sales figures and quote reviews of his work, but thinks little more deeply about it. A case can be made that he has had a greater impact on journalism than on his targets. John F. Kennedy remains a sainted name; Henry Kissinger and Dick Cheney enjoy rude health; the mogul Charles Bluhdorn stayed rich; the mob lawyer Sidney Korshak was never indicted; even Calley served but a token sentence.

Hersh's great *bete noir* is Kissinger ('The man lied the way most people breathed') and arguably his most momentous work the 700-page blockbuster *The Price of Power: Kissinger in the White House* (1983). But with the best will in the world, it is hard yakka. Hersh tells a story of shortly after the book came out walking into a Maryland swimming pool with his family and observing a sunbaking woman reading it. Half an hour later he looked back at her and she was asleep with the book over her face. Hersh is assuredly a reporter's reporter; with his wealth of unnameable sources and flair for conspiratorial conjecture, he has not always been so friendly for readers. He lost some of his faith in Remnick over the latter's relationship with Barack Obama: 'I had learned over the years never to trust the declared aspirations of any politician and was also enough of a prude to believe that editors should not make friends with a sitting president.' Which in its way is admirable, but also leaves him with nothing very much to believe in. One returns to the cover: a figure in shades of grey, now struggling to distinguish them.

# THE JOURNALIST AS GOSSIP

## *A review of Michael Wolff's* Fire and Fury (2018)

In his new account of Donald Trump's presidency *Fire and Fury*, Michael Wolff describes how Trump's 'adviser' Steve Bannon counselled fellow White House newbies to read *The Best and The Brightest* as preparation for their administration's tasks. Rarely for the mordant Bannon, his enthusiasm for David Halberstam's 1972 classic of the West Wing mandarinate who mangled the Vietnam War seems have been unfeigned and unironic. 'A very moving experience reading this book,' Wolff quotes Bannon as saying. 'It makes the world clear, amazing characters and all true.'

Is anyone likely to say the same of Wolff's rapid fire reportage of the Trump White House? Not in forty-five years, that's for sure; maybe, at a pinch, for forty-five minutes. The book has apparently already sold more than two million copies, benefiting enormously from Trump's reflex threats of legal action and suppression. Yet so extensively have its contents been parsed that the very little new in it already seems old, while the old lies dead on the page. Trump is a deluded solipsist surrounded by cretinous enablers and epigones. And, errrr...that's it.

*Fire and Fury* concerns less the presidency, or even politics, than rivalry – that between what Wolff calls 'Jarvanka', allies of the Trump family circle led by his daughter Ivanka and son-in-law Jared Kushner, and 'the Bannonites', led by the Manichean Bannon in loose alliance with chief of staff Reince Preibus and chief flak Kellyanne Conway. Some of these characters have intellectual pretensions; all are presented as rubes and naïfs in varying shades of stupidity and vulgarity. Only Bannon, as previously described in Joshua Green's *The Devil's Bargain* (2017), thought Trump had any chance at the election of November 2016. None were prepared for the day-to-day demands of political administration – what Weber called its slow drilling through thick boards. Instead they took the drills and boards and set about each other, while their boss wandered about in a self-pitying daze.

> He could not really converse...not in the sense of sharing information, or of a balanced back-and-forth conversation. He neither particularly listened to what was said to him, nor particularly considered what was said in response (one reason he was so repetitive). Nor did he treat anyone with any sort of basic or reliable courtesy. If he wanted something, his focus might be sharp and attention lavish, but if someone wanted something from him, he tended to become irritable and quickly lost interest. He demanded you pay him attention, then decided you were weak for grovelling.

That's Wolff writing about Trump; but, frankly, it could be Wolff writing about Wolff. Much has been made of his celebrity journalist's working method. Indeed, he makes much of it himself, claiming to have had a 'semi-permanent seat on a couch in the West Wing' and 'fly-on-the-wall status' for the duration of his research. The result is a fly-on-the-couch mess: people spoke to Wolff on a host of different bases with varying conditions of confidentiality and...well, bugger it...he just used what he wanted where he wanted to. Wolff is strangely reticent about inserting himself, identifying what he *saw*, what he *heard about*, and what he *guessed*. His being nowhere spreads him everywhere and the effect is strangely muteing and monotonous: much of *Fire and Fury* reads so unsurprisingly that it could have been tossed off without any access at all.

Now and again, Wolff gets in a good line. Trump is 'impetuous yet did not like to make decisions', has 'no interest in personnel problems, since they put the emphasis on other people'. Jared Kushner is 'what used to be called a Rockefeller Republican and might now more properly be a Goldman Sachs Democrat'; Steve Bannon is 'the equivalent of Trump's personal talk radio' (although why 'equivalent'?); Bob Woodward has written 'a long shelf of books in which even the most misguided presidential actions seems part of an epochal march of ultimate responsibility'. There's a few funny stories – they might even be too good to be true. The ten-day White House communications director Antony Scaramucci makes a memorably profane cameo; Bannon, Wolff reports, heard that 'The Mooch' had been sacked when a *New Yorker* fact checker rang to ask whether it was true that he sucked his own cock.

Despite the boast of being based on 'two hundred interviews', however, the reporting in *Fire and Fury* is diaphanously thin. Mike Pence and Neil Gorsuch barely feature; George Papadopolous, Rich Higgins, Ben Carson and Rick Perry don't. Scarcely any new light is shed on the administration's denials and admissions around contact with Russian emissaries; on occasions where testimony conflicts, Wolff lazily lays out competing versions without comment; on occasions where historical perspective or policy insight is required, he is embarrassingly lightweight. Where they offer limited colour and movement, key moments are overlooked. Wolff sniffs, for example, that Trump had no interest in the 'no-fun issue' of health care; he proceeds to echo the president's indifference by dismissing last year's collapse of the Republican push to 'repeal and replace' Obamacare, perhaps Trump's most mortifying policy setback, in a single sentence.

Worse, Wolff has a prose ear of the purest tin. His sentences are cantilevered with cliches: holy grails, silver bullets, magic bullets, domino theories, ground zeroes, road maps, smoking guns, feedback loops, free passes, quantum leaps and dead meats, with the occasional pretentious reaching for *ad hominem, beau ideal, ne plus ultra* and *joie de guerre* (no fewer than four times). In consecutive sentences, he likens Trump to a Delphic oracle, an energetic child and the Sun God; twice he likens Bannon to Cassandra; at one point Kushner gets 'saddled with an impossible hurdle', which you wouldn't wish on anybody. Simple sentiments such as that Trump and the media are mutually fascinated come out as: 'He was the whale against which media emotions, self regard, ego, *joie de guerre,* career advancement and desire to be at the centre of the story, too, all churned in nearly ecstatic obsession. In reverse regard, the media was the same whale, serving the same function, for Trump.' In other words, Wolff makes Kitty Kelley read like Robert Caro.

About the public who elected Trump, meanwhile, Wolff has the least to say of all. They are reduced to mere spectators: 'Perhaps never before in history – not through world wars, the overthrow of empires, periods of extraordinary social transformations, or episodes of government-shaking scandal – have real-life events unfolded with such emotional plot-thickening impact. That was the radical and transformational nature of the Trump presidency: it held everybody's attention.' Seriously? That's it? What about the clash of its ostensible economic populism with its beneficiation of the one per cent and assault on public-facing institutions? *Fire and Fury*, then, is the self-amused, morally-weightless salute of one hollow showman for another. Perhaps it is no better than Trump's cruel, mendacious and vituperative administration deserve. The rest of us could do with something other than *The Least and the Lightest*.

# THE JOURNALIST AS POLITICIAN

## *A review of Bob Woodward's* Rage *(2020)*

Tom Lehrer famously believed that Henry Kissinger's Nobel Prize for Peace rendered satire impossible. Has Donald Trump's presidency made the same true of political journalism?

This may sound counterintuitive. After all, Trump has been a boon for news outlets and book publishing as well as social media. Bob Woodward's *Rage* sold 600,000 copies in its first week. And that the dean of White House scribes herein abandons his trademark disinterest and pronounces authoritatively that 'Trump is the wrong man for the job' has been treated as news itself.

Yet so what? In the four years he has acted as America's id, journalists have repeatedly demonstrated that Trump is also an idiot – confirming more or less what anyone could tell from listening to him for five minutes. Yet for all that stupendous effort they have hardly shifted the dial by a degree, any more than seven million cases of COVID-19 and 200,000 deaths have. And *Rage*, sadly, hints why.

Woodward's stock in trade is the heavily 'reported', privileged-access, semi-official version of events, halfway between journalism and history, in which everyone gets their say, usually on a non-attribution 'deep background' basis. He departed that slightly for *Fear* (2018), his account of the first half of Trump's term, because Trump would not speak to him; he departs it here, too, because Trump does.

*Rage* becomes an uneasy mix of classic Woodward, in which the state's flawed but noble servants wrestle with events and nobody comes off too badly, and new formula Woodward, as the journalist sits through seventeen 'interviews' in which Trump rambles disconnectedly about obsessions that sometimes do not last the duration of a sentence.

The first half is mainly defence secretary Jim Mattis, secretary of state Rex Tillerson and national security advisor Dan Coats experiencing the 'almost irresistible call to presidential service' and living to regret it – ground already thoroughly traversed by Phillip Rucker and Carol Leonnig in *A Very Stable Genius* (2020). In the second half, Woodward is mainly just a dutiful stenographer, occasionally remarking on the 'vague, directionless nature of Trump's comments', the 'maddening, convoluted dodging', the 'stream-of-consciousness greivance', 'the rambling, repetitious, often defensive and angry monologues'.

Which, to be sure, they are, but they are nothing we have not heard before. Yes, prepare to be amazed. Trump unplugged sounds almost exactly the same as Trump plugged: scatter-brained, grandiose, self-pitying, a fashioner of sentences that collapse under the weight of their incoherence if they extend beyond five words, two of which will usually be 'tremendous' or 'unbelievable'. In listening so attentively, however, Woodward fails to hear something integral to Trump's appeal.

Not for Trump the self-protecting cloak of 'deep background'. He rings Woodward at all hours of the day and night, and either brags ('Here's the thing: I'm never wrong'; 'You know they talk about the elite. Really, the elite. Ah, they have nice houses. No. I have much better than them. I have better everything than them, including education') or bitches ('I have done a tremendous amount for the Black community. And, honestly, I'm not feeling any love'; 'I have opposition like nobody has. And that's okay. I've had that all my life'). Sure, Trump's brain is a garbage fire. But even a garbage fire supplies warmth.

Trump is a phony all right: the heir to a fortune who might as well have invested it in government bonds for all his actual commercial acumen but poses as a business genius; the self-styled strong man who prevaricates and postures rather than make actual decisions; the self-professed drainer of the swamp who has simply merged it with his own swamp of overt and covert self-dealing. But the act, as it were, is defiantly real, which to many makes him a refreshing antidote to decades of manipulation by machine politics and dirty dynasties (Bush, Clinton et al). Every now and again, there's some clusterfiasco – a bald-faced lie, a crude betrayal, a blown whistle, a legal snafu. Yet it blows over, or is dislodged by the next scandal du jour, Trump carries on like nothing has changed, and the impression is: he's indestructible, he's our guy.

This never seems to dawn on Woodward, who keeps straining to interpret Trump by the light of previous presidents. He tries fact checks, such as his earnest annotation when Trump invokes Antifa: 'Antifa, an abbreviation for "Anti-fascist", is a decentralised movement. It is not an organisation and does not have a leader or membership dues.' He tries introducing concepts like 'white privilege', which simply cause Trump to laugh: 'You really drank the Kool-Aid, didn't you? Just listen to you.' He tries pleading with Trump to pivot, to come up with a vision or a plan, to the extent of running past the president his own Woodrow Wilson-esque fourteen-point list of COVID policy objectives, which merely elicit Trump's condescension: 'I'm glad you told me.' *Rage* comes with a citation from the venerable Robert Caro calling Woodward a 'great reporter' who has 'never stopped seeking out facts'. But finding that facts here have no purchase, Woodward is reduced to pointless imprecations: 'It's a matter of the heart and the spirit.' Trump comes back, quite rightly, with: 'You don't understand me.' At last, Woodward sags: 'We were speaking past each other, almost from different universes.'

It is incidental comments in *Rage* that are most incisive. Of Trump's relationship with truth, Coats says: 'To him a lie is not a lie. It's just what he thinks.' Of Trump's objectives, COVID guru Anthony Fauci observes: 'His sole purpose is to get re-elected.' Of Trump's party, his creepily cynical son-in-law Jared Kushner observes: 'The Republican Party was a collection of tribes.' Trump, argues Kushner, has galvanised them: 'I don't think it's even about the issues. I think it's about the attitude.' In which case, what price political journalism, except as just another alternative in the market of attitudes? Emerson spoke of democracy as being 'a government of bullies tempered by editors'. But the message of *Rage* is that we are well past that stage, and that after twenty books Woodward is just another voice persuasive to no-one not already persuaded, that a president widely acknowledged to be an incompetent and ill-informed monomaniac who has subverted every democratic and institutional norm he has touched stands every chance of re-election in November. In which case what would become impossible is dystopian fiction.

# THE POLITICIAN AS CRITIC

## *A review of Lindsay Tanner's* Sideshow (2011)

Bill Clinton discouraged politicians from picking fights with people who bought their ink by the barrel. Mindful of that advice, Lindsay Tanner has waited until the end of a career dedicated to 'serious craft of politics' to remonstrate with the fourth estate about its fundamental unseriousness in reporting the democratic process.

The thesis of *Sideshow* can be summarised succinctly: that the media, under commercial pressure to entertain, regularly travesties weighty issues, both by wilful misreporting and compulsive trivialisation, forcing helpless politicians to dance to its tune with policies that are primarily about appearing to do something rather than actually doing it. The 2010 election campaign was this phenomenon in excelsis, both major parties tiptoeing delicately around matters of substance in favour of slogans, soundbites and stunts.

You're nodding, right? Journalism tacky and superficial? You betcha. Quality of public debate impoverished? With you all the way. Oh yes, there's much about the premise of *Sideshow* with which one's first instinct is to express wholehearted agreement, and to laud its author for speaking truth to power. These sensations do not survive the experience of reading it. *Sideshow* is a rambling, repetitive, question-begging book that belies the author's reputation as *un homme serieux* of Labor politics.

For a start, *Sideshow* more or less exonerates his peers, who only collude unwillingly in the debauching of debate, and who *only* practice their techniques of media management – 'spin' – in response to the media's 'need to entertain'. But politicians and media practitioners are born codependents, and natural collaborators. They live or die by their publics; they are both in the business of courting popularity, and in receipt of constant feedback about their fluctuations of fortune (politicians have polls, media outlets ratings and circulations); politicians might even be felt rather better off, in Australia at least, inasmuch as there is compulsory voting but no compulsory reading or viewing.

Political and media professionals move back and forth across a blurred frontier, media staff performing investigative work on political opponents, columnists acting as shameless shills. You can mount a respectable argument that reverses Tanner's – not that the relationship between politicians and the media is too adversarial, but that it is not adversarial enough, that both spend too long tickling one another, and insufficient time at loggerheads, brooding on their respective duties to the public. I've often felt that a giveaway of this collusion is the title of the ABC's Sunday morning journo talkfest *Insiders*. Whatever one may think of the show, journalists have no business being insiders, except on the most temporary of bases; when they forget that, they aren't worth a damn.

While Tanner acknowledges that 'there was no golden age of politics when politicians rigorously and objectively explained the strengths and weakness in their positions', he believes things are worse now than when he arrived on the scene twenty years ago: 'The media were central to national politics then, but they are much more dominant now.' Yet he also finds the volume of political coverage considerably diminished, and sees the besetting sin of *Today Tonight* and *A Current Affair* that they scarcely evince any interest in Canberra and its works at all. How does this correlate to dominance?

Tanner's abiding preoccupation is the Canberra press gallery, and with newspapers generally, despite his seeming awareness of their waning and frankly spent force. This is more telling of the state of Labor than of democracy in general. The Howard government prospered in spite of a frequently querulous and hostile gallery by selling messages direct to the public via live media like talkback radio, which Tanner doesn't get round to addressing until page 194 of *Sideshow* with a vague comment that it provides 'some hope'. When Tanner airily addresses 'new media', too, it's far from clear he knows whereof he writes because he groups newspaper websites and pay television in with 'blogs and tweets'.

*Sideshow* is also larded with more quotations than an Alan Ramsey column – quotations, moreover, often saying more or less the same thing, and stuffed in seemingly for the sake of parading the author's erudition, but at some stages constipating the narrative to the point of unreadability.

Quotations alone are not evidence; deployed here in such quantities, they steadily draw attention to Tanner's substitution of assertion for argument, and the book's one-note tone.

The effect is aggravated by Tanner's irritating stylistic tic of introducing each individual with a two- or three-word descriptor that is either bland ('British writer', 'American writer') or redundantly detailed ('inventor of the Ethernet and *Infoworld* columnist'). Robert Hughes is a 'cultural writer' – who knew? Jeremy Clarkson is a 'security commentator' – say what? Michael Parkinson is a 'popular interviewer' who thinks Australia is infected with a 'celebrity virus' – Tanner is somehow deaf here to the ear-splitting irony. Perhaps the most annoying is the framing of Daniel Boorstin as an 'American researcher'. What on earth is a 'researcher'? Boorstin was a superfine American historian and cultural critic whose analysis fifty years ago of the rise of the 'pseudo-event', *The Image*, traversed the terrain explored by *Sideshow* and far, far better.

Nor do Tanner's anecdotes and complaints always serve his argument. He cites, for example, a *Daily Telegraph* article in 2009 relying on figures from the government's AusTender site to the effect that spending on consultancies had increased during the Rudd premiership. In fact, complains Tanner, the data was not definitive: 'A change in reporting methodology, contracts between government agencies, multi-year contracts, and contracts incorrectly described as consultancies all made it impossible to rely on figures drawn from the website.' But why run a website with data it was 'impossible to rely on'? Those who knowingly make confusing information available have little right to complain when confusion arises.

Elsewhere, Tanner faults *Age* political editor Paul Austin for John Brumby's decision during the state election campaign to match his rival Ted Baillieu's commitment to increase police numbers while also claiming that crime rates were falling. 'If Brumby is right and Baillieu is wrong, why has the premier now decided to match the Liberals and promise an extra 1700 police?' asked Austin. 'The answer to this rhetorical question is simple,' Tanner responds tartly. 'Given the way the media cover these issues, John Brumby clearly believed this was an argument he could not win, irrespective of the facts.' Turns out that the 'facts' were dodgy, and Austin was right to intuit a contradiction.

The quaintest judgement of all is Tanner's conviction that Kevin Rudd was a 'victim' of the 'sideshow syndrome', of 'the dominance of media imagery and the machine politics it encourages'. Tanner here leaves out too many steps. For most of his ascendancy, Rudd was a huge beneficiary of the superficiality of political journalism. The gallery was dazzled by his poll numbers, and deaf to his growing unpopularity among colleagues. What was the 2020 Summit but the phoniest of pseudo-events? Who can forget that photograph of Rudd sitting on the floor, all studied informality and faux humility, as Australia's Great Brains studiously inched their way to ineffectual conclusions? It wasn't fear of 'irresistible media pressure' that doomed his prime ministership; rather was it his lack of factional support when the public twigged belatedly that he stood largely for his own prestige and advancement.

Lastly, Tanner takes for granted the idea that a fully-informed and engaged electorate is integral to democracy. But there are grounds for believing that Australia's democracy has been so successful and continuous precisely because we have seldom cared much for politics or politicians; it is in a covetousness of power and an intense attachment to ideology that lie the seeds of corruption and tyranny. A switched-off citizenry may, it is true, tend to shy from grand reform and creative change, but it may also counteract tendencies among its political elites to adamantine certainty and grandiosity.

Tanner's arguments against compulsory voting – which on balance he decides he *just* favours – overlook regular evidence in Australia for the wisdom of crowds. Time and again, it seems to me, voters in this country get it just about right. They worked out that John Hewson was a dreary cipher; they sensed that Paul Keating was a busted flush; they guessed Kim Beazley's laziness, Mark Latham's nastiness and John Howard's eventual emptiness and inanition.

In Victoria, voters punished Joan Kirner's government for ineptitude, Jeff Kennett's for hubris and Brumby's for staleness; in New South Wales, they waited as long as it took the Liberals to promote someone besides a half-wit, then kicked the Carr-Iemma-Rees-Kenneally junta into well-merited obscurity. Their ultimate triumph was to award the last federal election to nobody, a verdict whose fairness Tanner can scarcely dispute.

In favour of Tanner's *Sideshow*, it should be said that it is a useful argument starter, and concerns a worthy subject. Because the media could and should *always* do better; it *has* encouraged gotcha journalism, elastic ethics and obsessions with the cosmetic and counterfeit; and there *are* unprecedented commercial pressures on key media institutions at the moment, even if I feel Tanner overestimates them as a daily contributor to the modern malaise: current affairs has *always* pitted reporter against reporter in a cliché competition, with the spoils to the contestant finding the shortest direct route to a pre-existing prejudice.

Tanner actually gets close to a perennial problem, before sadly sheering off in another direction: the poverty among journalists of specialist knowledge in the areas they write about. Lacking the qualifications and training to ask probing questions about science, the law, medicine, accountancy and other areas requiring actual expertise, political journalists default naturally to transacting in images, polls and quotes. For decades, media outlets have been hiring graduates with useless degrees in journalism, media studies and communications, as though journalism is itself a profession rather than essentially a technique or a knack. This conduces to a 'star system' in which individuals advance because they turn a pretty phrase rather than because they actually know or care about any of the policies they are pretending to evaluate.

Perhaps the only arena other than journalism in which one may rise to prominence without knowing all that much about anything in particular is... well...politics. Especially in Tanner's own party, members advance largely on the basis of ambition, patronage and influence, their involvement in the right union or a favoured faction; ministers span giant portfolios they can scarcely know in detail, and swap as soon as they attain the slightest familiarity with; they announce policies and read speeches prepared largely by others affecting voters they know chiefly by poll numbers, and into whom they bump every four years. Tanner might profitably have set his own house in order, in fact, before starting on criticising his neighbour's.

# THE MASTER GAME

## *The love of chess* (2009)

Marx was keen. Lenin talked of it in his sleep. Napoleon and Casanova were hopeless, and George Bernard Shaw loathed it, but Tolstoy, Turgenev, Pushkin and Canetti were completely smitten; likewise Lee Harvey Oswald, the Moors murderer Ian Brady, the Rillington Place killer John Christie and the diabolist Aleister Crowley. It inspired a Beckett play, a Borges poem, and short stories by Marquez and Zweig. Doing it helped Kubrick bond with his actors and Scott of the Antarctic to wile away polar evenings, but persuaded Marcel Duchamp to turn his back on art.

It is chess, antecedents of which have been traced back almost 1500 years to India – the country from which, after centuries of Russian and European dominance, hales its present world champion. And it is a game of entirely timeless appeal, sublime in logic, elusive in point; a martial and monarchical game in which the King is the feeblest piece; a game dominated by men in which the Queen is the strongest piece; a game of patience *and* of conquest; a game both stationary *and* enervating; a game whose rules are unchanged in more than six centuries, but never unchallenged. 'If you ain't cheatin',' said an enthusiast, the actor James Coburn, 'you ain't tryin'.'

I learned chess at school. My earliest memories are of beating my younger brother – after all, what are younger brothers for? – and losing to everybody else. The second memory is honoured to this day, usually on a chess set I bought in the Philippines thirty years ago, which has become a kind of confessional box, insofar as it knows me at my weakest, clumsiest and slowest. It's not that I don't hanker to improve, more that I struggle to subdue a nervous anxiety to move before I am quite ready. The chesserati actually have a name for this: *zugzwang*, the compulsion to move. I have my own names; they're not printable here.

This infacility is an odd one, for I am not otherwise noticeably impetuous, yet chess is frequently held up as somehow indicative of character or metaphorical for larger struggles. 'Chess is *like* life,' ventured world champion Boris Spassky. 'Chess *is* life,' corrected Bobby Fischer, his conqueror at Reykjavik in perhaps the most famous chess contest of all. 'Chess is my life,' insisted Fischer's successor as world champion, Anatoly Karpov. 'But my life isn't just chess.' Indeed not – one of the Soviet chess machine's greatest and most earnest products, he obediently listed his other interests as 'stamp collecting and communism'.

'Chess is life in miniature,' argued Karpov's long-time rival Garri Kasparov, a less obedient scion of the Soviet system, who finally abandoned chess for the bigger life of political opposition to the post-Soviet junta. 'Chess is most certainly not my life,' said the self-deprecating English grandmaster Tony Miles, which may be a reason he did not achieve quite as much as was expected of him.

Yet there is something in each of these assertions. What an absorption in chess does bespeak is a capacity for becoming interested, *really* interested – because nobody merely dabbles or kills time playing chess; it's not something you do to unwind, but a game of utmost focus. Unlike sport, where you might be able to blame a bad bounce or unequal opposition, the playing field is unyieldingly flat and the resources completely even; unlike gambling or the punt, where you might be distracted by money lost or won, there is nowhere to look but the board. Sooner or later, too, everyone screws up, everyone is humbled. As Dominic Lawson notes in *The Inner Game* (1993), his riveting account of that year's World Chess Championship involving Kasparov and Briton Nigel Short, handling that is itself a kind of skill: 'Chess grandmasters are not just masters of chess. They are also masters of the excuse for playing chess badly.'

As such, there's a certain seriousness to the undertaking of a game. You are saying: I will sit here, concentrate just on this and face the consequences. And in this distracted decade, of Facebook, Twitter, multi-tasking and multi-player games, that amounts almost to a subversive act. It is messing with the fates and toying with obsession, for chess does indeed contain its cautionary tales. Duchamp, for example, got hooked on chess while living in Buenos Aires in 1918, aged thirty, on hiatus from *The Large Glass*. That became his last major work, because pretty soon could think of nothing but his next game. 'I play night and day,' he confessed. 'I like painting less and less.' While his artist contemporaries were cleaning up through the next few decades, the guru of Dadaism, cubism and surrealism was ekeing out a modest existence as a chess journalist; while on honeymoon, he became so utterly absorbed in chess problems that his wife Lydie Sarazin-Lavassor glued the pieces to the board, then divorced him after six months. When he was rediscovered in the 1960s, the game still gripped him tightly. In the year of his death, he played a concert with John Cage where the sounds were generated by photoelectric cells beneath the board responding to their moves.

The intensity of chess obsession may be one of the reasons why a mastery is often correlated directly with intelligence, although this is undermined by the number of self-confessedly terrible players from Einstein and Alan Turing to John Ruskin and Stephen Fry, and even with cunning and shrewd rationality. The latter, in fact, played a fascinating role in the murder mystery beloved of every serious player.

One night in January 1931, fifty-two-year-old Prudential insurance agent William Henry Wallace arrived for a game in the Liverpool basement that was leased by the Central Chess Club. There the club captain gave him a telephone message from a prior telephone caller who had identified himself as 'R. M. Qualtrough', asking him to pay a visit the following evening to an address the other side of town. The address turned out to be confusing then non-existent, and when Wallace returned home he found his wife Julia bludgeoned to death in the front parlour.

Much weight at Wallace's murder trial was placed on his 'scheming chess-player's mind'; he was described, for instance, as 'a master player; a man with a mind as brilliant as it was perverted, trained to think ahead to the next moves, and to anticipate the moves which his opponent would make'. In fact, as he later confessed, Wallace was what is conventionally known as a 'patzer' or 'woodpusher': a seriously bad player. 'I suppose I could play better, but I feel it is too much like hard work to go in for chess wholeheartedly,' he said. 'Hence my lack of practice keeps me in a state of mediocrity.'

Wallace successfully appealed his death sentence, perhaps to the chagrin of the Central Chess Club member quoted in Jonathan Goodman's *The Killing of Julia Wallace* (1990) as saying that Wallace should have been 'hanged for being such a bad chess player', but to the pleasure of Raymond Chandler, who regarded the slaying as 'the nonpareil of all murder mysteries'. It might even be a consolation to the likes of myself, coming to terms with chronic lack of ability, that incompetence occasionally comes in handy.

# CARTOGRAPHOPHILIA

## *The love of maps* (2009)

In his book *Island of Lost Maps,* American journalist Miles Harvey describes himself a 'mapperist' – that is, 'an ecstatic contemplator of things cartographic'. It is a made-up word, yet it is surprising that the sensation has hitherto eluded naming. The business of collecting maps, after all, is a huge one. The US Library of Congress alone holds 4,250,000 map sheets, 53,000 atlases, 700,000 microfilm images, 300 globes, 2,000 terrain models, 1,600,000 aerial photographs and remote sensing images. W. Graham Arader III, the American dealer whose patented grading system governs the value of rare maps, has built a fortune of more than $US200 million out of a business that began in the back of his station wagon.

Above all, even the simplest map evokes the human need to locate oneself and make a mark. Landscapes abide, but geography is ever a work in progress, not least in a land like Australia, where white settlement is so relatively recent. In Cook's journal, one can still discern where the words 'Botany Bay' were substituted for 'Stingray Harbour'. It was the revered war historian Charles Bean who described this land as 'a big blank map', whose people were 'constantly sitting over it like a committee, trying to work out the best way to fill it in'.

From the first, cartographers have held a role akin to religious authorities, for following a map requires an act of faith in its maker. Cartographers, in turn, would push at the bounds of ignorance, fortifying themselves against the threat of the unknown with compasses, cartouches, crucifixes and creatures to fill the unexplored spaces. In the collection of world maps at the National Library in Canberra, one can study how Australia was made out over centuries like a crossword clue, starting as such speculative scribbles as Terra Australis Nondum Cognita, Magallanica, Nouvello Hollande and Ulimaroa.

An ancient atlas was as mind-expanding as the worldwide web today. Long-distance travel was slow, expensive, dangerous and discouraged, and education and literacy far from general. But while very few of those who examined Matthew Flinders' *General Chart of Terra Australis* ever visited Australia, the existence and estimation of an antipodes were an invitation to its exploitation. It was standing over a map of Africa that Belgium's King Leopold II uttered his famous apologia for imperialism: 'We must not miss out on a slice of this wonderful cake.'

Mapping was then a consolidation of the act of conquest, even if science was not so easily suborned. When Colonel William Lambton and his horse-drawn, elephant-mounted survey crews began dragging their half-ton theodolite across India in April 1802, the Honourable East India Company expected their Great Trigonometrical Survey to take five years; it took sixty, and proved a huge drain on profits. Lambton displayed 'no symptom of more than common powers', said his successor George Everest, yet 'when he aroused himself for the purpose of adjusting the great theodolite, he seemed like Ulysses shaking off his rags'.

Science also pushed mapmakers in unexpected directions. William Smith devoted almost twenty years of his life to the first geological survey of a country, and finally published 400 copies of *A Delineation of the Strata of England and Wales* in 1815. Drawn at the scale of five miles to the inch, its fifteen sheets measured 182 * 274cm. Simon Winchester's book about Smith calls it *The Map That Changed the World*; it certainly changed Smith's life, so consuming his resources that he was sent to a debtor's prison.

The poor themselves were the subject of one especially celebrated work of social cartography: the *Labour and Life of the People of London*, published by the Victorian social reformer Charles Booth, which starkly delineated social stratification of the city's streets, grading them in seven classifications ranging from 'Upper-middle and Upper classes, wealthy' to 'Vicious, semi-criminal'. It was a work of statistics rather than surveying, and its goals were political rather than personal.

Perhaps the zenith of the map as a political tool, however, was the peace conference at Versailles in 1919, where the contestants of World War I congregated to divide the spoils of strifetorn Europe, making and remaking national boundaries to suit whomever's voice was loudest and most insistent. 'How fallible one feels here!' lamented the British diplomat Harold Nicolson.

'A map – a pencil – tracing paper. Yet my courage fails at the thought of the people whom our errant lines enclose or exclude, the happiness of several thousands of people.'

'It would take a huge monograph,' wrote two American delegates, 'to contain an analysis of all the types of map forgeries that the war and peace conference called forth...It was in the Balkans that the use of this process reached its most brilliant climax.' Some perpetrations took generations to unravel: the effect of the padding of the borders of the old Serbia with the inclusion of Bosnia, Montenegro and Slovenia plus parts of Bulgaria and Albania was not played out until the dissolution of Yugoslavia in March 2002. The world is still dealing with the constituting of Palestine and the cobbling together of Iraq.

Not that the map for mass use is value neutral either. The very first tourist map, printed 500 years ago by a Nuremburg compassmaker Erlaud Etzlaub, was *Rom Weg*: The Way to Rome. Marking 800 towns, and using familiar German rather than esoteric Latin, it was designed to encourage Catholic pilgrims to make the journey to the centre of their faith. In a similar way, oil companies began publishing free road maps a century ago to encourage motoring, and public transit authorities images of their own routes to discourage it. There probably isn't a better known map in the world than that of the London Underground, designed to coincide with the foundation of London Transport in 1933, and inspired by the circuit diagrams with which electrical engineer turned draftsman Harry Beck was familiar. The world map in your in-flight magazine is there to inform but also to excite – just think of all those places you haven't been...

On the vague or unfamiliar, the map imposes order, which makes it an ideal *deus ex machina* in fiction. Geography is the key to resolving several of Arthur Conan Doyle's Sherlock Holmes mysteries: a map of Brunton in the Hurlstone Library assists unraveling 'The Musgrave Ritual', a map of the region round 'The Priory School' helps explain the disappearance of Lord Saltire; there is a map on the body of the Mafia cutthroat Pietro Venucci in 'The Six Napoleons', and a cycle map of Sussex in the hotel room of the vengeful Scowrer, Ted Baldwin, in *The Valley of Fear*. Robert Louis

Stevenson's *Treasure Island* not only foregrounds a map but was inspired by one – a map being painted by his stepson Lloyd Osbourne:

> Stevenson came in as I was finishing it, and with his affectionate interest in everything I was doing, leaned over my shoulder, and was soon elaborating the map and naming it. I shall never forget the thrill of Skeleton Island, Spyglass Hill, nor the heart-stirring climax of the three red crosses! And the greater climax still when he wrote down the words 'Treasure Island' at the top right-hand corner!

In fiction, the map usually acts as a certification of authenticity, such as the minutely imagined representations of Middle Earth, Thror, Wilderland and Bleriand in *The Lord of the Rings*. American artist Adrian Leskiw has given this a twist by creating road maps of imaginary countries. His book *The Map Realm* offers such fictional locations as The Treaty States of Aultica, and the neighbouring Canadian provinces of Brampton and Cardin, in such loving detail that their non-existence is disappointing.

More harmful have become the obsessions of those to whom maps become a meal ticket. Miles Harvey's book is an account of the life and crimes of Gilbert Bland, who suited his name in every respect save his kleptomania where maps were concerned. For twenty years he stalked the world's great atlases, visiting libraries so that he could whip maps from them with his trusty razor blade. Not until 1995 when he was caught with three maps he had just purloined from Baltimore's Peabody Library did his activities come to light.

Ten years later, the discovery of an X-Acto knife on the floor of the reading room in the Beinecke Rare Book and Manuscript Library at Yale University led to the arrest of one of the map world's most respected members. In September 2006, Edward Forbes Smiley III was sentenced to three and a half years in jail for the theft of 97 rare maps originally valued at $US3 million. While Bland had been an asocial misfit, the genteel world of map dealing was stunned by the verdict against Smiley, apparently the map-happiest of mapperists. Mind you, it is not unfitting that a discipline all about a faithful representation of the earth should also reflect the full gamut of human natures.

# FED UP IN THE AIR

## *The love of airline food* (2013)

In Stanley Kubrick's *2001: A Space Odyssey* (1968), a lengthy scene-setting sequence is devoted to scientist Heywood Floyd's transit to the moon, where he has a date with a mysterious alien monolith discovered at Clavius crater.

The space race was at the time coming to its heady peak, with Neil Armstrong then in training for his landmark lunar mission aboard *Apollo 11*. To convey that mankind by 2001 would have moved on from such high-stakes adventures, Kubrick entrusts Floyd to a more prosaic carrier: Pan American Airways. As the Pan Am Aries 1B cruises through space, Dr Floyd is fussed over by two stewardesses who negotiate the zero gravity environment in shoes designed to grip the floor. 'We see that space has been conquered,' observed reviewer Joseph Morgenstern in the *Wall Street Journal*. 'We also see it has been commercialised and, within the limits of man's tiny power, domesticated.'

It is an undemanding, nearly lighthearted section of a movie that grows ever more sombre and mystical, and over one particular item Kubrick dwells with special enchantment: the customised food tray, a straw jutting from each self-contained Liquipak, each promising a taste of fish, carrots, peas, corn, coffee and so on. The rigmarole of fetching the tray from an electronic dispenser is lovingly documented, the hostess appearing to walk up the wall and round the ceiling – an effect created by a rotating set. The novelty of letting the tray go so it drifts in midair is the subject of a sight gag – an illusion achieved with subtle wiring. Another broad joke has Floyd poring over minute print outside the zero gravity toilet ('Read instructions carefully').

These are not merely the fruits of the imagination of the great auteur, who, ironically, was himself profoundly averse to flying. Pan Am was one of a number of aerospace concerns that shared their futurological speculations with Kubrick during his research for *2001*, and far happier with the outcome than IBM, which withdrew permission to use their name when the HAL

9000 became the villain of the film's second half. The message was that there was no need to fear the future: while many things might change, airline food would be there awaiting us, meeting abiding human needs, served by comely uniformed maidens in instantly recognisable roles.

By the year 2001, the movie's prophecies had gone the way of most. Routine lunar shuttling and nuclear-powered spaceflight had not eventuated; high art aliens were nowhere in sight; Pan Am was defunct and Kubrick dead. But airline food had an identity as robust as ever, served with weightless and automatic smiles by what were now called flight attendants. It was still in the movies too: James Bond (Pierce Brosnan) ordered his signature martini in first class on British Airways in *Die Another Day* (2001), and Hannibal Lecter (Anthony Hopkins) commented with asperity on his inflight meal in *Hannibal* (2001): 'It's not even food, as I understand the definition. Which is why I always travel with my own.' And while airline food might never have made it into space, it is as of today a highly successful $40 billion global industry, churning out more than a million meals a day – a miraculous 'sliver of modern capitalism' that is also emblematic of the economic system's predicament, as columnist Chris Berg put it recently, inasmuch as it works so well that we pay it no attention 'unless we're complaining about it'. Because the assumed tastelessness and tediousness of airline food is also, as surely nobody is unaware, a vein of humour mined almost to exhaustion.

To sum up, technology historian Guillaume de Syon has called airline food an 'essential ritual of flying' that 'passengers expect and even welcome' while also being resigned to disappointment. They keep serving it, we keep poking at it, all at 30,000 feet. But what might it teach us about our changing relationships with food, and with flying?

Airline food hides in plain sight – for something so ubiquitous, its literature is thin. Books about airlines tend to be about planes, routes, bold entrepreneurs, nerveless pilots; they are about flying, rather than being flown, or the quotidian experience of flight in the passenger cabin. Books about food tend to be about...well, food.[1]

If there were an authoritative history of airline food, it would begin a century ago, when flight was the prerogative of monied elites, and the cuisine reflected it. The first victuals carried aloft by commercial aviators, for the delectation of twenty-three journalists on the June 1910 maiden flight of the zeppelin *Deutschland*, were caviar and champagne. How much was consumed is unknown, although it probably wasn't much, as the *Deutschland* went down in a gale over the Teutoberger Forest, fortunately without loss of life. But in its four years running pleasure flights between large towns and resorts in Germany, the Deutsche Luftschifffahrts-Aktien-Gesellschaft (German Airship Transportation Company) strove for the maximum opulence. A menu from the *Deutschland*'s sister ship *Schwaben* offers caviar, lobster, capon and Westphalian ham, washed down with Rhine wine and champagne, cognac from 1842 and 'sherry pale very old'.

Service standards on airships remained high. Fare grew a little plainer as journeys lengthened: a luncheon menu from the *Graf Zeppelin* preserved at the Paris Aerospace Museum promises honeydew melon au citron, goulash, asparagus vinaigrette and eclairs. But the settings grew more splendid: in the 75-square-metre, ten-table dining room of the *Hindenburg*, passengers ate their fattened duckling and venison cutlets off blue and white chinawear with silver cutlery while a pianist played a superlight aluminium baby grand covered in yellow pigskin; they then adjourned to a pressurised smoking room accessed through an airlock where they could also sip a signature cocktail, the Maybach 12, named for the craft's mighty engines. Weight was of the essence on lighter-than-air craft, but food was never stinted on: on its ten transatlantic journeys, the *Hindenburg* stowed two and a quarter tons of produce in three store rooms next to a galley staffed by a chef and five assistants.

Operators of heavier-than-air craft were initially far less ambitious. In October 1919 the *Aeroplane* reported what appears to have been the first offer of inflight refreshments on fixed-wing aircraft: three luncheon 'baskets' containing 'six sandwiches and fruit and chocolate' on twin-engined Handley Page O/7s being flown between London, Brussels and Paris. Refreshment was scarcely necessary on flights seldom longer than two hours, and barely even feasible: in flimsy, unpressurised, unheated compartments, passengers assailed by cold, noise, smell and vibration were less likely to eat than to do the opposite. The intention instead was to introduce a degree of normality to conditions, like the custom of appropriating terms familiar from sea transportation such as crew, cabin and (air)liner. In 1922 Daimler Airways introduced 'cabin boys' to perform tasks like distributing blankets and hot water bottles to passengers; in 1927 Imperial Airways recruited 'stewards' and 'pursers' for the Armstrong Argosies on its London–Paris 'Silver Wing' flights – aviation's first 'branded' route. It was not the same as dining at the captain's table on the *Queen Mary* or the *United States* when Imperial, France's Air Union and Germany's Lufthansa all began offering rudimentary hot meals in the second half of the decade – for one thing, the food was cooked on the ground, preparatory to sealing in thermos flasks, vacuum bottles and ice chests. But the intention was not dissimilar: to invest flight with an aura of calm, comfort and safety – plus just a hint of indulgence.

In Europe, inflight comfort was taken to new levels by Imperial Airways, precursor to BOAC. In 1931 Imperial introduced the Handley Page 42, with its distinctive corrugated aluminium fuselage, four wing-mounted engines, and a roomy galley separating twin cabins for thirty-eight passengers sharing full-course dinners on fixed tables facing fore and aft – an attempt to re-create the amenity of a first-class railway carriage and the ambience of a London club. Four years later, Imperial commenced flying boat services to Australia lavish in their splendour: one surviving menu promises pâté de foie gras; roast chicken, ox tongue and York ham with Russian or green salad; peaches and sauce melba with golden figs; Cheshire cheese or camembert, with 'Toast Imperial' and 'Airway Cocktail'. Qantas followed this example when it commenced its own flying boat service in March 1938 with a chief steward from Imperial, and a menu to match.

> Here is a genuine hotel breakfast menu – grapefruit, followed by a choice of two cereals. Poached eggs and grilled bacon. Brown and white bread rolls with tea, coffee and cocoa. And the whole wonder is that it is hot – piping hot.
>
> Would madam prefer roast mutton with peas and crème potatoes? Or would she prefer ham or pressed beef or ox tongue with vegetable

> or green salad? Then perhaps you may be tempted with pêche melba or cherry flan, and cheese and fruit before your coffee.

Nothing like the same instincts were at work in the United States, where government subsidies made mail more attractive than passengers. Not until 1928 did an American operator try operating a passenger-only service with superior inflight trimmings, and then only as an experiment with financial support from the Guggenheim Foundation for the Promotion of Aeronautics. Western Airways Fokker Trimotors flying between Los Angeles and San Francisco had cabins lined with mahogany and laid with light pile carpet, in which were served juicy thick-cut sandwiches prepared at the glamorous Hollywood diner the Pig'n'Whistle. Universal Air Fokker Trimotors marketed as 'Sky Diners' on routes between Chicago and Minneapolis-St Paul serving such delicacies as 'Under the Wings Chicken à la King' and 'Aviator Fruit Cocktail' were similar in intent. Both ventures ended the same way too: in failure.

Airlines built their initial niches instead by the fast, the frequent and the punctual. Eastern Air Lines launched the first successful trunk route from New York to Miami in 1932 not with the offer of an airborne banquet but with a promise to convey passengers 'From Frost to Flowers in Fourteen Hours'. Meals were eaten on the ground at landing strip lay-bys: the flight stopped at Philadelphia, Baltimore, Washington and Richmond, where lunch was served; then Raleigh, Florence, Charleston, Savannah and Jacksonville, where dinner was served; an additional call was paid at Daytona Beach before the last destination.

The chief American inflight innovation lay not in *what* was served but in *who* served it. In May 1930, Ellen Church, a 25-year-old nurse from Cresco, Iowa, bitten by the flying bug, wrote to Boeing Air Transport, a precursor of today's United, seeking the job of pilot. Flight was still thought rather too racy and unpredictable a field for women, but Church astutely turned this on its head with a couple of questions: 'Don't you think it would be better psychology to have women in the air? How is a man going to say that he's afraid to fly when a woman is working on the plane?' On a hunch,

Boeing hired Church as a 'stewardess', making her the template for seven others: all were registered nurses, none were older than twenty-five, heavier than fifty-two kilograms or taller than 162 centimetres. Their duties were varied, extending to hauling luggage on board and refuelling the aircraft, but the accent of their employment fell on the tone they brought to flying. 'Remember at all times to maintain the respectful reserve of a well-trained servant,' their handbook laid down. 'A ready smile is essential. Wind the altimeters in the cabin, sweep out the plane and dust the windowsills, swat flies in the cabin and warn passengers against throwing lighted cigar butts out of the windows. Passengers who wish to remove their shoes should be assisted and the shoes cleaned by the hostess before returning them.' Nor should the help that stewardesses offered to a fledgling industry of marginal profitability be overlooked: young women were cheap, willing and eager to serve. After the hiring of the first stewardesses, bookings at Boeing Air Transport are said to have grown by 30 per cent.

No food in the world could have done that. When civil aviation resumed after the Second World War, it was still unclear which version would prevail: fewer paying more or more paying less. At first there was simply excitement at the possibilities of smoother sailing at higher altitudes over longer ranges offered by new pressurised airliners, such as the Boeing 307 and the Lockheed Constellation. But other changes were afoot. In March 1946 Pan Am, which the ravages of war had left as the market leader among international airlines, foreshadowed a new system of food handling, which would make cumbersome thermoses and flasks a thing of the past. During the war, William Maxson, a former naval officer turned inventor, had built a modest business selling three-part frozen meals to his old service; now Pan Am adopted the Maxson Food System for its new Constellation 'Clippers', with meals cooked on a partitioned plate, flash frozen at 20 degrees below zero, then stored in a pre-chilled balsa box before reheating in two on-board electric ovens run off 24-volt DC motors. Pan Am suddenly began offering passengers, including Americans who hitherto had seldom done much better than sandwiches, such menus as these:

*Half Grapefruit Maraschino*
*Celery & Olives*
*Sirloin Steak with Sauce*
*Baby Lima Beans*
*Potato Boulinger*
*Hearts of Lettuce with Russian Dressing*
*French Pastry*
*Coffee-Tea-Milk*

Easily handled, mass-produced, mass-appeal meals were a precondition of the other signal development for which Pan Am was responsible: the offer of lower fares. In September 1948 Pan Am separated some of its Constellations into 'President' seating and 'Rainbow' seating – the antecedents of first/business and economy/tourist/coach classes. For airlines were gradually twigging that they could no longer rely solely on the wealthy and the privileged – something a correspondent in the *Aeroplane* in January 1950 explained in food terms: 'The sooner air transport grows out of the salmon and champagne era and gets down to kipper and tea traffic the sooner it will justify its existence,' he wrote, helpfully defining 'kipper and tea' as meaning 'packing as many paying customers as decently possible into one's aeroplane'. So it was that air travel in the next two decades came within the reach of almost everyone, especially in the United States, which historian Daniel Boorstin noted was 'the first nation in history so many of whose citizens could go so far simply in quest of fun and culture'.

Airline food helped shape and was shaped by this gradual democratising of commercial aviation. Mass air transit calls for simple meals to suit the widest possible tastes that can be eaten with elbows tucked in, tasted in rarified atmospheres and digested in confined quarters. It is a dining genre ruled by iron laws of economics unheard of in restaurants with their 200–300 per cent mark-ups; when cost is paramount, portion control is king. If it is dismaying to look down a row of seats and watch everyone chowing down on the same thing, you are also observing the workings of a very specific political economy.

These developments set airlines a distinct commercial challenge: how to distinguish themselves in an environment of growing homogenisation. Along with its exclusivity, flying was losing its cachet and romance: how could one prevent it growing completely mundane, its providers indistinguishable and its customers indifferent? The answer was no single thing, but perhaps an accumulation of many, with one being the quality, the attentiveness and, frankly, the attractiveness of inflight staff.

In the 1950s and 1960s the comely, worldly air hostess was an alluring figure, part geisha, part mother, all at once glamourising and civilising the clouds, and beloved by popular culture.[2] 'You know, an aeroplane is more than just a piece of metal,' gushes perky Marcy Lewis (Jane Wyman) in the rom-com *Three Guys Named Mike* (1951). 'It's like a home in the air.' A middle American small town girl, Marcy is so euphoric on her first flight that she forgets the box lunches and needs the plane to turn back for them – a none-too-subtle reminder that she's there to care for others rather than enjoy a career of her own. Inevitably, too, when all the plots and subplots are played out, her successful suitor is a home town boy, redomestication drawing her adventures to a close. But between times there is plenty of fun and frolic, not to mention advertising of American Airlines, which astutely provided aircraft and other sets free of charge.

Soon after, American made Marcy's career trajectory semi-official by announcing that it would ground unmarried stewardesses at thirty-two, based on the assumption that women any older were unable to meet the job's 'established qualifications' of 'attractive appearance, pleasant disposition, even temperament, neatness, unmarried status and the ability and desire to meet and serve passengers': by the time such stipulations were struck down by Type VII of the *CivilRights Act* more than a decade later, almost two-thirds of American airlines would have them. This was, by some measures, the 'golden age of the air stewardess', to use the subtitle of a history of the British variant, Libbie Escolme-Schmidt's *Glamour in the Skies* (2009). In their own way, though, they were just another thing to be consumed: an aesthetic extra, a fantasy bonus.

That applied not least in Australia, where the basic homogeneity of air travel was statutorily enshrined in the so-called two airlines policy. In September 1967, Ansett-ANA went as far as making a 22-year-old hostess from Balwyn, Susan Jones, the face of their inflight service, having her skills enumerated in a campaign designed by J. Walter Thompson: 'She knows how to serve a gin and tonic, stop a nose-bleed, massage a bruised ego, distract children, quietly put a pillow under your head, light your cigarette, hand you your paper – and how to say the word that cheers you after you've had one hell of a day.' A photograph of petite Susan was framed by the question: 'How can both airlines be the same? We've got Susan Jones.' Not, however, for long. The final advertisement in March 1968 featured Susan showing off the engagement ring she had accepted from JWT executive Bob Foster, and revealing that she was the 842nd Ansett hostess whose career had been terminated by marriage. Susan Foster Jones later returned to the air, with Qantas in 1979, but only after her divorce.[3]

Additions generally became the name of the game, assuming they could be had at minimal cost, and the experience of flying long distances became a steady drizzle of hot towels and cold collations.[4] Pre-recorded entertainment packages were made possible by magnetic tape, inflight movies by the development of affordable lightweight film projectors, and the serving of booze was freed up by changing social mores. Established during Prohibition, airlines in the United States had kept a puritan distance from alcohol through the 1930s and 1940s, before catching up with a vengeance. American became so famous for its Bloody Marys that it made tycoons of an enterprising couple from Southern California, Herb and June Taylor, originators of Mr and Mrs T Bloody Mary Mix. Airlines in the Bible Belt held out longest, Delta scorning liquor until 1958 in favour of more genteel touches like complimentary corsages for women and free cigars for men. But the South soon shed all inhibitions too. In becoming one of aviation's great success stories, Texas's Southwest also became the state's biggest distributor of Chivas Regal.

In the sleek and silvery jet age, airline meals retained their initial purpose as a reassurance of normality. A time-honoured dictum of stewardesses spying nervous passengers was to 'feed them first' on grounds that 'blood cannot be in two places at once' – that is, meals drew blood from stress areas, reducing tension in the body. But they also acquired meaning as a modest but pleasant perquisite, with a semblance of choice provided by the standard offer of one meal or another – by convention, 'the meat' or 'the fish'. That was a recognisable enough meme by the late 1950s to provide the basis of the plot of the aviation thriller *Zero Hour!* (1957), which unfolds aboard an Air Canada DC-4 en route from Winnipeg to Vancouver after the pilots opt for the grilled halibut over the lamb chops. Soon enough, the halibut eaters are doubling over with botulism, which Dr Baird (Geoffrey Toone) explains to stewardess Janet Turner (Peggy King) can mean only one thing:

> Baird: There seems to have been contaminated seafood brought on the plane.
>
> Turner: How could the fish be contaminated? The airline checks all foods prior to departure.
>
> Baird: Possibly because of an undetected bacteria strain or untreated cleaning processes of the seafood...but that's not important right now!

What *is* important, explains the doctor, is the life-or-death scenario: 'The life of everybody on this plane depends on just one thing – finding someone back there who can not only fly this plane but did not have fish for dinner.' A traumatised wartime fighter pilot partial to lamb chops, Ted Stryker, reluctantly comes to the controls and saves the day – salvaging his rocky marriage in the process.

If the plot sounds familiar, that's because it was exuberantly spoofed by the Zucker brothers and Jim Abrahams for *Flying High* (1980), after they accidentally taped *Zero Hour!* while harvesting television commercials to parody at their Kentucky Fried Theatre. Many of the same lines are used, both in deadly literal earnest and as the basis for catchphrases, by characters including Dr Rumack (Leslie Nielsen) and stewardess Randy (Lorna Patterson).

> Dr Rumack: You'd better tell the Captain we've got to land as soon as we can. This woman has to be gotten to a hospital.

> Stewardess Randy: A hospital? What is it?
>
> Dr Rumack: It's a big building with patients, but that's not important right now!

One element in the film goes strangely underdeveloped. As the denouement approaches in *Zero Hour!*, Turner adjourns to the galley for a soothing cup of joe, and quips: 'Remind me never to travel on this airline again. They have terrible coffee.' It is as close as either movie comes to commenting on the quality of airline cuisine – a surprising lack in a film like *Flying High* that allows no gag to go uncracked for 100 minutes. Too simple? Too obvious? So just when did airline food become a form of proto-joke that barely requires elaboration?[5]

Airline food will always struggle to be anything better than average. As previously observed, its intent is less about being good than about not being bad. Anything too attuned to one palate is bound to elicit an equal and opposite reaction from another. Airline food must perforce walk the middle of the road, and a narrow middle it must sometimes seem, given the breadth and variety of human preferences.

In the conditions under which their food is to be consumed, the designers of airline meals also face peculiar physical and social demands. The dry air aloft both instantly cools meals down and nullifies olfactory senses, while accentuating certain acidities and astringencies; low cabin pressure causes the digestive tract to swell, contributing to a general sense of discomfort. Airline food is also stripped of what on the ground adds so much to the pleasure of eating: the companionship of the table. At altitude, one eats like a prisoner in solitary confinement, staring at the back of another seat, somehow the lonelier for the proximity of one's fellow diners. In such circumstances, it might even be disturbing to eat too deliciously or nourishingly. The English restaurant critic Fay Maschler once postulated that airline food involved a kind of ritual self-abasement:

> Despite the fact that it would be perfectly possible to assemble a fine picnic and take it with one onto the plane, remarkably few people do.

> They need the partitioned trays, the plastic cutlery, the polythene glasses, the salt and pepper packaged like tiny tampax, because they realize that flying is not something that comes naturally to man and the food must in the end betray that fact.

But above all, because its cost is usually priced in to the value of a ticket, the quality of airline food will always be susceptible to the vagaries of profit margins in civil aviation. There is something poignant about the vision that opened this essay, with Kubrick acting as eyewitness to the technological optimism of Pan Am, circa 1968. The airline was then at its zenith, flying to no fewer than eighty-five countries, and about to take delivery of its first Boeing 747s; *2001* was emblematic of its confidence. 'Every new hire Pan Am pilot went to see the movie,' reports journalist Robert Gandt in his *Skygods* (1993). 'In 1968, no one had yet flown to the moon, nor was anyone seriously thinking about commercial lunar flight. But it was assumed, even in science fiction, that if anyone were to fly a scheduled lunar service, it would be, of course, Pan Am.' Pan Am was flying blind into its doom. Its new planes would prove too expensive, its old routes too difficult to defend from aggressive competitors. Fuel was about to become more expensive, bankers more militant, investors more demanding, halving Pan Am's market value during the 1970s.

Pan Am wasn't alone. Facing austerity for the first time since the Second World War, airlines pruned networks and services, including all those extras they had begun laying on in the 1950s. Drastic solutions were countenanced: as the industry bore the brunt of the first oil shock, Robert Timms of the US Civil Aeronautics Board suggested that airlines simply do away with offering food altogether, because their other costs such as staff and fuel were inelastic. In fact, the Civil Aeronautics Board was something else airline food outlasted, as it was abolished under the Airline Deregulation Act of 1978. But as serial crises roiled, the new heroes of American aviation would prove to be those who kept their seatbelts tightly fastened, such as American's Bob Crandall, a former department store finance executive who famously saved the airline $20,000 by deleting olives from all salads, and United's Richard

Ferris, a hotelier by background who replaced the airline's generous steak and chicken portions with cheaper lines such as pasta, noodles and fish for which he dreamed up such exotic names as *sole bonne femme*. Additions and bonuses now came more frequently in arithmetical form: frequent flier points, the first scheme of which was launched by United in 1972, spread quickly. Inflight comforts were scaled back: between 1980 and the mid 1990s, per passenger food expenditures on airlines in the United States roughly halved – thus, perhaps, postdating *Flying High* ever so slightly.

The situation in Australia, which deferred deregulation longer, was not quite so extreme. No sooner had Rupert Murdoch taken over Ansett in partnership with TNT's Sir Peter Abeles in January 1980 than he dragooned his *Woman's Day* culinary ace Margaret Fulton into reviving the airline's moribund menu. In her memoir, *I Sang for My Supper* (1999), Fulton describes being given two hours at the airline's kitchen to whisk up the open sandwich for a 'picnic-style meal in a box' that became Ansabox – its biggest local effort to brand inflight service since 'Susan Jones'. But the inexorable progress of 'open skies' policies around the world, shaving margins as they bore down on prices, caused most airlines to economise on food, some by outsourcing to catering firms. This was actually an old idea whose time had come. In 1937 the proprietor of a chain of food and root beer stands, J. Willard Marriott, was surprised to find long queues for his Hot Shoppe outlet at New York's Hoover Airfield, discovering that they were Eastern Air Lines passengers accumulating snacks for their Miami flight: as mentioned, Eastern on that route only served meals on the ground. Marriott persuaded Eastern's famous founder, fighter ace Eddie Rickenbacker, that Hot Shoppes should become the airline's external caterer. The result was not only the original aviation industry outsourcing deal, Host Marriott Services Corporation becoming the market leader, but also the basis of the accumulation of a great hotel chain, on which Marriott began spending his catering cash flows. From the 1980s, airlines that had built their own catering businesses also began touting to serve others. Thus the big four of today: Gate Gourmet, formerly part of Swissair; SATS, once part of Singapore Airlines; LSG Skychefs and SA Servair, still arms of Lufthansa and Air France respectively.

Airline food, then, is a faithful reflection of an industry that in the last forty years has known as many bad times as good, as can be inferred from an alphabet of sizeable airlines that have joined Pan Am in the boneyard in that time: Ansett, Braniff, Continental, Dan-Air, Eastern, Flying Tiger, Global, Jet America, Lone Star, Malev, Mohawk, Northwest, Olympic, PSA, Republic, Swissair, TWA, UTA, Varig, Western. And after all that, Kubrick was prescient: *2001* did prove to be a date with destiny for airlines, those in the United States losing more than US$7 billion in the year after 9/11, and those in Europe and Asia suffering almost as grievously. At the time, it seemed that everyone had it in for the industry. Canadian management guru Henry Mintzberg published a popular philippic, *Why I Hate Flying* (2001), lamenting the industry's inadequacies, of which food was an egregious example: 'Do you think the airlines have designated workers to make the food taste bad? (I'm told they're called 'Accountants'.)' And Dutch graphic designer Marco 't Hart created a website dedicated to inflight food, airlinemeals.net, which at first seethed with complaints. 'I started two months after 9/11 and it was a time many airlines were cutting, trying to reduce costs,' says 't Hart. 'Quantities got cut back; there were more boxes, more buy-on-board meals. Metal cutlery was going for safety reasons. Glasses were disappearing and everyone was drinking from plastic cups. There were lots of bad experiences.'

Yet here's a paradox of airline food: that as flying has grown more routinised, what we will be served has become almost the only surprise left, and contains as a result an almost unique scope for delight. 't Hart started airlinemeals.net for fun, because he was flying a lot, and because his mother asked him what food he was being served. He soon found that there were many people like his mother – curious, even passionate about the inflight eating experience. At first, 't Hart solicited contributions by posting on rec.travel newsgroups: 'If you are flying and you happen to have a camera with you, please take a picture of your meal and send it to me.' Not only was he immediately deluged with images but he also received enquiries from *USA Today*, the *NewYork Times*, the *Wall Street Journal*, the *Chicago Tribune*, and was even interviewed on CNN. 'When it [airlinemeals.net] started, it was a bit like an early version of social media,' 't Hart observes. 'People could share their images and their experiences at this platform – and complain too. You'd try to complain to airlines and you could never get through. So to make your complaint, you needed another part of the internet.'

Not surprisingly, initial interest was in the worst meals. But after the general negativity of the first torrent of contributions, the tone began changing, with contributors revelling in airline food as a horizontal slice through culture – at 30,000 feet. They had Kit Kats on Mongolian Airlines? All Nippon served hot dogs with pickles? Who knew? The most engaging feature of the site – which now features around 28,000 images from 650 airlines and receives 300,000 visits a month – is the depth and variety of the comments, which range from the lugubrious ('always the omelette ... always the same'), the enraged ('It would be hard to find this 'quality' of watered down coffee and stale biscuit even at the worst truck stop on route 66') and the resigned ('I was hungry so I ate it. I think it looked worse than it was') to the appreciative ("The best beef I've ever had at 38,000 feet!'), the expert ("The salty proscuitto and blue cheese went with the bitterness of the rocket and sweetness of the fig') and the downright jubilant ('I'll take this caramel torte any day!'; 'I especially loved the brownie which I requested for one more and the flight attendant gave me 3 more! Awesome!').

Some contributors have sent hundreds of postings – one, who signs him/herself as 'Airline Freak', even photographs cabin crews in action. And the man who has perhaps seen as much airline food as anyone is confident in his conclusion. 'It's definitely getting better,' argues 't Hart. 'Quantities are increasing, and quality too. There's more variety than there used to be. A lot of airlines are using local products, trying to give tastes of the culture they're part of. They're hiring top chefs and really working at their menus, so it's no longer just microwaved chicken and pasta.'

Qantas can claim to have been ahead of this last trend, having appointed Rockpool's Neil Perry as its first-class culinary consultant more than fifteen years ago, although probably the original program was what Singapore Airlines introduced as World Gourmet Cuisine in September 1998: a refreshment of all its menus using recipes from France's Georges Blanc (GB Parc & Spa),

American David Burke (DB Kitchen), Swiss-Australian Dietmar Sawyere (Forty-One, Berowra Waters Inn), Peter A. Knipp from Singapore (Raffles Hotel) and Yoshihiro Murata of Japan (Kikunoi, Kiyamachi). Murata is still involved, on a nine-member culinary panel of celebrity chefs including New York's Alfred Portale (Gotham Bar and Grill), Sydney's Matt Moran (ARIA) and the irrepressible Gordon Ramsay.

British Airways (Hestor Blumenthal and Simon Hulstone), Air France (Joel Robuchon), Air New Zealand (Peter Gordon), Lufthansa (Juan Amador) and Qatar Airways ('four chefs with seven Michelin stars between them') have also tapped into modern gastroculture, and there is a new preparedness to cater for different types of food consumption as well. For the fussy, more than eighty airlines, including Air France and KLM, now offer pre-ordering of meals: a website, inflightfeed.com, allows easy comparison. For those partial to fast foods, Starbucks products are available on United, All Nippon, Easyjet and Horizon Air, while Japan Airlines even offers KFC.

In part, this reflects an industry on the rebound, post 9/11, post GFC, now buoyed by improving revenues and growth prospects – whether as a trend it would survive a big spike in fuel costs is perhaps debatable. But it is also an outcome of more demanding, better informed consumers, seeking more from their airlines than a commodity experience, prepared to survey the scene online and demand with specificity. The need to reassure passengers about safety has all but gone; what we have been left with is boredom, and in especially acute form, given that everyday means of distraction such as phones and the web are unavailable in the air.

'Mile-high meals: a feast at 30,000 feet', read a headline in the *Age* in April, reporting that 'top chefs and national dishes are making bad airline food a thing of the past'. Premature? Of course. But airlines appear to have grasped that when there is almost nothing to do *but eat*, the experience is intensified, and pleasure obtainable out of all proportion – even for someone like Henry Mintzberg, caustic detractor of all things airborne, who nonetheless found himself seduced by a solicitous flight attendant's offer of 'omelet / or / poached / eggs' on a flight over Africa:

I take the omelet. She smiles: I think she is sincerely interested in my choice. Then she asks clearly if I want coffee or tea – 'coffee / or / tea' – and when I reply neither, she understands. 'Could I have some orange juice instead?' I ask. She replies I can have orange juice and coffee or tea. Wow! Then I get a brilliant idea. 'Could I have two orange juices?' Again, she smiles an honest smile. So do I. I'll bet no-one ever took two orange juices in an airplane before. So, here I sit, my omelet / and / veal / sausage framed by a glass of orange juice on each side, feeling ever so individual. Maybe there is hope for flying after all.

1. The only non-technical book I can identify as concerned entirely with airline food is an appealing compilation of historic airline recipes called *Dinner in the Clouds* (1985). Otherwise, it most often features in the margins of commissioned histories of airlines and general works about civil aviation.

2. There is a delirious variety of air hostess–related pop culture. Fictional representations range from Bernard Glemser's *Girl on a Wing* (1960) and *The Super-Jet Girls* (1971) to the sixteen books in a Nancy Drewesque series for children named for its plucky protagonist Vicki Barr of Worldwide Airways (1947–64). Most successful of all were the four *Coffee, Tea or Me?* 'memoirs' (1967–74), saucy romps allegedly written by two pseudonymous stewardesses but actually written by Donald Bain, a prolific penny-a-liner later responsible for the *Murder, She Wrote* series.
   Movies updated the image from the chasteness of *Air Hostess* (1949) and *Three Guys Named Mike* (1951), to the more knowing sauciness of *Come Fly with Me* (1963) and *Boeing Boeing* (1965), to the production-line porn of *The Swinging Stewardesses* (1971). For all this and more, see Kathleen Barry's *Feminity in Flight* (2006) and Victoria Vantoch's *The Jet Sex* (2013).

3. Trivial digression: Ansett released a four-track EP of the song 'Susan Jones', written by Pete Best. On the strength of his performance, the teenage vocalist was rewarded with a contract by EMI – which is how Johnny Farnham came to record 'Sadie the Cleaning Lady'. Farnham then completed a curious double by recording '(You'll Get a Little Bit More) The Friendly Way', which Ansett's rival, Trans Australian Airways, devised in response to 'Susan Jones'.

4. *In Pax, Slips and Dunlops* (2003), a chatty, anecdotal account of '65 years of inflight service on Qantas', the hot towel is credited to a steward, Charlie Pollard, who had seen them in use in Tokyo restaurants. Alas, no substantiation or further detail is offered, but you can see a picture of him at http://acms.sl.nsw.gov.au/item/itemDetailPaged.aspx?itemID=87771.

5. Wheels within wheels. The screenplay for *Zero Hour!* was the first success for Arthur Hailey, who adapted it for the novel *Flight into Danger* (1958). As a bestselling novelist, Hailey later wrote the original mass-market novel of airborne disaster, *Airport* (1968), whose screen adaptation also features a set-up involving airline food, with the passengers on their Trans Global flight seen enjoying a snack and appetisers before a mad bomber strikes. Leslie Nielsen, meanwhile, also starred in *2001: A Space Travesty* (2000), which spoofs the inflight scenes of *2001: A Space Odyssey* (1968) mentioned earlier at rather painful length.

# LEND ME YOUR EARS

## *The love of speechmaking* (2009)

Swine flu is the work of sinister pharmaceutical multinationals now engineering a man-made 'fish flu'; new investigations should be opened into the assassinations of Abraham Lincoln and John F. Kennedy, the latter of whom was a victim of Israel's machinations: Libya's Muammar Qaddafi was in characteristically farouche form at the rostrum of the United Nations General Assembly on 23 September 2009. Yet when it came to recounting his scattergun address, reporting focused unanimously on its length, Qaddafi having thrown proceedings into disarray by rattling on for 100 minutes, and causing the breakdown of an Arabic translator who had to be replaced after an hour and a half. A hundred minutes? The eccentricity of the effort was paralleled with Qaddafi's habit of sleeping in an air-conditioned Bedouin tent.

Times have changed, and what constitutes good speechmaking with them. Lincoln's Gettysburg Address, with its instantly recognizable opening ('Four score and seven years ago…'), is still held up as an example of timeless oratory. What few people realize, however, is he was not top of the bill: the president had been asked only for 'a few appropriate remarks' in response to a speech by Edward Everett, a rather undistinguished former senator nonetheless widely renowned for his rhetorical powers, whose flowery, free-flowing account of the Battle of Gettysburg lasted two hours.

That was then the custom and, in its time, Everett's 13,607-word speech, with its references to 'these broad fields reposing from labours of the waning year' and 'the mighty Alleghanies dimly towering above us', was held to be the masterpiece; Lincoln's 278-word epilogue was first celebrated only on his death, in the eulogy by Senator Charles Sumner identifying it as 'a monumental act'. Since then, its resonance has grown and deepened, to the extent that one of the few political speeches of comparable fame, Martin Luther King's 'I Have A Dream', delivered on the steps of the Lincoln Memorial, began with a direct homage: 'Five score years ago, a great American, in whose symbolic shadow we stand today, signed the Emancipation Proclamation.'

Any search for immutable rules of rhetoric, in fact, is open to this challenge: rules and customs are always changing. In his *Doing Our Own Thing: The Degradation of Language and Music, Why We Should, Like, Care* (2003), the Columbia linguist John McWhorter compares the ringing, declamatory speeches in Congress in Washington in December 1941 demanding war with Japan to the halting, stumbling, colloquial justifications sixty-one years later for war with Iraq. He describes the difference between past and present speechmaking practices as between that of 'speaking', involving some 'effort or nicety', and 'talking', involving 'no conscious effort, no striving toward any ideal, just doing what comes naturally'. It is, he says, a perverse outcome of the age's alleged egalitarianism: 'The modern American speechmaker tends strongly to operate under a guiding imperative not to sound too high a note. For the author invited to "share their thoughts", the speaker at a business convention etc, the tacit running message is "I'm just like you". No one expects the speaker to bring potato chips or take off their shoes, but the speaker seeks, and is praised for, maintaining as much warmth and familiarity as possible despite the formal nature of the occasion.' Not only is brevity the soul of wit today, but ingratiation precedes inspiration.

It's arguable, further, that the great speeches of the past have made up their own rules. Probably the most important political speech of the twentieth century made Qaddafi's look like a toast. In delivering 'The Personality Cult and its Consequences' at the Twentieth Congress of the Soviet Communist Party in the Grand Kremlin Palace on 25 February 1956, Nikita Khruschev spoke for four hours with one intermission; nonetheless, his 23,000-word denunciation of Stalin, for everything from mass murder to military incompetence, which had earlier caused both its researcher and the stenographer who took Khruschev's dictation to break down in tears, was received initially in what one delegate described as 'a deathly silence; you could hear a bug fly by', then in uproar. Nor did the speech gain wide circulation, not being reported in the *New York Times* until June, and remaining unpublished in the Soviet Union until twenty years ago. To Mikhail Gorbachev, however, then a young Komsomol official in Stavropol, it represented 'the first blow struck at what had seemed an unshakable totalitarian system'.

Similar in scope although slightly different in intent was Nelson Mandela's opening address at his trial, facing the death penalty for acts of sabotage as the leader of the African National Congress's armed wing Umkhonto we Sizwe, on 20 April 1964. It was not the speech of a firebrand or insurrectionary, but a painstaking 11,000-word factual and philosophical elaboration of the manner and method of black resistance to apartheid, delivered by all accounts with utmost gravity, betraying emotion only in its famous conclusion: 'During my lifetime I have dedicated myself to this struggle of the African people. I have fought against white domination, and I have fought against black domination. I have cherished the ideal of a democratic and free society in which all persons live together in harmony and with equal opportunities. It is an ideal which I hope to live for and to achieve. But if needs be, it is an ideal for which I am prepared to die.' Here, publicity certainly was the objective, albeit publicity of a particular kind. Not for Mandela a florid embrace of martyrdom; by showing a lawyer's respect for the law as well as a campaigner's zeal for his cause, he strove for intellectual and moral legitimacy.

Such speeches, relying on content for their impact, are now exceptional. Today, more often than not, speechmaking is aimed chiefly at conveying a few simple messages rather than news – what modish teachers now call 'the take away'. Here the trend setter was probably John F. Kennedy's speech on the occasion of his inauguration on 20 January 1961, best known for its reverberating injunction: 'And so my fellow Americans, ask not what your country can do for you – ask what you can do for your country'.

At 1364 words, it is the fourth-shortest such speech in history. Indeed, it was designed so to be. On display at Boston's Kennedy Memorial Library is a handwritten list, compiled by Kennedy's chief speechwriter Ted Sorensen, containing the number of words in a selection of prior inaugural addresses, including those by Woodrow Wilson, Franklin Roosevelt and Dwight Eisenhower inter alia. Kennedy could not do quite as well as FDR, who celebrated his 1940 re-election with only 1281 words, but was considerably more economical than his predecessor Ike, who took 1730 words to mark his re-election sixteen years later.

Also on display in the library is a shorthand version of the address that Kennedy dictated ten days earlier to secretary Evelyn Lincoln while aboard the family aircraft *Caroline*. As Thurston Clarke describes in *Ask Not: The Inauguration of John F. Kennedy and the Speech That Changed America* (2004), the speech then went through multiple iterations in order to arrive at the punchy, polished and relentlessly balanced phrases – such as 'Let us never negotiate out of fear, but let us never fear to negotiate' – that became Kennedy's verbal signature. The succinctness proved to have another benefit. The day on the inauguration was so bitterly cold that thought was given to abandoning the ceremony: as it was, guests were grateful not to be kept outdoors too long.

Kennedy's belief in the efficacy of brevity had an obvious impetus. By winning the first televised presidential debates, he had launched his presidency in a cathode ray halo. The salient audience was suddenly no longer in the room, the hall, the parliament, the congress: it was unseen, distant, massed, fickle. The difference was fundamental. All of a sudden, it was no longer the audience being invited by the speaker but the speaker being invited by the audience – and pretty soon shown the exit, via the remote control, if he or she failed to please. Messages grew accordingly simpler, more allusive, less specific. By 1972, Gough Whitlam had condensed his to two words: 'It's Time'. By 2008, Barack Obama had made even this look verbose: 'Hope'.

The tyranny of the soundbite has had a compressing and also a diluting influence on political rhetoric. Kevin Rudd's apology to the stolen generations was, by modern standards, very long, but at 3875 words it was not thrice the length of Kennedy's inaugural, despite being puffed up with 21 uses of the word 'future' and half a dozen 'new beginnings'. These days the UN General Assembly enforces a time limit of 15 minutes on speakers, after which a red light flashes to encourage their winding up; it flashed on and on during Qaddafi's speech, to his conspicuous indifference. There are now additional technological exhortations to concision in the restrictions imposed by SMS and Twitter: the 140-character State of the Union Address may not be far away.

Content, too, has slipped from being a secondary consideration to very nearly an irrelevance – detail is the stuff of budget papers, policy statement, departmental briefings, and can safely be dispensed with. In politics, one concentrates on what Paul Keating called 'the big picture', which tends to suit not just politicians but journalists who report them and voters with no particular wish to be troubled by either. As Qaddafi droned, confused, raved and maddened his way to a conclusion in September, he also prompted some mischievous speculations. How would other modern political leaders handle 100 minutes at the rostrum? And how many of them would you elect afterwards?

# AUTOMATIC WRITING

## *The love of doodling* (2010)

In 1801, a gentleman renting a house on the Yorkshire moors paid a visit on the manor of his landlord. Snowed in, he was compelled to stay overnight, and, finding himself tossing and turning in a freezing bedchamber, began exploring the room's few musty and dilapidated books. In these, he was astonished to find that the pages of the margins teeming with scarcely intelligible notes and symbols. 'Some were detached sentences; other parts took the form of a regular diary, scrawled in an unformed, childish hand,' he recalled. 'At the top of an extra page...I was greatly amused to behold an excellent caricature of my friend Joseph – rudely yet powerfully sketched.'

Most readers will recognise the foregoing as Lockwood's discovery of the library of Catherine Earnshaw in Emily Bronte's *Wuthering Heights* (1847); they are also an early example of the mystery and allusiveness to be found when a wandering mind with a writing instrument strays into blank space. Catherine's scrawlings don't quite fit the category of what we now deem doodling, but they do exhibit several of its key characteristics: spontaneity, mystery, an intimacy to the creator, and an apparent invitation into their unconscious mind.

At the turn of the nineteenth century, when books were scarce and often circulated among friends, the custom of multiple marginal commentaries was widespread; it was called 'marginalia', a word imported to English by Samuel Taylor Coleridge when he actually published a collection of such commentaries in 1819. The custom was curtailed by the rise of lending libraries, which naturally frowned on such habits, but the older instinct to fill any empty space at hand, dating back at least as far as Erasmus, who drew comical faces in the margins of his manuscripts, survived and prospered, exerting a strange fascination, especially when associated with a well-known perpetrator. A doodle of Ronald Reagan's was sold in 1986 for $10,000. Most coveted when Marilyn Monroe's books were auctioned in September

1999 was a copy of *The Little Engine That Could* containing 'childish scrawls at the end', rumoured, somewhat dubiously, to have accompanied her to John F. Kennedy's Birthday Ball.

The custom and its curious thrall are the outcome, in the twentieth century at least, of developments in technology and medical science. With the rise of white collar work and the spread of inventions like the telephone, there arose the capacity and the opportunity to perform multiple tasks simultaneously. With the popularisation of the speculation of Freud and others about the subconscious, meanwhile, came an interest in unfocused thoughts: the so-called 'Freudian slip', free verbal association, stream of consciousness prose, and what the American psychiatrist Anita Muhl studied in her pioneering book *Automatic Writing* (1930).

If anyone is entitled to be considered the dean of doodling, however, it is Russell Arundel, journalist and Capitol Hill staffer of the 1920s and 1930s. 'Place a pencil and pad near the telephone of any human of more than primeval intelligence and the bet is ten to one that he'll doodle during his next telephone call,' he stated confidently. 'While doodles appear to be aimless pixillations, they are in reality accurate pictures of the subconscious mind. They are psychic blueprints of man's inner thoughts and emotions that have slipped from the deeps of memory onto paper.'

Arundel traced his fascination to a 1929 visit to Washington by the Prince of Wales. Standing among a throng of reporters flinging questions, he noticed the Prince uneasily scribbling on the back of an envelope. Seeing the item discarded, he went to retrieve it, and found that the shape of a triangle around which had been shaped a number of concentric rings. The symbolism was obvious, he thought: the Prince was 'shy' and disliked being 'in the midst of crowds'. To what other insights might he be privy if he set to collecting the unconsidered trifles of the famous?

Arundel was something of an eccentric: a fox hunter and steeple chaser who later in life paid $20,000 for an island off Nova Scotia which he proclaimed the 'Principality of Outer Baldonia'. But in the accumulation of the doodle collection that formed his *Everybody's Pixillated* (1937), he was at one with the emergent culture of celebrity, whose chief impetus had been Charles Lindbergh's epic trans-Atlantic flight. Lindy's fame thereafter was such that two women in a restaurant famously came to blows trying to souvenir the bone of a chicken drumstick he had eaten; the Prince was one of Lindy's few rivals for the title of world's most photographed man. Arundel's delightful book, which contains the 'work' of eighty prominent doodlers and quaint psychological speculations on each, is a testament to the ubiquity of doodling: even the blind senator Thomas Gore was an addict, a furious cross-hatcher. But the book is also an early artefact in the perennial enquiry: 'The famous: what are they really like?'

During Arundel's Washington years, the White House was occupied by some genuinely compulsive doodlers. Warren G. Harding was almost a graphomaniac, with an energetic art deco aesthetic; Herbert Hoover, with a draftsman's background in engineering, created hugely intricate and geometric patterns. One of Hoover's designs, in fact, was adapted as the pattern for a line of children's rompers; another ornate scrabbling, plucked from a wastebasket by a visitor and sold to collector Thomas Madigan, made it onto newspaper front pages, where it was analysed by various experts. 'Generally this man is highly efficient, a man who figures things out and who is at his best tackling difficult tasks,' stated one expert in the *Chicago Tribune*, which turned out to be wishful thinking as the Depression unfolded.

Hoover was displeased by the publicity surrounding his doodling, perhaps because it conveyed the image of an idle, unfocused mind, but was fighting a losing battle. When Franklin Roosevelt endowed the first presidential library in 1939, he created a cult of collection round the presidency, consecrating everything the chief executive touched. The best of the genre is surveyed in *Presidential Doodles* (2006) by David Greenberg of *Cabinet* magazine, some of it inescapably fascinating. When the CIA toppled Jacobo Arbenz in Guatamala in June 1954, for example, Dwight Eisenhower drew a slim but buff self-portrait against a backdrop of gunboats with the cursive notation 'Internal security' heavily marked and underlined.

John F. Kennedy, meanwhile, was a vividly impatient man in meetings: his fingers, recalled his amanuensis Arthur Schlesinger, were in constant motion, 'drumming the table, tapping his teeth, slashing impatient pencil lines on a pad'. But the former naval officer Kennedy eschewed bristling gunboats in favour of serene sailboats, especially his sloop *Victura*. On an undated piece of White House stationery from the Cuban Missile Crisis, Kennedy wrote and ringed an emphatic 'Blockade Cuba!', then in the corner sketched a ketch with '62' on the sail.

Least of White House doodlers was Richard Nixon. 'The president does not doodle,' presidential aide H. R. Haldeman told his White House colleague William Safire when the latter asked for a sample of their boss's scribblings. Haldeman then paused, Safire narrates in his classic *Before The Fall* (1975), and asked: 'Should the president doodle?' It is probable that Nixon would have done so had he not been so prey to paranoia, for he once explained that it was his custom in meetings to 'always watch my opposite number to see how they doodle'.

Yet in some respects, important, busy people are the last to whom one should turn for doodling. Doodling is more characteristic of boredom and listlessness; it is activity amid inactivity, like wheels spinning on a frictionless surface. Sometimes this is simply self-amusement. The eminent Japanese financier Tokushichi Nomura was famous for his habit of industrious note taking in board meetings – or at least, he *was* famous until a colleague took a peek one day and found that he was sketching comic caricatures of colleagues. On occasion it is more calculated: in his memoirs *Howling at the Moon* (2004), maverick record producer Walter Yetnikoff describes undermining a despised CEO at CBS Records management offsite by ostentatiously drawing pornographic sketches on the soles of his shoes during an earnest presentation about *In Search of Excellence*.

Just every so often, though, something seems to come from nowhere that might not have emerged from a focused mind, and to drop like a penny into a slot. It was in a bored doodle on the pad of Nobuhiko Kawamoto, then a gifted young engineer but a chief executive in the making, that originated one of Honda's first and best racing car designs. It was while absent-mindedly circling prime numbers on a grid during a scientific conference that the émigré Polish mathematician Stanislaw Ulam noted their spiral pattern: the graph became the basis of what is now called the Ulam spiral. It was on an envelope in the back of a cab that British cabinet minister Michael Heseltine arrived at the structure of his Ministry of the Environment: he was given the envelope back by his civil service staff when he departed.

Researchers, in fact, have moved on from the idea that doodles are glimpses of a submerged psyche to exploring their association with memory. In a recent experiment, psychologist Jackie Andrade of the University of Plymouth found that a sample of people listening to a list of names on a recorded message achieved significantly better degrees of recall if they were doodling at the time. The results published last year, said Andrade, were the 'first experimental test…of the prediction that doodling aids concentration'.

It was not, however, the first such story. In 1917, a young Maryland soldier bound for the western front, Private Marvin Shores, cautiously liquidated his assets and buried the proceeds in the form of gold and silver bullion on the farm owned by his grandfather, confiding the location in the old man. This act of prudence went badly awry: Shores, badly shell-shocked in the trenches, lost his memory; in his absence, the grandfather died.

For the six months after his repatriation, Shores wandered the farm digging hopelessly, finally giving up. But sometime in the early 1930s, he took a phone call while playing cards, and as he spoke began drawing apparently meaningless patterns on the cover of a magazine. By coincidence, one of Shores' card-playing cronies had just read Anita Muhl's *Automatic Writing*, and suggested that Shores comb the house for other such scrawls; studying them, a psychiatrist noted the recurrent figure of a bunny. Yes, the bullion lay beneath the hutch Shores had built for his pet rabbit just before his enlistment. For Shores at least, doodling was assuredly what others have claimed for it: buried treasure.

# THE READER STRIKES BACK

## *The love of libraries* (2017)

If you wanted to see the ideals of democracy in action, and its dismaying and seedy modern local government reality, a good vantage point last week was the council chambers of my home town in Geelong.

Since the Andrews government turfed out its council last year, the City of Greater Geelong has been run by a bunch of hand-picked apparatchiks who effectively rule by decrees. One of these decrees last month was to announce, without consultation, with barely an explanation and without right of review, the closure of three well-used and well-loved local libraries, at Chilwell, Highton and Barwon Heads.

This could not be right, said residents who depend on these libraries. They have mounted a campaign – a model of civic engagement, in fact, representative, organised and courteous. Three hundred residents attended the council meeting, holding superb home-made placards, presenting bible-thick petitions containing thousands of signatures.

Fifteen individuals, having gone through the rigmarole of registering online, took turns at the microphone asking questions of such detail and logic, replete with usage statistics, demographic data and compelling quotations from the council's own documents, that one wished they were journalists.

The closures will generate minuscule savings. They will undermine carefully nurtured communities. They will deprive of resources nearby primary schoolchildren without their own school libraries; they will hurt the elderly who depend on them for social contact. They form part of the steady chipping away of the city's amenities. Just over 10 years ago, Chilwell's library was 'merged' with neighbouring Newtown's; it is now the area's last remaining community hub.

In these hurried, hustling times, where it seems impossible to find a place simply to sit without someone trying to sell you a $1 coffee for $4.50, libraries are one of the last remaining bastions in our cities and towns of repose and sanctuary. Victoria has 2.1 million public library members who paid them more than 30 million visits last year.

Anyway, so compelling were the questions as to seem unanswerable. And that's exactly what happened. The administrators didn't answer them. Not one.

The chairwoman hadn't turned up anyway. Instead, her ineffectual locum curtailed the questions, granted a few additional weeks of after-the-fact 'consultation', recited some boilerplate about 'service models' and '21st century blah blah', and moved the meeting clumsily on to matters more congenially irrelevant.

Their idea is that people can just breeze along to the city centre's $45 million flagship library, very impressive from the outside but with all the appeal of a hotel lobby inside, with space for a cafe that's never been used, and around which a car park is prohibitively expensive even assuming you can find one.

So the chamber emptied – quite enough democracy had been permitted for one night.

What do you do about that? There is not even the satisfaction of voting the imperious administrators out: although apparently they wanted their sinecure to extend a couple of extra years, they finish in October, after the slated closure dates.

The state government purports to love libraries. 'Libraries are so important to local communities,' claims Local Government Minister Natalie Hutchins on every other press release. 'That's why we're investing to build and upgrade libraries across our state.' Yet when the affected Geelong residents wrote to Hutchins, they received one of those chill pro-forma 'not our affair' responses so characteristic of the Andrews government.

You might consider seeking support from the Geelong Football Club, a powerful influence in the city, and the beneficiary of many taxpayers' and ratepayers' dollars over the years. Yet the Cats, too, replied with a 'not a cause we can commit to' message. Maybe the footballers' children don't read.

You might turn for solace to the State Library of Victoria, equally awash with cash. I did. Donuts.

The ABC took an interest – in fact, nothing could have illustrated so effectively why people are protective of their national broadcaster. A hard-working local radio/television/online reporter came to the council meeting, interviewed the parties, produced valuable content. Jon Faine invited the administrators on: they claimed to be too busy with their 'second stage' of consultation, after the first stage that didn't happen.

Otherwise it seems that unelected officials can exercise unilateral powers profoundly affecting the quality of life of thousands of people, and damn all can be done. And for what? To loosen up some real estate for development? To justify a prestige project that is better at impressing than serving?

The administrators talked grandly of a 'vision', yet clearly had not the glimmer of a plan – they were simply holding the line until, come October, it will be someone else's problem. But it's everyone's problem, even if you have never been to these libraries and don't live in these areas. When good citizens walk away disillusioned and disgusted by those meant to serve them, it is a loss we all share.

NB: Gratifyingly, this admirable community campaign, for which I was ersatz 'media manager', succeeded in its objective. The libraries were reprieved and, four years later, flourish.

# THE FUTURE OF THE PAST

## *The love of history* (2018)

Time present and time past
Are both perhaps present in time future,
And time future contained in time past.
– TS Eliot, 'Burnt Norton'

Fifty years ago last month, the eminent Cambridge historian Sir John Plumb delivered three famous lectures at New York's City College, subsequently forming his book *The Death of the Past*. In them, Plumb drew an Hegellian distinction, between the past, primitive and pre-industrial, entangled in myth, religion and superstition, and history, rational and scholarly, undergirded by documentary evidence and disinterested analysis.

Plumb was sanguine. He foresaw that the rapidity of cultural change would inevitably weaken the hold of the popular past, which had tended to be 'the handmaid of authority', preluding its replacement by the professional productions of scientific and objective historians, who might genuinely 'serve the multitude'.

'Nothing has been so corruptly used as concepts of the past,' claimed Plumb. 'The future of history and historians is to cleanse the story of mankind from those deceiving visions of a purposeful past.' He concluded optimistically: 'The old past is dying, its force weakening, and so it should. Indeed, the historian should speed it on its way, for it was compounded of bigotry, of national vanity, of class domination...May history step into its shoes, help to sustain man's confidence in its destiny, and create for us a new past as true, as exact, as we can make it.'

*The Death of the Past*, wonderfully readable and ceaselessly erudite, might be seen as marking a zenith in the confidence of the discipline of academic history – justified in a way by Plumb's life as a disciple of GM Trevelyan, as a contemporary of EH Carr and Joseph Needham, and as an influence on the likes of Norman Stone, Richard Overy, Simon Schama and Roy Porter. But like so many predictions made, as it were, at the top of a market, it proved almost completely wrong.

History in the academy has faded and fragmented, eaten away from the right and from the left as part of the general eclipse of the liberal arts education. History at school has slipped into a parlous state, crowded out by ever-growing, relevance-obsessed curricula. History in politics is just a Punch and Judy Show, another area in which resentments fester and histrionics flourish.

Over us, however, in forms such as tradition, heritage and nostalgia, and in expressions such as the urge to explore origins and to venerate heroes, to conserve the natural environment and to preserve the built, the past exerts an ever firmer hold. Even when we wish to repudiate or condemn previous generations, by toppling a statue or removing a painting we find uncongenial by present standards, we are testifying to its imaginative thrall. So while Plumb's powers of prophecy can be doubted, his distinction remains abidingly useful; it might be argued that the past is flourishing at history's expense, as a form of therapy for the exigencies of a present accelerating at rates undreamed of half a century ago. And in addressing the Future of the Past in this address, I want to keep it in mind. Another paradox of our surge into the future is that it is rendering the past unprecedentedly accessible and recoverable – in ways that, in my curiosity about the world, I find exhilarating. But to the implications of these, in an age where so many of our contemporary debates seem to involve appeals to history, we'd do well to remain alive.

There's no doubt that we're living through an age of extraordinary intersections between futuristic technology and bygone culture – the change may be as profound as the spread of print and of mass literacy at the expense of oral tradition in the nineteenth century. Some compare it to the original linkage of the software of the Greek alphabet with the hardware of papyrus more than 2000 years ago. Every day carries news fascinatingly enlarging our ideas and understandings. Think of the DNA testing that identified a skeleton beneath a Leicester carpark as Richard III. Think of the pattern recognition technology that placed an eighteenth century exploration text aboard Blackbeard's flagship the *Queen Anne's Revenge* from a single word on a scrap of paper found in the breech of a cannon recovered from the ocean bed.

*National Geographic* recently announced the discovery of no fewer than 60,000 Mayan structures under the jungles of northern Guatalamala, radically enlarging the speculated scale and interconnectivity of Mesoamerican civilisation – palaces, pyramids, towns connected by roads, fields watered by irrigation. The discovery was the fruit of airborne laser mapping – a spin-off from the technology of self-driving cars. *The New York Times*, meanwhile, reported the discovery that seven plays of Shakespeare borrowed liberally from an obscure treatise, 'A Brief Discourse of Rebellion and Rebels', by an Elizabethan courtier. Researcher Dennis McCarthy is not a literary scholar but a computer scientist; he did not thumb a first folio, but submitted the canon to an open-source plagiarism software comparing the incidences of words and phrases between George North's manuscript and a database called Early English Books Online, containing 17 million digitised pages of nearly every English language work published between 1473 and 1700.

Sometimes, the scope seems limited only by one's imagination.

In Henry James' novel *The Sense of the Past*, youthful historian Ralph Pendrel dreams of communion with the dead and lost, hankering for a knowledge that is tactile and sensual as well as cerebral and scholarly: 'He wanted the very tick of the old stopped clocks.' Such is his fervour that a mysterious cousin bequeaths him an old house in London, at 9 Mansfield Square, whose threshold he crosses in 1910 and finds himself...in 1820, where the past envelopes him like 'an extraordinarily strong odour inhaled – an inward warm reach'. Since its publication a hundred years ago, *The Sense of the Past* has generally been grouped with James' gothic, supernaturalist fictions, alongside 'The Turn of the Screw' and the 'The Private Life', but it now reads more like steampunk. Might Ralph Pendrel's legatees have just such an experience, enabled by virtual reality and psychotropic drugs to step into a simulacrum of favoured former worlds?

Augmented reality has already been pressed into service at museums in the US, UK and Asia. Apps allow you to tour the Globe Theatre and wander ancient Rome; the BBC last year showed schoolchildren exploring a virtual Somme. Or perhaps where my generation paid pilgrimages to Sovereign Hill, the next will visit the like of *Westworld*. 'Are you real?' asks one character of another in the acclaimed HBO drama. 'If you can't tell, does it matter?' comes the reply.

In a way, though, such gee whiz stories are by the by: the truly revolutionary change lies in the sudden *ubiquity* of resources available to access the past. A generation since the Netscape browser, the world wide web is the first port of call for virtually every historical enquiry. And why not? Wikipedia contains 5.6 million user-generated articles, Wikimedia Commons 45 million usable media files. Google Books has scanned 25 million books, Google Cultural Institute has absorbed roughly ten million items: in December, its was the most downloaded app on iTunes, partly because it enabled you to take a selfie and find a doppelganger among 45,000 artworks gleaned from more than sixty museums. Even the venerable *Australian Dictionary of Biography* is now online, all 12,000 exquisite profiles. Bunch in true crime examples like *Bowraville* and *Wrongful*, and in the last five years there have probably been more than a hundred Australian podcasts prodding the past, from *Australian Naval History*, prepared by the Naval Studies section of UNSW Canberra, to *The Familiar Strange*, from anthropologists at ANU. Latest addition is the Australian Museum's *Treasures*, launched last month. *Kick to Kick*, a chatty podcast about the history of Australian rules football, since 1858, recently hit 1914. *That Was The (Greatest) Season That Was*, a podcast dedicated to a round-by-round recapitulation of the 1993 AFL season, has just begun.

That's just the free stuff, for elsewhere the past is being monetised. A hundred million American households receive the History Channel: circulations of mainstream history magazines, like those of the BBC, *National Geographic* and the Smithsonian Institute, are buoyant. Last year, NBC reported that the second biggest hobby in the US after gardening has become family research, thanks to the advent of Ancestry, MyHeritage, Rootsweb, 23andMe and other online genealogy services. On Ancestry alone, which boasts 20 billion records of births, deaths, marriages, immigration and military service, there are 90 million family trees and 75 million daily searches. Flagging an IPO last year, the company was valued at $2.6 billion.

Genealogy is the original form of history: the book of Genesis offers effectively the first family tree. It has bound castes and clans, determined rulers and nobles. But in our generation it has turned into something altogether more popular, and populist. You can think of the shift in televisual terms, from *Antiques Roadshow,* around for forty seasons, to *Who Do You Think You Are,* a franchise in the UK, US and Australia in the last decade. Formerly we apprehended the popular past chiefly by object; now, perhaps, we discern it firstly in ourselves.

There's also been a revolution at history's taproot, sources. Museums, libraries and other collecting institutions have spent modest fortunes over the last quarter century providing search engines with stuff for their bots to bump into. The creation of digital facsimile from analog artefacts has been seen as a crucial step to making collections more public facing, widening the audience of their potential interpreters; within institutions there also exists a duty of care towards physical objects coherent with minimising their handling. The National Library of Australia and State Library of Victoria have led the way, each digitising close on two million images. CSIRO is embarked on digitising a natural history collection of fifteen million items. The State Library of NSW has foreshadowed plans to digitise 20 million images in the next decade, at considerable expense – $40 million in the first five years.

Results have varied, in part because the programmes have been resource-dependent and thus spasmodic. High-end cameras, flatbed scanning and optical character recognition do not come cheap; nor does the labour inherent in what remains a heavily manual activity. Users of smaller libraries would be entitled to ask whether such projects offer wise use of scarce funds when operating budgets are under such stress. But remarkable achievements have been dangled from veritable shoestrings, with help from an unanticipated budget stretcher: the public.

The history of history, as it were, has been the science of the document – the primary source professionally interpreted. Since the mid-1970s, the American term 'public history' has been used to refer to its amateur counterpart: extra-academic exploration of the past, commonly around museums and galleries, historic homes and sites, but also in the development of local historical societies and chapters. In Australia, that distinction has been strikingly blurred, notably in natural history, with spin offs from the

CSIRO's eight-year-old online project, the Atlas of Living Australia, and partly inspired by giant citizen science initiatives like the galactic census undertaken by Galaxy Zoo.

An example is Digivol, the world's first open platform cataloguing project, which went live at the Australian Museum in May 2011, allowing volunteers access to collections for digitisation and manual distance transcription. More than 3000 volunteers have participated, the most prolific having digitally catalogued 150,000 different items. Most notably, Digivol is open platform. Any collection needing transcription can post records on Digivol: beginning with a trial run to digitise the museum's cicada collection, it has since moved on to encompass everything from the minute books of the City of Parramatta to the registers of a Brisbane orphanage.

The signal triumph of all Australian collecting institutions has been Trove, the National Library of Australia's online library database aggregator and faceted search engine – probably the single most valuable development in the humanities in Australia since the postwar expansion of the universities. Trove is first of all a catalogue of catalogues, encompassing 563 million resources, from books and pictures to maps and music, linking big libraries and museums with private and local history collections: who would have thought that the photographic collection of the Australian Paralympic Committee and the Cyril Kett Optometry Museum could be so interesting? But it is also a community, in that it has made available more than 21 million pages and 200 million digitised articles from 1300 Australian newspapers, 260 million lines of which have been corrected by more than 50,000 citizen volunteers. With but a few keystrokes, one can sift terabytes of data for results that roll out in the familiar fashion of a Google relevance ranking.

For the last five years, it has been possible to use application programming interfaces as a back-end channel to Trove data, allowing for its ready crunching: the library has so far issued fifty so-called API keys for the study of subjects such as patterns of the spread of Spanish flu in South Australia, and changing populations of Platypus in Tasmania. In Griffith University's Prosecution Project, historians are linking newspaper stories on Trove with digitised court registers, court calendars, trial briefs and police gazettes from interstate archives in order to allow study of the criminal justice system. On ANU's database To Be Continued, associate professor Katherine Bode has provided an entirely new history of Australian literature before World War I by culling Trove for fiction serialised in newspapers – a genre vastly more substantial than fiction published in novel form. The site provides a full text archive and bibliographic index for thousands and thousands of hitherto unknown stories of more than 10,000 words in length. Among the takeaways: serials, vigorously syndicated, were as much a feature of provincial as metropolitan newspapers; far from exhibiting a colonial cringe, local writers were exuberantly Australian in their themes and characters, including making extensive use of indigenous figures. Among the spin offs: a new volume of works by the novelist Catherine Martin, *How I Pawned My Opals and Other Lost Stories*.

We're at the heady early stages of our embrace of big new data sets, and still fascinated by really pretty basic things, like the incidence of words, which I frankly find a bit banal and uninformative. Further, the short cuts that digitised surrogates for actual artefacts and documents offer us should be recognised as such; if we grow accustomed to short cuts, we can easily lose sense of the charms of scenic routes and rugged terrains. To compose her classic works on the French revolution, *Subversive Words* and *The Vanishing Children of Paris*, the social historian Arlette Farge spent decades perusing records of ordinary life as it was documented in the 1700s before the courts and by police. I love her evocation of the exhilaration that comes from slow, fastidious research:

> A whole lifetime would not be enough to read the entirety of eighteenth century judicial archives. But instead of being discouraging, this fact can stimulate your desire to consult them, disorder and all, perhaps even without a specific goal, out of the sheer pleasure of being astonished by the beauty of the texts and the overabundance of life brimming in so many ordinary lives…One cannot overstate how slow work in the archives is, and how this slowness of hands and thought can be the source of creativity.

This strikes a strong chord. I recently had to go looking for a single piece of a paper, an official police report of a 1920s sexual assault, which I actually couldn't be sure existed, in a very large and poorly dated series at the Public Record Office which nobody will ever digitise and which I had no choice but to pore over, box by overstuffed box. It took me two weeks to find the record – frankly rather uninformative, if nice to have. But the education I got along the way was exactly as Farge describes it. What people reported as lost and stolen to the police in the 1920s, for example, was powerfully evocative, of times of scarcity, of deference towards the law, and of language's elasticity; other assaults I found myself studying told such a story of the period's sexual mores, and of investigators' trepidation and incomprehension, that I was in constant danger of forgetting my actual task. You'll know this yourself if you've ever toiled in big record series, that the most prosaic and insignificant detail is often the hardest won, and also that the journey almost invariably outshines the destination. The cumulative experience actually shaded some of my views by confronting me with additional factors to consider and ideas to conjure with – something that simply doing a key word search and locating a scanned document would not have. As Barbara Tuchman noted: 'Nothing can compare with the fascination of examining material in the very paper and ink of its original issue.'

To be fair, this is a counsel of perfection. And nobody who's ever used Trove for more than fifteen minutes has failed to come away with much more than they bargained for – something they hardly knew existed, a previously unconsidered link or dimension. Perhaps we are entering an age fulfilling the promise, first expressed in the 1930s by the American Carl Becker, that every man can be his own historian, in which the tools of trade have been radically democratised, in which the deposits of cultural memory are open to all? I'm all for it.

I'm also wary. About what exactly is being transacted in, I think we do need to be mindful of Plumb's distinction twixt history and the past. Merely accessing a source does not a historian make, otherwise watching the football would make you a football historian. In our anxiety to hug the past to ourselves, we overlook the melancholy reality that we actually can't. 'Ancestry inspires the assumption that our forbears being our own flesh and blood are somehow more accessible, as well as more important to us than other dead people,' writes Graeme Davison in his *Lost Relations*. 'At the end of our pilgrimage we imagine ourselves sitting in a room with our ancestor, as we would with a lost relation, joined by an unspoken bond of understanding... However, our distant forebears were not people like us in period costume. They were inhabitants of another country, the past, where they did things differently.' And while I'm myself an amateur genealogist, I'd argue that 'family historian' is a contradiction in terms. Research on the scale of the family may recover fact and produce narrative but it is not on its own broadly meaningful – or at least as meaningful, I think, as history should ideally be. We might call it family journalism, were the latter word not so debased by constructions such as 'lifestyle journalism' and 'celebrity journalism'.

Perhaps the hardest thing to guard against in the digital universe, meanwhile, is the hubris arising from the impression of universal knowledge. You can call it the Google effect – whereby what's 'on Google' becomes the extent of the universe of knowledge – although it is arguably older. Historical sources have always distorted the past. Put simply we place weight on those that survive, can do nothing about those that don't – we struggle with indigenous history, for example, because of its officially fragmentary and personally intimate documentary record. Digital sources will in the future inevitably eclipse analog in a hierarchy of accessibility. At risk is not a widening of available knowledge but a narrowing, for cost and convenience's sake.

Trove innocently lends itself to this right now in what I've heard referred to as the *Argusisation* of Melbourne: time and again in Melbourne stories, you'll see *The Argus* quoted more than any other masthead. Because it is the paper best digitally represented, it has, sixty years after its closure, become Melbourne's paper of historical record. We're apt to forget that there were a host of other papers – I sometimes think that a history of Melbourne written using *Truth* as its primary source would change a helluva lot we think we know about this city, as well as being massively entertaining.

As yet, in fact, only a minuscule proportion of our cultural heritage has been rendered digitally accessible, and those that have unavoidably express the partialities and prejudices of the digitisers. In a recent talk, hacker historian Tim Sherratt produced a fascinating graph of digitised newspapers articles on Trove, with an observable peak around 1914 (https://plot.ly/~wragge/303/trove-newspaper-articles-by-year/). It faithfully reflected, Sherratt noted, how the approaching centenary of World War I had become a focus for resources: in a way invisible to users, then, Trove reflects the frankly burdensome conservative *idee fixe* with Australia's qualifications as a nation of martial traditions. And as Sherratt asked: 'With dollars for digitisation becoming increasingly scarce we can expect more "project based" funding responding to particular events or anniversaries. Will this simply reinforce the limits of our digital horizons?'

Speaking of horizons, so far I've emphasised only one direction in which technology is leading history – towards a sort of cherry picking at the level of individual persons, and objects, and documents. I'd like to touch briefly on a second, as different as the telescope from the microscope: the macrohistory popularised by the likes of Jared Diamond and Ian Morris that describes the past in great sweeps, synthesising what was once called natural history with evolutionary biology, environmental science, astrophysics, geology and cosmology.

The History Channel paid its Australian guru David Christian the tribute of a 10-part series five years ago; Bill Gates has sponsored Christian's Big History Project to spread the gospel in schools. Its technological drivers are not data bases and search engines, but radio carbon dating, gene mapping and gee-whiz tools like ChronoZoom, a free open source project devised at University of California visualizing time on the broadest possible scale, from the Big Bang to the present. I don't have the time or scope here to explore Big History in depth. Personally, and it is entirely a personal prejudice, I find its insights uninvolving, and its philosophy reactionary, precluding all thought of culture, civilisation and community; not that I expect anyone to agree with me, its materialism, molecularity and minimisation of human agency leaves me feeling dragged back to the fatalism of the Middle Ages, although it is science enthroned rather than God.

I mention it here mainly because of the extraordinary oppositeness of its scale compared to what I discussed earlier. When inquiry is skewing between magnification of the minuscule and the abbreviation of the infinite then I think some concerns must exist around the centre. I wonder whether there has been a kind of recoil from exercise of the historical imagination in favour of a past either scaled down and acutely personalised or massive and completely impersonalised. In fact, notwithstanding splendid work that has been produced, I'm struggling to think of a work of Australian history that has left a major mark on the culture since *The Fatal Shore*.

Perhaps it is the effect of decades execrating history as nothing but the shoring up of pale patriarchal penis people, the dogma of theory, the pugilism of the culture wars, the tyranny of the corporate university – I make no finding. But in this environment of khaki-coloured storytelling and billion dollar war memorials, we glimpse the advantage the past enjoys, in that it can be shaped to comfort us; history, with its scope for interpretation, makes more demands, of our imagination and intelligence, of our capacity for self-reflection and sympathy.

Technology must be factored in here, in that the declining marginal cost of facts has enhanced the scope for their promiscuous, inexpert and sometimes cynical usage. It is increasingly easy to generate content with the veneer of history but none of its weight, content straining for authority while lacking real rigour – content, in fact, that is actually more political than historical, more concerned with advocacy than inquiry. Former East Germans have an expression, *Ostalgia*, referring to fond recollection of aspects of life before the fall of the Berlin Wall; Australia has developed a similar *Ozstalgia* for periods of imagined prosperity, social cohesion and national achievement from which we're imagined to have tailed off, and maybe also a *Hostilgia* for a concomitant aversion to anything construed as patriotic celebration and ancestor worship.

Seeking to determine whether history is 'good' or 'bad' has always seemed as pointless to me as addressing whether one's life has been happy or sad. But the past is today in more or less constant peril of political recruitment, to the extent that historical inquiry has grown less about curiosity about what is not known than a desperate attempt to shore up what is already felt: a 'cosy blanket of half-remembering and convenient forgetting' that the British historian David Andress has called 'cultural dementia'. Observes Andress: 'People, and especially people from privileged groups, do not want to listen to historians telling them bad things about their treasured identities.' And one needn't stray far from the mainstream online track to encounter murks of tendentious conjecture and paranoid conspiracy, with the tell tale being that throat clearing proposition: 'History proves...'

It's a challenge to everyone working in this area, then, to harness their powerful new tools to fruitful and enlightened ends, to recommit to inquiry that is rigorous and revelatory. Plumb's thesis of fifty years ago may have been found wanting, but his concluding remarks resonate with me as much as ever. 'The historian cannot be free from either moral or political judgements any more than the scientist can be,' he said. 'But he can do his best to form both in the light of history, flickering and feeble though it may be. There are human truths to be derived from history, and truths well worth the telling, some general, some technical, some large, some small.'

Let's go find them.

# About the Author

Gideon Haigh has been a journalist for almost four decades, published more than 40 books and contributed to more than 100 newspapers and magazines. His cricket books include *The Cricket War, The Summer Game* and *On Warne*; his other works span business, medicine, media, social history and true crime. His books *Asbestos House: The Secret History of James Hardie Industries* and *The Office: A Hardworking History* won multiple non-fiction awards. His most recent book is the acclaimed *The Brilliant Boy: Doc Evatt and the Great Australian Dissent*. He lives in Melbourne.